Illinois Studies in Communications

Illinois Studies in Communications

Series Editors
Sandra Braman, James W. Carey, Clifford G. Christians,
Lawrence Grossberg, Thomas H. Guback, James W. Hay, John C. Nerone,
Ellen A. Wartella, D. Charles Whitney

Books in the Series

Fifties Television: The Industry and Its Critics
WILLIAM F. BODDY

Hollywood and Broadcasting: From Radio to Cable
MICHELE HILMES

The American Radio Industry and Its Latin American Activities
JAMES SCHWOCH

The American Radio Industry and Its Latin American Activities, 1900–1939

The American Radio Industry and Its Latin American Activities, 1900–1939

James Schwoch

University of Illinois Press   Urbana and Chicago

© 1990 by the Board of Trustees of the University of Illinois
Manufactured in the United States of America.
C 5 4 3 2 1

This book is printed on acid-free paper.

Library of Congress Cataloging-in-Publication Data

Schwoch, James, 1955–
    The American radio industry and its Latin American activities,
    1900–39 / James Schwoch.
            p.   cm.
    Includes bibliographical references.
    ISBN 0-252-01690-4 (alk. paper)
    1. Radio broadcasting—Economic aspects—Latin America—History.
2. Capitalism—Latin America—History.   3. Radio-broadcasting—
Economic aspects—United States—History.   4. Capitalism—United
States—History.   I. Title.
HE8699.L29S39   1990
384.54'4'0973098—dc20   89-20197
                                                                          CIP

To Mimi

Contents

Acknowledgments

This book could not have been written without the help of many individuals, and I am thankful for this opportunity to express my appreciation to all my friends and colleagues who have supported my research over the years. My appreciation begins with many people whose names I do not even know—the multitude of curators, archivists, librarians, clerks, and staff at the National Archives, the Library of Congress Manuscript Division, the Herbert Hoover Presidential Library, the State Historical Society of Wisconsin, and the libraries of the University of Wisconsin and Northwestern University. Without their assistance, many of the collections and records used in researching this book may have gone by unexamined. I had the opportunity to get to know a few of these individuals during this project: Dane Hartgrove and Ron Swerzek at the National Archives, Carolyn Mattern at the State Historical Society of Wisconsin, and Catherine Heinz at the Broadcast Pioneers Library all helped me grow as a scholar. Everett Needham Case is in a class by himself, and the week I spent working with him reading the Owen Young Papers in Van Hornesville, New York is one of my most pleasant memories associated with this book.

Outside of the libraries came a wealth of assistance as well. While I was a graduate student at Northwestern University, my dissertation committee of John Gartley, Nathan Godfried, Manjunath Pendakur, and Chuck Kleinhans offered invaluable encouragement and support. Nathan Godfried was particularly responsible for introducing me to the vagaries of diplomatic history. Clarence Ver Steeg and the Graduate School offered financial support and encouragement. John Allyn and the Allyn Foundation offered important support at the earliest stages of this research; without him, this project may not have ever been started.

The Broadcast Education Association awarded writing prizes for early versions of chapters 2 and 3 of this book, and I am grateful for their appreciation of this research.

During my three years at Marquette University, I was fortunate to receive the full support of David Buckholdt, Lynn Miner, and Thaddeus Burch. The assistance from Marquette's Office of Research Support was outstanding. Michael Price and the Department of Broadcast and Electronic Communications also supported this project. I gratefully acknowledge the support of the National Endowment for the Humanities in my research; their support came through a travel grant in 1986 and a summer stipend in 1987 that provided the uninterrupted time necessary to finish a complete draft of the manuscript.

At University of Illinois Press, my greatest debt is owed to Lawrence Malley, who fully supported this project and kept his faith as it went through its incarnations. Bobby Allen, Dan Leab, and Jim Carey, through a full range of comments, criticisms, and suggestions, significantly improved the manuscript. Mary Giles did a superb job of copyediting, especially the difficult and lengthy footnotes. And I am also thankful to Richard Wentworth for his support and for his help in guiding this project through the final stages of publication.

Last but not least, the community of colleagues, friends, and family that has supported me as I labored at this project deserves hearty thanks. Robert Pepper, James Baughman, Lawrence Lichty, Ellen Seiter, Thomas McCormick, William Lafferty, Herb Terry, William L. Bird, Thomas Guback, Richard DeCordova, James Capo, Vance Kepley, Julianne Burton, Vincent Mosco, Susan Reilly, William Uricchio, Eileen Meehan, and Dana Polan all read portions of the manuscript and offered suggestions and support. Fred Fejes and Kathy Woodward both read the entire manuscript at critical moments; without their support, I would have been lost. Lauren Rabinovitz, Greg Easley, Emily Martin, and Nils Varney all offered their hospitality during research trips to the Herbert Hoover Library near Iowa City. Mark Tolstedt always kept his eyes open for helpful sources of information. Maria Uribe convinced me of the significance of video piracy in contemporary Latin America. Michael and Jean Miller never let me stop thinking like a revolutionary. Pam Falkenberg made many contributions, including showing me the importance of open territory. My parents,

Glenn and Harriet, offered their love and the convenience of living near Madison, Wisconsin. My in-laws, Bernard and Ruth White, gave their affection as well as the convenience of living near Washington, D.C. Finally, most of all I thank my wife, friend, and colleague, Mimi White. Her contributions are the most valuable of all, because they come simultaneously from both the mind and the heart.

Introduction

The first four decades of the twentieth century saw a global emergence and growth of radio promoted by American private corporations, as well as the American public sector. In this volume, radio is discussed in a variety of applications, beginning with its first uses as a method of point-to-point communication through the best known use of radio technology, that of broadcasting. Thus, this book explores aspects of twentieth-century history from technological, political, social, economic, and cultural perspectives in American and global contexts.

The primary geographical region of analysis herein is Latin America, although the Caribbean, Canada, Europe, and indeed the entire world often enter the narrative. The discussion covers the beginnings of radio inventions and innovations around 1900 to the coming of World War II. Although this is an arbitrary period, it is a manageable section to examine because it was between 1900 and 1939 that radio first emerged as a means for point-to-point communications, was disseminated into maritime and commercial commerce, advanced technically as a reliable means of global communications, exploded culturally into the phenomenon of broadcasting, and spread via a variety of applications or services—from military and government uses through commercial and cultural manifestations—into every last corner of the globe, whether rich or poor, advanced or backward, industrialized or underdeveloped. Like the cinema, radio arrived on the world scene concurrent with the last great wave of global exploration. And like the camera, radio went everywhere: not always easily, and of course not for the same reasons, but nevertheless radio's development marked the end of an age based largely upon human expansion through exploration and settlement and the beginning of an age based largely on mechanical expansion through technology and information.

As the previous sentence suggests, the concept of expansion—economic, political, and cultural—is a major theme of this study. The question of expansion begins with the historical expansion of the United States as a nation on the world scene. There was a growing relationship between radio and the maturation of the United States as a global power of the highest magnitude in politics, economics, and culture. Radio as a means of international communication became a key element in the global expansion of American political and economic influence in the first two decades of the twentieth century. By the 1920s, the world's former dependence on European systems of international telegraphy and underseas cables had finally been circumvented, and the independent control over a means of global communications (radio) meant that the American political economy subsequently achieved a heretofore unrealized level of success in the world at large. But the story does not end with politics and commerce; modern American consumer culture also progressed, as by the 1920s radio broadcasting—particularly in its American-style incarnation (that is, private ownership of stations, offering popular entertainment and supported with advertising)—had quickly spread through Latin America and much of the world. A study of radio shows the cultural component, even the frequently cultural priorities, of a system of global influence.

The question of expansion does not end with a chronicling of the rise of American influence. The latter half of this book goes beyond the conflict of nation-states, and the continued dominance of the United States over Latin American nations throughout the twentieth century, and discusses the theory and practice of capitalism. Thematic questions shift away from an examination of modern American power as elaborated by American revisionist diplomatic history (e. g., the work of William Appleman Williams) and into the work of world-systems approaches, especially the writings of Fernand Braudel. Historical analysis using the concept of world systems recognizes the fundamental changes capitalism began to bring to social systems in the 1500s, when social systems above and beyond the boundaries of any one nation began to be linked by relations of economics, culture, and politics. Economic activity is a catalyst in the formation of a world system, and the economic activity of a given world system is confined within a recognizeable geographic area and contains a center. In addition, a heirarchy of zones from center through middle spaces to peripheries are discernible throughout the system, not only in economic activity, but also in politics and culture. In this model, the capitalist process of accumulation and uneven development can be discerned within the system as a whole and not only within its individual political components. Finally, although the scale and scope of a world system reaches far beyond the boundaries of even the most powerful nation-state or other political entity found at its center, beyond the perimiters of world systems exist neutral zones, or open territory. This open territory shifts and changes in its geographical location and in its range of political, economic, and cultural activities over the passage of time. Thus a world-systems approach recognizes the heirarchical nature of capitalism while at the same time allowing a certain conceptual flexibility not always found in American diplomatic history (whether revisionist or mainstream).

The aim is not to suggest these two bodies of literature are disparate so much as intertwined. The historical narrative of this study veers away from the theme of globally developed radio as a key element in American expansion and moves toward the theme of globally developed radio as a manifestation of the long history of capitalism and a world system. Therefore, the final three chapters of this book discuss the global rise of broadcasting through the theme of competing nation-states and then the global rise of broadcasting as a manifestation of capitalism in a world system. What results is not an "either/or" preference for historical narratives and themes, but rather the value of a dual approach that accounts for both competing nation-states and global capitalism as explanatory factors. These factors share some common roots yet have their own distinct identities. The goal is not to discard either the idea of American power as a nation-state or the influential work of American revisionist diplomatic history, but instead to demonstrate that American global influence truly has its roots in an older, more discreet, always-international system of capitalism dating back at least five hundred years and built upon very old structures of global relations. The ability to reveal these roots is one of the values of a dual history.

The development of any form of mass media at the global level, whether it be newspapers, magazines, books, radio, film, or television, is a complex, contradictory, back-and-forth process.

Growth is not a straight-line phenomena; in the case of radio, global growth occurred for the most predictable and also the most unpredictable reasons. Further, although a number of private and public institutions from around the world successfully encouraged growth, the attempts of a greater number of institutions were unsuccessful. In the United States, American public and private policymakers ultimately enjoyed success in achieving their visions of the nation as a world power and radio as a component of that power, but often that success took unexpected turns, as in the unforseen development of radio broadcasting. And in the short run, American designs for growth often met resistance and a host of problems in Latin American societies.

In general, the policymakers who brought radio from a technology held within the domain of small businessmen and individual entrepreneurs to the world of the global industrialists never really considered the possibilities of a broad-based, culturally inspired dissemination of radio signals; broadcasting was primarily the creation of amateur radio enthusiasts. Yet the aspiring American architects of radio technology and world communications quickly seized broadcasting and tried to bend it to their will, both domestically and globally. While we must admit (from our privileged viewpoint of the late twentieth century) that although these architects have more often than not been successful in controlling the cultural aspects of radio technology, this success is never permanent but in fact the very opposite; cultural domination is a constant struggle, whether it be in the world of radio broadcasting in the 1920s, the world of videotape distribution in the 1980s, or any material and temporal world before or between. The global history of radio, and by extension the continuing story of modern media culture, is therefore not so much deterministic as dialectic.

Broadcasting and consumer culture were not the only terrains of contention concerning radio at the global level from 1900 to 1939. Questions of technology, global commerce, military applications, and international cooperation for the use of the electromagnetic spectrum also occupied global policymakers interested in radio questions (as they continue to dominate the policy of electronic communications and the information age today). This forty-year period coincides with the formation and enunciation of an American policy consensus regarding global communications and information. The decisions, positions, and ideology reached during this period continue to dominate contemporary American policy positions. The value of private enterprise as the leader of policy formation in the communications sphere was discovered, protected, and promoted by American policymakers during this period. As a part of this ideology, American public and private policymakers began to trumpet incessantly the primacy of new technology as a determinant factor in global decision making, as well as the promotion of American manufacturing in electronic communications equipment as the highest standard achievable. The push for new technology has led to a consistent domination of decisions for new uses of the electromagnetic spectrum by private corporations, who are the major developers of new technologies, and so a single, shared global resource fell under the domain of private enterprise, and another milepost arose in the rise of multinational corporations as global leaders. The worldwide promotion of American electronic communications equipment encouraged American exports, then American branch manufacturing, and finally direct American investment in foreign corporations to develop into major components in the global structure of electronic communications. Radio was at the center of these developments because many of the questions concerning American policy for international communications issues were first faced in radio.

Much of this American activity with regard to radio and international communications has been acted out less in Europe and the industrialized world than in the third world and the underdeveloped world. Like many scholars who work in American international relations, I have come to believe that American relations with non-European nations—both before, during, and "after" the cold war—are at least as important and significant as relations with England, France, or the USSR, despite the apparent domination of domestic and world attention that U.S.-European relations seem to command. A minute or two of speculation on the state of U.S.-third world relations over the past two decades brings back memories of such events as the Vietnam War, the Arab oil crisis, the Iranian hostage situation, the *Pueblo*, the *Mayaguez*, the *Achille Lauro*, and the *Stark*, the deployment of American military forces in Lebanon, Grenada, Central America, Libya, and the Persian Gulf, the Iran-Contra affair, American corporate investment in South Africa, Ferdinand Marcos, Manuel Noriega, and "Baby Doc" Duvalier, and the complex relationship between American financial institutions and third-world debt. These events are exemplary of the confusion, misunderstanding, frustration, and even anger from the American public over third-world relations. The historical roots of these relations run back to the beginnings of the United States—to the American colonies—to the European expansion into the Western Hemisphere—and, finally, to the emergence of capitalism in Europe and its subsequent expansion on the world scene. Although the world of thirteenth-century Italy may seem far removed from a world of satellites, computers, video, and databases, the chapters that follow try to lay out the paths and trails readers might navigate in order to better understand our past.

This book takes a different view of the political economy of international communication. By proposing a world-systems model as an explanatory factor to take its place alongside the model of competing nation-states, this analysis also takes up questions of short-, medium-, and long-term business cycles at local, regional, national, and international levels. Short-term analysis demonstrates the growth and then collapse of local media economies that first resist and then capitulate to, or collaborate with, international corporations. The long-term trend has been the progressive domination of local economies by the predatory giants of international capitalism, yet local economies continue to survive by maintaining a forward momentum with the advance of media culture. Therefore, the local economies continue as an area of resistance in the long-term, although the actual field of struggle (radio in the 1920s, videocassettes in the 1980s) is always subject to abandonment by local economies in favor of opportunities that new manifestations of media culture might offer.

This study opens with radio's beginnings as a viable industry in the United States, and with the attempts by early American radio entrepreneurs to expand into the global economy. From roughly 1900 to 1913, attempts to expand American radio—such as it was—into Latin America met with a few successes and a large number of failures. The exploits of two companies are examined in detail: United Fruit and its successful establishment of wireless services in Central America, and U.S. Rubber's failed attempts to establish a wireless system in Brazil. These represent but two of a score of American business attempts to use wireless in Latin America as an adjunct to their global activities. United Fruit and U.S. Rubber were chosen for detailed investigation because they represented two of the largest investments by American corporations into Latin American wireless activities.

American reactions to World War I, as well as American and European designs in the Western Hemisphere during this period, dominated events from 1914 to 1918. The period marks the coalescence of radio manufacturing under the domain of large American corporations such as American Telephone and Telegraph, General Electric, and Westinghouse. The entrance of these corporations into radio, their relations with the American public sector, and the emergence of an American-controlled world communications system based on radio technology are discussed in detail. As a part of this discussion, the rise of the modern American military-industrial complex, its attendant discourse, and the use of radio as the incipient technology of military intelligence and electronic survelliance are also examined. Second, American control and influence over hemispheric communications in both public and private spheres come into play. American policymakers believed that the threat of European control over hemispheric communications in the new radio technology was one of the most important global policy questions of the era.

A desire to prevent European control of radio communications in the Western Hemisphere was one of several motivating factors that led to the shaping of American policy for international communications conferences in the postwar period from 1919 to 1939. During that twenty-year period, public and private policymakers interested in the global growth of American radio moved from initial discord and mistrust to a united front that efficiently and effectively promoted the global interests of the American radio industry concurrent with the interests of the American government. Achievement of this united front was not straightforward or simple; a number of private meetings and acrimonious albeit closed debates occurred before American private enterprise successfully convinced the public sector that industry should lead the state in both domestic and global radio matters. Putting the past behind them, the American public and private sectors then embarked on a remarkable period of global entrenchment and expansion that culminated in the 1930s with American dominance over the international decision-making process concerning the electromagnetic spectrum and the world system of electronic communications.

The tensions and dynamics between nation-state models and world-systems models are discussed in chapters 4 and 5, which alternatively explore American involvement in Latin American broadcasting. Along with providing details, images, and answers about the global growth of broadcasting, I try, in these chapters, to ask new questions about nation-states, global capitalism, and modern media culture. Detailed examination begins with the modern American nation-state and its radio-related activities. The "carpenters" of the global expansion of the American radio industry are the exporters, traders, salesmen, drummers, consuls, attaches, and embassy workers who encouraged the penetration, protection, and promotion of American radio in their various Latin American territories. The particular specialities of the U.S. State and Commerce Departments are explained; the Commerce Department's consuls and attaches usually concentrated on the development of Latin American nations as equipment markets for American radio manufacturers, whereas officials of the State Department expended their energies on promotion of the broader American style of broadcasting. That style was based on private ownership of stations, popular entertainment for broadcast programming, and advertising support as a method of financing operations. This promotion of the American style included facilitating the availability of American popular culture in the form of sheet music, recordings, personalities and performers, and literature explaining how to broadcast.

Chapter 5 introduces the rise of global capitalism as a competing narrative theme and the role of "radio capitalists" regardless of their nationality as a new set of protagonists. The ties between the rise of the powerful American nation-state and long-term global capitalism are discreet and difficult to perceive because the concept of the nation-state at times is a rallying point, at other times a smokescreen for relations between global capitalists and government policymakers. Radio broadcasting is an appropriate case study to better understand this connection because radio was a key element in the rise of the powerful American nation-state. When radio became truly global (indeed, in order to become truly global), it was also subject to the vagaries of capitalism, vagaries not dependent wholly on its modern manifestations in twentieth-century America, but also dependent on an older, deeper, subterranean structure of international trade, finance, speculation, credit, monopoly, anti-market, and power.

Therefore, a study of the American radio industry and its Latin American activities from 1900 to 1939 not only reveals the power of the modern American nation-state; it also helps to show that modern American global influence is dependent on an older world system of capitalism, with its attendant promise and problems. The United States may in the twentieth century represent itself as the land of freedom, promise, and opportunity; perhaps it really is. However, such a representation does not mitigate against or somehow neutralize the nation's dependence and reliance on the peculiar powers and history of capitalism to make it what it is. But despite historical power, there are also open territories and ongoing historical resistance against international capitalism and the culture of a world economy, as an examination of radio and media culture reveals.

In the pages that follow, media studies and American diplomatic history will be examined, along with the process of historical analysis and the role of history in society's self-awareness. This examination involves questions concerning the simultaneous descriptive and ideological nature of history and the relationship of history to narrative analysis. The investigation of the American radio industry, U.S.-Latin American foreign relations, and the process of historical writing culminates in an examination of the coming of capitalism to the American radio industry, as well as the narrative of capitalism in historical writing. What finally emerges is a study balanced between theory and practice that hopefully will allow readers the opportunity to empower themselves with greater knowledge about global media culture. Such an empowerment may then yield new questions, fresh perspectives, and continued work on questions of media, politics, culture, and society.

Whenever possible, I have tried to avoid antiquated technical terms and other specialized vocabulary and jargon. In this book, *wireless telegraphy* (or simply *wireless*) refers to the use of radio not as a broadcast or mass medium but instead as a communication device for point-to-point communications. This was the major application of radio technology from approximately 1900 to

1920, and the signal was not by voice, but in Morse code. *Wireless telephony* refers to voice and music experiments that used radio before the coming of broadcasting around 1920. An early system of transmission was known as *spark-gap*, which was inefficient and which varied the radio wave by interrupting the signal. Spark-gap was soon replaced by *continuous wave*, which created varying signals through oscillation and allowed for more efficient use of the spectrum. *Radio* refers to all the various uses of radio technology, whereas *radio broadcasting* singles out the most familiar use of radio technology. *Amateur* radio enthusiasts, who were very important in the early development of radio broadcasting, were somewhat akin to today's ham radio operators. *Shortwave* broadcasting became popular in the 1930s and used sections of the electromagnetic spectrum that allowed for the intercontinental reception of broadcast signals on a regular basis (however, Latin American radio audiences regularly listened to standard American broadcast signals in the 1920s and 1930s prior to the widespread use of shortwave). *Undersea cables*, the major technology for global electronic communication before radio—and a concept that is returning under the technology of fiber optics—connected the continents via large, specialized underwater telegraph lines. In discussions of international communications diplomacy, *conference* signifies the actual meetings, negotiations, and sessions that took place, whereas *convention* refers to the agreements reached at various conferences.

1

American Corporations and the Wireless Abroad, 1900–1913

The earliest days of the American radio industry were dominated by small-scale business interests and individual entreprenuers experimenting in electricity and technology, rather than large corporations specializing in the manufacture of established electrical products. Although the research and innovations generated within the laboratories of major corporations such as General Electric, American Telephone and Telegraph, and Westinghouse had a direct bearing on the nascent work in wireless telegraphy, these corporations did not immediately show direct and significant interest in radio's emergence. Radio experimentation, research, and development in the early 1900s, at least in the United States, remained in the domain of small-scale inventors and entrepreneurs.[1]

If the large American corporations involved in electrical manufacturing at the turn of the twentieth century did not have an immediate working interest in radio, that did not mean radio research languished in the United States. Experimenters abounded at the hobbyist and small-investor levels. In part, this interest exemplifies the tradition of Yankee ingenuity. Rather than describing any particular ethnocentric trait, this phrase recognizes the widespread interest among Americans (primarily white male Americans) in inventions and technical devices. Kits, journals, and plans for radios were everywhere; experimentation at a simple level was relatively cheap. *Scientific American* ran its first advertisement for a complete radio kit—the Telimco for $7.50—in December 1906. In addition, inventors enjoyed celebrity status in American popular culture as they regularly made headlines; some inventors, for example Thomas Alva Edison and Henry Ford, became household names, particularly when they became industrialists while still retaining their popularized images as inventors.

In the new world of radio as it existed around 1900, Gugliemo Marconi usually reigned as the household name associated with this new technology—that is, if any name was associated at all. In the latter half of the 1890s, Marconi had put into practice many of the principles and theories of wireless electrical communications. He organized his first British corporation in 1897 (eventually calling it the Marconi Wireless Telegraph Company, Ltd., commonly known as British Marconi) and came to the United States in 1899 on a wave of publicity. Marconi parlayed the attention surrounding his reporting of the America's Cup races in 1899 into another wireless corporation, the Marconi Wireless Telegraph Company of America (American Marconi).[2] For the next fifteen years, Marconi would enjoy both the image of dominant inventor and the position of dominant wireless corporation in the United States and in the rest of the world. Of course, Marconi was by no means the only inventor associated with radio, nor the only inventor who attempted to build radio into some sort of international corporate entity. Two American inventors, Lee DeForest and Reginald Fessenden, made important contributions to American radio research, actually breaking new ground rather than merely duplicating the work described in journals. Both started large-scale wireless companies, and both eventually experienced failures in their corporate endeavors.

Fessenden's lasting contribution to radio research remains his recognition of the importance of continuous-wave transmission, integral to sending voice and music through the electromagnetic spectrum and still the basis of all electromagnetic transmissions today. Fessenden did attempt to expand the National Electric Signalling Company beyond its domestic market into the global economy by challenging the dominance of Marconi in transatlantic wireless communications. Global expansion seems to have at least been a constant if not always primary goal; he occasionally visited embassies in Washington, D.C., to suggest how his radio technology could serve as an alternative to undersea cables, and he corresponded with individuals and potential investors throughout the world.[3] After successfully conducting a well-publicized voice transmission in December 1906, Fessenden and National Electric Signalling Company began to construct and operate a transatlantic wireless telegraphy relay. In 1907, he set up a receiving station in Scotland, but the station was unfortunately destroyed in a storm. However, by 1910, Fessenden was regularly operating a system in the United States that communicated between the Boston area (Brant Rock, Massachusetts) and New Orleans, a span of about 1,800 miles. On the basis of this achievement, the British Post Office, empowered with monitoring and regulating wireless activities in the United Kingdom, promised National Electric Signalling Company a fifteen-year license for transatlantic communication. Although the license could have put National Electric Signalling Company into direct competition with Marconi for transatlantic business, Fessenden split with his financial backers over the right to enter the Canadian market, particularly the rights to a Canada-England circuit, which Fessenden tried to set aside as his own and not a part of National Electric Signalling Company. A suit brought by Fessenden against National Electric Signalling Company investors was decided in his favor in 1912, netting him a settlement of $406,000 and making him a relatively wealthy man, but also forcing National Electric Signalling Company into insolvency. The Marconi companies became the major beneficiaries of the results of the squabble.

The story of Lee DeForest, a contemporary of Fessenden, at times seems to border on the fantastic. In general, his lasting image as an early radio inventor who so often lost control over the commercialization of his own genius is overly romanticized by his autobiography, although less personalized accounts bear out DeForest's singular hardships, however to a lesser degree.[4] While the various wireless companies DeForest was a part of in the early 1900s seemed to come and go with the wind, he was directly involved in at least five corporations aimed exclusively at overseas markets, including the DeForest Wireless Telegraph Company of Canada, capitalized in 1903 at $2,500,000; the International Wireless Telegraph Company, capitalized in 1903 at $7,500,000; the Dominion DeForest Wireless Telegraph Company (Canada), capitalized in 1903 at $1,200,000; the Canadian Radio Telephone Company, Ltd., which was part of the DeForest Wireless Telegraph Syndicate (British), capitalized in 1905 at 120,000 pounds; and the Oriental and Occidential DeForest Wireless Telegraph Company, established in 1906 (capitalization unknown).[5]

The only certainty about all of these companies is that they existed on paper; their actual function as business entities is largely unknown.[6] They may have been little more than the promotional techniques of DeForest's chief financial backer, Abraham White. White, the quintessential high roller, kept DeForest supplied with cigars, occasional $100 bills, and a vision of worldwide wireless dominance. Backers solicited by White heard of plans for subsidiaries in Canada, England, Europe, Africa, Asia, Australia, and South America.[7] These subsidiaries were, in fact, little more than pipe dreams. Almost all the DeForest companies, domestic and international, were capitalized for much more than they ever returned in revenue or tangible assets. Although DeForest went to Europe several times after his Eiffel Tower experiments of 1908 (during which his transmissions of phonograph records were received several hundred miles away) in hopes of drumming up investors, nothing ever came of his voyages other than earning the distrust and animosity of Marconi and the Marconi investors. And although the domestic market held promise for a time, a series of stock fraud investigations and a mail fraud trial concerning the major DeForest company, United Wireless Company, resulted in the receivership of United Wireless in 1911 and led to jail terms for several salesmen in United Wireless. Although jurors exonerated DeForest (who had distanced himself from United Wireless and formed new companies), the brouhaha eventually took its toll on other DeForest companies, especially North American Wireless. The Marconi companies again became the immediate beneficiaries, as they purchased the assets of United Wireless for $650,000. This purchase was in essence a takeover that allowed American Marconi to reaffirm its position as the dominant wireless corporation in North America.[8]

As capitalists promoting their own technological developments, DeForest and Fessenden failed to expand the American radio industry into the global economy. However, as suppliers of radio equipment to other corporations, they were both involved in a number of American-led investments in overseas wireless telegraphy systems before World War I. By far the majority of American-led promotions of wireless telegraphy overseas took place in Latin America, where a number of corporations operating in those areas experimented with the uses of radio as an adjunct to their communications needs. The initial round of American investment in Latin American radio development began in Brazil in 1901 with the advent of American-backed radio experiments in the Amazon valley. These experiments would lead to the formation of a subsidiary corporation in the valley owned by the United States Rubber Company—the subsidiary being the Amazon Wireless Telephone and Telegraph Company.

A leader at U.S. Rubber in developing a radio subsidiary was E. C. Benedict, a board member since 1901 and an experienced Wall Street finance capitalist.[9] U.S. Rubber's interest in better management of wild rubber forests increased during 1902 and 1903. Supply agents hired by U.S. Rubber explored much of the Amazon basin and established purchasing agencies for raw rubber in the state of Para and in Manaus, both on the Amazon in Brazil, in 1903. The company's annual report hinted that further plans were underway: "We have also laid the foundation in another direction for acquiring and handling generally our very large requirements of crude rubber. We are confident that these steps and facilities will give us special advantages and facilities never before possessed by this Company and not enjoyed by any other consumer of rubber."[10] The advantages referred to in the report were in fact the establishment of Amazon Wireless.

The impetus toward Amazon Wireless began in 1901 when two Americans, Richard Mardock and Charles Archer, began a series of experiments in the Amazon area using Fessenden-designed radio equipment.[11] The governor of the state of Amazonas granted a concession on September 29, 1902, to Mardock or any company he should form for fifteen years of operation and waived the standard requirement for investment by a Brazilian national. In 1903, Joaquim Gonclaves de Lalor, a Brazilian agent for Amazon Wireless, received a thirty-year concession for the company from the governor of the state of Para. The authorization of concession by state governors was deemed proper under a clause of the Brazilian constitution that granted that all power of concession not authorized to the federal government automatically became the power of concession from state governors, and Brazil had not enacted specific legislation at the federal level concerning wireless concessions. The legal position of the Amazon Wireless concessions, tenuous at best, would be a source of future problems.

Much of the early engineering and technical work by Amazon Wireless proved fruitless, and achievements were slow in coming. The unusual atmospheric conditions in the tropics made transmissions and receptions difficult, and engineers did not immediately recognize that electromagnetic spectrum characteristics differed slightly in various regions of the world. Perhaps the truest assessment came from American Consul to Para William Pickerell, who wryly observed in 1911 that "since 1904, work on this company has been almost continuous, but for various reasons very little was accomplished."[12] The company had difficulty sending a signal more than fifty miles. The Fessenden system was abandoned and Amazon Wireless contracted with the International Telegraph Construction Company, formed by Henry Shoemaker in 1902 around his radio patents. Shoemaker was the first to recognize fully the unusual atmospheric and spectrum problems associated with tropical locations, and thus achieved better results for Amazon Wireless.[13]

U.S. Rubber faced competition in the radio field as well as in the rubber industry. In 1905, a French cable company applied for a concession from the Brazilian federal government to install and operate a wireless system between Para and French Guiana. This concession was granted in 1907, and E. M. Backus, president of Amazon Wireless, traveled to Rio de Janeiro and met with the Brazilian minister of industry and with American Minister Irving Dudley, asking Dudley to discuss the case with Brazilian Foreign Minister Baron do Rio Branco.[14] Amazon Wireless had invested more than $225,000 in construction costs and the French system, if built, threatened to cause interference problems. The transmitting equipment (spark-gap instead of continuous wave) as well as the portion of the spectrum used at the time meant that two stations in the same region often cancelled each other out, and no message could get through to either station during simultaneous operations. Amazon Wireless stuck to its position that its state concessions were valid in the absence of federal legislation concerning wireless.

The Brazilian government seemed intransigent, and a federal commission ruled in August 1905 against allowing Amazon Wireless to carry on interstate transmissions. Amazon Wireless conveniently ignored the commission and continued to work, installing a new station far inland at Santarém. The success of the American rubber manufacturing industry demanded expansion of raw rubber supplies, and the rubber harvesters could only expand their output by pushing farther and farther into the rain forest. This situation would worsen until 1912, when harvesters could no longer maintain the previous year's output. In 1905, however, pushing into the interior was a priority, and getting reports from the interior could help in industrial planning and perhaps even make U.S. Rubber less vulernable to market speculation in raw rubber prices.

Backus was not the only Amazon Wireless official to visit Brazil in 1905. Benedict himself had gone to the Amazon valley and met with state officials from Para and Amazonas. When the Brazilian federal government approved the French concession, Benedict wrote Secretary of State Elihu Root to blame the entire affair on the contradictory behavior of the Brazilian government, but he left the door open for indemnification. Benedict argued that Amazon Wireless could be a key element in the expansion of the American rubber industry, and included written opinions from five Brazilian lawyers in support of Amazon Wireless. Backus wrote Root four days later, pointing out that Amazon Wireless was having credit problems and its stock value was dropping due to problems with the Brazilian government.[15] Meanwhile, the Brazilian government was becoming more interested in wireless activities, particularly in activities carried out by its own federal agencies and branches. In 1904, the Brazilian Telegraph Administration set up a system between Rio de Janeiro and Grande Island, a link of about seventy miles. Much of the administration's work took place in populated coastal areas rather than the Amazon valley and the interior. Brazil also accepted the guidelines of the 1906 Berlin Wireless Conference (which shored up the involvement of the Brazilian navy in wireless), and several bills to regulate radio at the federal level were introduced in Congress although all failed to pass.

The State Department doubted the strength of the Amazon Wireless legal position. Root advised Backus to continue negotiations with the Brazilian government and warned against hoping for too much in light of the confusing concessions situation.[16] Amazon Wireless was ready to begin daily operations in the spring of 1911. Wireless plants would be operated by Brazilians assisted by American and European experts. Progress was in part attributable to yet another equipment switch, this time to German-manufactured Telefunken equipment. Finally, the Brazilian government gave authorization in April 1911 for Amazon Wireless to operate in Brazil. Benedict was jubilant, praising the governors of Para and Amazonas and recalling their "Brazilian embrace" from his last visit, but his joy was short-lived. The Brazilian government turned around in August and rescinded the authorization, leading to a protest from the State Department.[17] Benedict could not believe it. He told Assistant Secretary of State Huntington Wilson that "[our] case was not one where we are forcing ouselves upon an unwilling community and asking our government to lend its hand to some questionable measure . . . any action to reinstate our rights to serve the people in those states would meet with the hearty approval of their Governors, Mayors, Chambers of Commerce, the press and the people . . . an inquiry would surprise you in the unanimity of welcome we have received."[18]

The State Department seemed unable to accomplish anything to Benedict's satisfaction, so he went on another trip to Brazil in February 1912. He met with Brazilian President Marshal Hermes de Fonseca, who revealed the nation's plan for its own national wireless system.[19] Benedict came away from that meeting aware that Amazon Wireless would always face opposition from the Brazilian Telegraph Administration, and began plans for turning over Amazon Wireless to the Brazilian government, optimistically noting that stockholders would receive a fair indemnity. However, Benedict had problems even with his bailout. The *Correio Da Manha* of Rio de Janeiro—which George Rives told his superiors at the State Department was a "daily of rather large circulation but of decidedly bad reputation"—claimed in its issue of March 19, 1912, that Benedict was trying to "hoodwink" the Brazilians: "It is rumored that for the three stations which the Commodore, the intrepid Benedict, seeks expropriation, he requests as indemnity a pile of dollars. . . . Political graft has installed its best in the Foreign Office. Diplomatic intervention has been the means of accomplishing many deals which have been ruinous to national finance and have reflected shame on our administration."[20] This kind of publicity did not make things easier, and Benedict left Brazil with no firm plans for Amazon Wireless. Whether his demands were excessive is hard to tell, because no one had operated in the Amazon valley. In fact, the work of Amazon Wireless had, if nothing else, proven that wireless could work in the most remote and inaccessible areas of the world, areas even the aggressive Marconi company had previously thought were virtually impossible.[21] All this was of little compensation to stockholders, however.

In November 1912, Benedict told the State Department that he wanted $1,500,000 in indemnity for Amazon Wireless. He based this amount on both construction costs and future revenues, claiming that the work of Amazon Wireless not only provided a valuable service but also advanced the Amazon region to the threshold of a new and modern era. If Brazil truly desired control of all internal uses of radio, as seemed the case in 1912, then Benedict and Amazon Wireless were willing to cooperate for proper recompensation. Finally, in March 1913, Brazil offered $680,000 for expropriation. U.S. Ambassador Edwin Morgan advised that Amazon Wireless accept this offer rather than begin a court fight that would undoubtedly last for several years. Benedict reluctantly accepted, received an additional $6,343 in operating expenses for April 1913, and American investment in wireless telegraphy for the Amazon valley temporarily ended.[22] Fortunately for U.S. Rubber, their plantations begun in Sumatra in 1909 had out-produced the wild rubber harvest for the first time during the same year Brazil expropriated Amazon Wireless. An unusual chapter in American business history closed.

The entire incident was not only an unprofitable investment for Amazon Wireless stockholders, but also a disapointment for government representatives who had become involved in the affairs of the company. The rubber industry and its subsidiaries symbolized all American industries dependent on control of overseas raw materials,[23] and the inability to protect and promote Amazon Wireless certainly must have been felt a failure in the hearts and minds of State Department officials. Brazil had been able to do almost anything it pleased, and by 1913 was rapidly moving toward a government-owned and operated domestic wireless system. If Latin American nations could not be influenced by American corporations and the American government to allow American corporations the right to own and operate wireless systems within their own borders, perhaps American foreign policy would have to accept or even promote government ownership in Latin America and push for American companies merely as radio equipment suppliers.[24]

U.S. Rubber was only one of nearly a score of large American corporations that experimented with wireless telegraphy as an adjunct to their operations in Latin America in the early 1900s. Virtually all of the companies were wholly or partially built around the development and distribution of primary resources and raw materials, such as agriculture or mining. The individuals and corporations trying to construct and maintain wireless systems encountered many of the same problems as did E. C. Benedict, and the Amazon Wireless experiences serve as a fairly typical (if somewhat drama-laden) example of setbacks and inconsistencies. In Uruguay, the federal government closed all privately operated stations in 1912, preferring instead to encourage the Uruguayan military to own and operate all means of radio communications.[25] United Wireless, National Electric Signalling Company, and American Marconi all attempted to secure concessions so they might operate in Cuba; United Wireless also tried to set up shop in Mexico. However, the U.S. Navy was generally disposed against Cuban investments and at best preferred that any concessions given in Cuba be of a short duration, lessening the value of any agreements that the companies might reach. Any chances of success in Mexico were scotched by the internal corporate problems at United Wireless in 1911.[26]

A number of American mining corporations set up wireless systems in Mexico. The American Smelting and Refining Company conducted a number of radio experiments in the early 1900s.[27] The Lluvia de Oro Gold Mining Company had installed a system so it might communicate with its headquarters in the United States. However, the station received little cooperation from the revolutionary Mexican government, and the revolutionaries tried to shut down the wireless system.[28] Other American-owned wireless systems in Mexico included the system of the Cananea Consolidated Copper Company and a system at the Chispas Mine, both in northern Mexico. The Cananea system was shut down in 1914 by order of the Mexican government, but the receiver at the Chispas Mine was allowed to remain. This latter installation had been in place since at least 1907; the operators once told the American consul in Nogales that they had listened in on President Theodore Roosevelt's order to send the American naval fleet on a world cruise.[29]

Not all American corporations were stymied in their efforts to build wireless systems in Latin America. For example, although regulations in Venezuela mitigated against private ownership of wireless systems, the Canadian-Venezuelan Ore Company had been granted a waiver and installed a wireless system in 1912.

Despite its name, it was an American corporation headquartered in Philadelphia.[30] Probably the best-known example of a successful American corporation using wireless in Latin America as an adjunct to their overall operations during the early 1900s is the United Fruit Company. United Fruit began wireless experiments around the same time as Amazon Wireless; in 1903, they established a system between Port Limon, Costa Rica and Bocas del Toro in Panama. The link spanned about seventy miles and was the first in a growing chain of stations between North and Central America.[31] Central America did not enjoy the reliable undersea cable communications more common to the rest of the Western Hemisphere, and reliable and rapid communications would be essential to shipping produce on a regular basis and meeting the shifting demands of North American and European markets. United Fruit had been an early purchaser of Lee DeForest's equipment; for the first few years, progress was again slow, and static problems were common. In 1908, United Fruit began adding equipment purchased from Reginald Fessenden and National Electric Signalling Company, in part because of the clear signal given out by Fessenden from his experimental station in Brant Rock.[32] A major effort toward expansion and modernization came in 1912 with the purchase of the Wireless Speciality and Apparatus Company, which held patent rights to the crystal detector, one of the simplest and most effective reception devices available through the mid-1920s.[33] United Fruit then formed a new subsidiary, the Tropical Radio Telegraph Company, in 1913 and invested $700,000 in equipment. That same year, the company launched its "Great White Fleet" of passenger steamships. By 1921, annual expenditures in radio averaged more than $260,000, with installations in Colombia, Costa Rica, Panama, Cuba, Guatemala, Honduras, Jamaica, and Nicaragua.[34]

Why did United Fruit eventually succeed and U.S. Rubber fail in their efforts to maintain and expand a privately owned wireless system in Latin America? In part, the problems of U.S. Rubber can be traced to the extreme difficulties of working in the Amazon valley. Not only was transportation and erection of equipment difficult, but the vagaries of the electromagnetic spectrum in that part of the world also puzzled radio engineers for years. Almost a decade elapsed before Amazon Wireless transmitted intelligible signals on a consistent basis. Although United Fruit also operated in remote areas, they did not generally experience problems of physical environments to the degree of Amazon Wireless. However, logistics and the spectrum variance cannot fully account for the relative success and failure of the two systems.

Another factor that must be considered is the nature of the products the wireless systems served. For United Fruit, plantations were immediately established rather than any dependence on wild harvesting (if such a thing were even possible). This meant that United Fruit could rely on a relatively stable production base each year, and could promote expansion by known methods of acquiring and clearing land and adding labor. The political and social inequalitites and problems these methods caused at a local level were generally not a concern of popular consciousness and corporate public relations as is the case today. When United Fruit introduced a passenger steamship line, the new subsidiary meshed nicely with the company's growing wireless system because wireless and maritime commerce were clearly inseparable by the 1910s. In North America, the United Fruit wireless system eventually became the major commercial wireless alternative to the European-operated systems of Marconi and Telefunken of Germany such as American Marconi and the Atlantic Communications Company, a Telefunken subsidiary.

U.S. Rubber, on the other hand, tied its wireless system to a raw commodity that could not be controlled by any known production methods. The wild rubber harvest in the Amazon valley was a dicey proposition at best. No one could be sure which trees were tapped out, or how far gatherers would have to penetrate the rain forest. Each new station trying to keep up with the wild rubber harvest promised to be an exercise in frustration. To their credit, Benedict and others saw that Amazon Wireless could play a greater role in the regional economy beyond coordinating the rubber needs of the parent company, and as an economic entity could possibly become interdependent of the annual rubber harvest. However, a complicated concession arrangement and the protectionist stance of the Brazilian government in favor of the Brazilian Telegraph Administration reduced the fate of Amazon Wireless to a question not of whether to submit to expropriation, but of how much indemnity to hope for.

Finally, the differences in American foreign policy execution from Central to South America played a part in the success of

United Fruit and in the failure of Amazon Wireless. United Fruit operated and prospered in the one area of the world where U.S. influence undoubtedly dominated: Central America has a continuing history of U.S. economic, diplomatic, and military intervention in the internal affairs of the various nations.[35] The overwhelming influence the United States generated over Central American affairs proved beneficial to the new interests of United Fruit in several areas. The company never faced any significant opposition from European wireless companies, although this would change during World War I. No indigenous companies surfaced to challenge the dominance of United Fruit. Finally, no Central American governments offered opposition. This absence of governmental opposition meant that United Fruit never faced legislation that would drastically alter expansion of its wireless system. Any legislation that did exist was invariably based on American legislation or drafted with the advice of American officials. In addition, United Fruit could depend on the cooperation and support of American military forces, whether through intervention to protect corporate interests or technical cooperation from the wireless work of the U.S. Navy.[36] The American military presence in Panama and the Canal Zone certainly did not harm the United Fruit Company. Although American influence did not completely control all affairs of the region, influence was so dominant that it created a vacuum or void in which United Fruit channeled its interests and grew accordingly. This void was in fact an excellent environment for the company could prosper.

The situation in the Amazon valley—and in all of South America— was quite different. American diplomacy had yet to approach the levels of influence in South America that were the custom in Central America. Despite a growing American presence in the region's global relations, South America remained the domain of European (especially British and German) diplomacy and finance. Undoubtedly, American business and government leaders saw South America as an extremely important area for promotion of American interests, but the gains were inconsistent and all too often temporary. As a by-product of diplomatic inconsistencies, Amazon Wireless faced strong competition from European wireless concerns including Marconi, Telefunken, and various French companies. Strong competition also emerged from indigenous developments, such as the work of the Brazilian Telegraph Administration. In turn, the Brazilian Telegraph Administration received strong support from the other branches and agencies of the Brazilian federal government. In the face of a confused situation in wireless concessions, American diplomats simply could not push the Amazon Wireless position through, and admitted as much to Benedict. Neither could the State Department procure an expropriation fee that was close to the original demands of investors. Finally, American military presence in Brazil and South America was occasional at best. Although it is true that the U.S. Navy made forays in the areas during problems such as the Brazilian naval crisis of the 1890s, and the State Department played a vital role in opening the Amazon River to international commerce in the 1870s and 1880s, the effectiveness of American governmental leaders in supporting and promoting American investments in Brazil and South America did not match their successes in Central America.

The problems and ineffectiveness of American diplomacy in South America did not suddenly appear during the trials and tribulations of Amazon Wireless. Indeed, shortcomings were recognized by some, such as Secretary of State William Henry Seward, soon after the American Civil War, and became more acute during the economic upheavals that shook the United States between approximately 1870 and 1890.[37] A series of boom and bust cycles had led to increasingly unstable manufacturing and agricultural industries, spurring longer and longer periods of mass unemployment that promoted labor unrest. The upheaval was caused by a new development in the American economy: for the first time, the domestic economy could not regularly come close to absorbing most of the agricultural and industrial output of American commerce. The new inability to absorb growth in production caused business upheaval, unstable employment, and labor unrest. The foundations of American social structure were at least shaking, if not indeed crumbling.

What was to be done? In the early 1890s, a new consensus—not specifically tied to any single presidential administration or political party but instead fostered by a wide variety of business, government, and social leaders—had fully emerged. The social and economic crises of the past twenty-odd years could only be surpassed through the development of a strong export market and global commerce. If the rest of the world could be encouraged and/

or induced to absorb American "surpluses"—that of course would then no longer be surplus—in agriculture and manufacturing, the American domestic populace would then no longer bear the burden of absorbing such a large percentage of that entire output. New American growth would now occur in areas such as commerce and technology, extending the ideology of manifest destiny beyond the American domestic frontier that had, as Frederick Jackson Turner argued in 1893 to the American Historical Association, finally been conquered. At the same time, global and technological expansion meant that American industry and agriculture could run at or near full capacity, thereby assuring full or nearly full employment and quelling labor unrest.

The means for accomplishment of this task seemed clear to American policymakers of the era: rather than a mimicry of European models of colonialism, a so-called empire of trade might prove to be the "balance wheel"[38] for the American economy. Certain territorial expansions and acquisitions, particularly ports and islands, would prove beneficial in building a trade system into Latin America and Asia, although a full-scale colonization system such as Europe maintained in Africa was both moral and fiscal anathema. So the United States proceeded through the Spanish-American War of 1898, gaining Puerto Rico and the Philippines and controlling Cuba; annexed Hawaii in 1899; inspired the Panama revolution of 1903; picked up Midway, Wake, Guam, and Samoa along the way; and between 1890 and 1905 sent American forces to intervene in Argentina, Haiti, the Bering Sea, Chile, Hawaii, Brazil, Nicaragua, Korea, China, Colombia, Samoa, the Philippines, Honduras, the Dominican Republic, Syria, and Morocco.[39]

Public and private policymakers throughout the United States responded positively to this new consensus. The State Department had begun a vast reorganization in 1890, designed for efficiency in promoting American business overseas. Part of this reorganization included a slowly growing recognition of the importance of controlling the means of global communications as a key element in both domestic and global economic expansion. Although by 1913 much of this reorganization was complete, including a new cabinet-level office with a vision for radio (the Department of Commerce), the changes came too late to help E. C. Benedict. However, American failures in Latin American radio such as Amazon Wireless were about to become the exception rather than the rule.

Notes

1. Susan J. Douglas, *Inventing American Broadcasting 1899–1922* (Baltimore: Johns Hopkins University Press, 1987); also see Hugh G. J. Aitken, *Syntony and Spark: The Origins of Radio* (New York: John Wiley and Sons, 1976) and *The Continuous Wave: Technology and American Radio 1900–1932* (Princeton: Princeton University Press, 1985); Leonard S. Reich, *The Making of American Industrial Research: Science and Business at G.E. and Bell, 1876–1926* (Cambridge: Cambridge University Press, 1985); George Wise, *Willis R. Whitney, General Electric, and the Origins of U.S. Industrial Research* (New York: Columbia University Press, 1985).

2. Douglas, *Inventing American Broadcasting*, pp. 3–22, 65.

3. Ibid., p. 86; Aitken, *The Continuous Wave*, chap. 2; Gleason Archer, *History of Radio to 1926* (New York: American Historical Society, 1938) and *Big Business and Radio* (New York: American Historical Society, 1939); Helen M. Fessenden, *Fessenden* (New York: Coward-McCann, 1940); Rupert Maclaurin, *Invention and Innovation in the Radio Industry* (New York: Macmillian, 1949); Paul Schubert, *The Electric Word: The Rise of Radio*, (New York: Macmillian, 1928).

4. Lee DeForest, *Father of Radio* (Chicago: Wilcox and Follet, 1950); Douglas, *Inventing American Broadcasting*, pp. 29–66; Aitken, *The Continuous Wave*, pp. 162–85; Samuel Lubell, "Magnificent Failure," *Saturday Evening Post*, January 17, 24, 31, 1942; Maclaurin, *Invention and Innovation*; Gerald Tyne, *Saga of the Vacuum Tube* (Indianapolis: Howard W. Sams, 1977); Georgette Carneal, *Conqueror of Space: The Life of Lee DeForest* (New York: Liveright, 1930).

5. Maclaurin, *Invention and Innovation*, provides a chart of DeForest companies on pp. 86–87. In addition, the North American Wireless Company included the United States, Mexico, and Canada; it capitalized in 1910 at $10 million and declared bankruptcy in 1911.

6. Douglas, *Inventing American Broadcasting*, contains one of the most thorough and accurate accounts of the early DeForest companies; unless otherwise indicated, most of the following information on De-Forest is based on Douglas's research. DeForest was associated with at least as many domestic wireless companies as foreign corporations. Douglas also clearly reveals the important contributions to radio research that DeForest received from his fiancee and wife, Nora Stanton Blatch— assistance DeForest never acknowledged in his writings (pp. 173–77).

7. Lubell, "Magnificent Failure."

8. Douglas, *Inventing American Broadcasting*, pp. 183–85.

9. Most of the information on U.S. Rubber and E. C. Benedict comes from: Frank R. Chalk, "The United States and the International Struggle for Rubber, 1914–1941," Ph.D. diss., University of Wisconsin, Madison,

1970; Glenn Babcock, *History of the U.S. Rubber Company* (Bloomington: Indiana Business Reports, 1966); James Lawrence, *The World Struggle with Rubber 1905–1931* (New York: Harper and Row, 1952); Howard Wolf, *Rubber* (New York: Convici-Friede, 1936); U.S. Department of Commerce, "Rubber Production in the Amazon Valley," Trade Promotion Series no. 23 (Washington: Government Printing Office, 1925); Lawrence W. Hill, *Diplomatic Relations Between the United States and Brazil* (Durham: Duke University Press, 1932); Henry Hall, ed., *America's Successful Men of Affairs* (New York: New York Tribune, 1895); Robert Sobel, *The Curbstone Brokers* (New York: Macmillian, 1970); *Who's Who in America 1906–1907*, p. 129.

10. U.S. Rubber Company annual report for 1904, p. 8.

11. Victor Berthold, *The History of the Telephone and Telegraph in Brazil 1851–1921* (New York: American Telephone and Telegraph, 1922); E. C. Benedict, Amazon Wireless, to Secretary of State Elihu Root, 11 May 1907, Record Group (RG) 59, numerical file no. 7175, Department of State, National Archives, Washington (DSNA); Edwin Morgan, U.S. Ambassador to Brazil, to State Department, 8 October 1912, RG 59, (decimal file) 832.74am1/32, DSNA.

12. American Consul to Para William Pickerell to State Department, 13 July 1911, RG 59, 832.74am1/5, DSNA.

13. E. M. Backus, Amazon Wireless, to Root, 22 January 1908; Benedict to Root, 18 January 1908, both RG 59, no. 7175, DSNA. International Telegraph Construction Company was a supplier to many government wireless systems, including the U.S. Navy, before its purchase by United Wireless in 1908.

14. U.S. Minister to Brazil Irving Dudley to State Department, 11 May 1907, RG 59, no. 7175, DSNA.

15. Benedict to Root, 18 January 1908; Backus to Root, 22 January 1908, both in RG 59, no. 7175, DSNA.

16. Root to Backus, 12 May 1908, RG 59, no. 7175, DSNA.

17. Transcript of discussion between Amazon Wireless investors and State Department, 23 August 1911, RG 59, 832.74.am1/7, DSNA. Also see Benedict to Assistant Secretary of State Huntington Wilson, 24 August 1911, RG 59, 832.74am1/8, DSNA.

18. Benedict to Wilson, 24 August 1911, RG 59, 832.74am1/8, DSNA.

19. George B. Rives, American legation, Rio De Janeiro to State Department, 9 February 1912, RG 59, 832.74am1/21, DSNA.

20. Clipping from *Correio Da Manha*, Rio de Janeiro, 19 March 1912, in Rives to State Department, Washington, 20 March 1912, RG 59, 832.74am1/24, DSNA.

21. U.S. Ambassador to Brazil Edwin Morgan to State Department, 8 October 1912, RG 59, 832.74am1/32, DSNA. In the final symbolic quest, wireless reached Antarctica in 1912 during an expedition led by the Australian Douglas Mawson. See Roland Huntford, *Scott and Amundsen* (New York: Putnam, 1979), p. 304n. Although Amazon Wireless is probably the most poignant example, the score of American corporations

experimenting with the uses of wireless as an adjunct to their business operations in Latin America during this period all helped to advance the growth of wireless into the third world. On the importance of Brazilian business communications, see Eugene W. Ridings, "Business Interest Groups and Communications: The Brazilian Experience in the Nineteenth Century," *Luso-Brazilian Review* 20 (Winter 1983): 241–57.

22. Morgan to State Department, 14 November 1912, RG 59, 832.74am1/34; Benedict to Secretary of State Philander Knox, 26 December 1912, RG 59, 832.74am1/35; Morgan to State Department, 20 March 1913, RG 59, 832.74am1/47; Benedict to Second Assistant Secretary of State Alvey A. Adee, 22 March 1913, RG 59, 832.74am1/48; Adee to Benedict, 12 July 1913, RG 59, 832.74am1/63; all DSNA.

23. Chalk, "The International Struggle for Rubber," discusses the symbolic importance of the rubber industry to the State Department.

24. In fact, this viewpoint served as policy for a short time during and after World War I, as is discussed in later chapters.

25. American consul to Uruguay Frederic Gooding to State Department, 20 April 1912, RG 59, 833.74/4, DSNA.

26. American Minister to Cuba John Jackson to State Department, 6 May 1910, RG 59, 837.74/-, DSNA; Adee to John Griggs, American Marconi, 22 July 1912, RG 59, 837.74/28, DSNA; Gaston Schmitz, American consul, Aguascalientes, to State Department, 5 April 1912, RG 59, 812.74/2, DSNA.

27. Schmitz to State Department, 5 April 1912, RG 59, 812.74/2, DSNA.

28. Thomas Littlepage, Merchantile Trust Company of St. Louis (the parent corporation the Lluvia de Oro Gold Mining Company) to Secretary of State William Jennings Bryan, 15 May 1915, RG 59, 812.74/36, DSNA. Littlepage asked for Bryan's help, noting "this station is not in any sense a Mexican government station. It is a private station, belonging to the mining company, and the only necessity for its use is for communicaton between the mining company and its American office and other points in the United States strictly on business matters . . . it hardly seems fair that the owners of this property should be deprived of the only possible means of communication with it."

29. W. E. Chapman, American consul, Nogales, to State Department, 19 April 1917, RG 59, 812.74/79, DSNA.

30. American Consul Thomas Voetter to State Department, 23 December 1912, RG 59, 831.74/3, DSNA. In 1916, a group of Russian investors, claiming to have the backing of William Randolph Hearst, attempted to gain permission to build a number of wireless stations in Venezuela. See American Minister to Venezuela Preston McGoodwin to State Department, 9 September 1916, RG 59, 831.74/11, DSNA.

31. The work of the United Fruit Company in radio is discussed in a number of standard broadcast history texts, including Christoper Sterling and John Kittross, *Stay Tuned: A Concise History of American*

Broadcasting (Belmont: Wadsworth, 1978), chap. 2; Archer, *History of Radio*; Schubert, *The Electric Word*. Also see the annual reports of the United Fruit Company from 1900–1929 for capsule summaries of their radio activities.

32. Douglas, *Inventing American Broadcasting*, pp. 95–97, 161.

33. The crystal detector was eventually surpassed by improvements in vacuum tubes and reception devices that utilized feedback, such as the heterodyne. Crystal detectors remained a staple of hobbyists and amateur radio enthusiasts and still are often included in radio kits and hobbyists' packages.

34. United Fruit Company annual report for 1913; "Report on United Fruit Radio activities," file 11–14-5, Box 85, Owen D. Young Papers, Van Hornesville N.Y. (hereafter Young Papers).

35. Walter LaFeber, *Inevitable Revolutions: The United States in Central America* (New York: W. W. Norton, 1983).

36. Susan J. Douglas, "The Navy Adopts the Radio, 1899–1919," in *Military Enterprise and Technological Change*, ed. Merritt Roe Smith (Boston: MIT Press, 1985).

37. The following analysis of American diplomatic history during the latter third of the nineteenth century generally follows the narrative construction advanced by the revisionists of the 1950s and 1960s. This school of thought is perhaps best exemplified by the work of a number of scholars at the University of Wisconsin during the period, especially William Appleman Williams, although it is by no means confined to that university. Seminal works include William Appleman Williams, *The Tragedy of American Diplomacy* (New York: Dell, 1959); William Appleman Williams, *Empire as a Way of Life* (New York: Oxford, 1980); James Weinstein, *The Corporate Ideal in the Liberal State 1900–1918* (Boston: Beacon, 1968); Richard S. Miller, ed., *American Imperialism in 1898: The Quest for National Fulfillment* (New York: John Wiley and Sons, 1980); Thomas McCormick, *China Market: America's Quest for Formal Empire, 1893–1901* (Chicago: Quadrangle, 1967); Richard Werking, *The Master Architects: Building the United States Foreign Service 1890–1913* (Lexington: University Press of Kentucky, 1977); Walter LaFeber, *The New Empire: An Interpretation of American Expansion 1860–1898* (Ithaca: Cornell University Press, 1961); Martin J. Sklar, "Woodrow Wilson and the Political Economy of Modern United States Liberalism," in *A New History of Leviathan*, ed. Ronald Radosh and Murray Rothbard (New York: Dutton, 1972); Carl Perrini, *Heir to Empire: United States Economic Diplomacy 1916–1923* (Pittsburgh: University of Pittsburgh Press, 1969). For analyses of the revisionist historical approach, see Thomas McCormick, "Drift or Mastery? A Corporatist Synthesis for American Diplomatic History," *Reviews in American History* 10 (Winter 1982): 318–30; and David W. Noble, *The End of American History: Democracy, Capitalism, and the Metaphor of Two Worlds in Anglo-American Historical Writing, 1880–1980* (Minneapolis: University of Minnesota Press, 1984).

38. A term coined by Wilbur Carr, an early secretary of commerce. See Werking, *The Master Architects*.

39. This list of interventions from 1890 to 1905 is from Williams, *Empire as a Way of Life*, pp. 108–10, 136–38.

2

Radio and the Rise of an American Military-Industrial Discourse, 1914–18

As 1913 ended, the Brazilian Telegraph Administration continued to formulate plans for a national wireless telegraphy system. The Brazilians envisioned sixty new radio stations by the end of the decade, although, as U.S. Ambassador Edwin Morgan commented, "the installation of the 60 stations . . . will cost in the neighborhood of 13 million dollars and there is no immediate prospect that the work will be undertaken in the large scale which has been sketched."[1] Further, Morgan saw no dangerous competition for established American and European cable companies, which meant that American business interests in Brazil—and by extension Latin America—could continue to rely on the communications services already in operation. However, a growing recognition of the inadequacies of such systems frustrated public and private policymakers, especially because these inadequacies seriously hampered the otherwise bright prospects for American expansion into Latin American national economies.

The heightened resolve of American diplomats and business leaders for global expansion led to greater cooperation between American businessmen and American government representatives in Brazil. This new cooperation spread into aspects of Brazilian cultural activities. In 1913, the American consul to Rio de Janeiro, Albert Gottschalk, met on several occasions with the director of the Commercial Museum of Brazil to discuss the establishment of a permanent exhibit of American-manufactured goods and new American industrial innovations. Gottschalk believed that "if an exhibition of such goods were organized and handled properly, a market in many articles now unknown in Brazil could be created here."[2] The Commercial Museum was designed to display objects from several nations, and Gottschalk also hoped that young Brazilians working in local importing houses would recognize the comparative quality of American products.

The American group in Rio de Janeiro did not end their work with the museum exhibit; in May of 1915, a movement began within the group that led to the formation of a local chapter of the United States Chamber of Commerce. Local American business representatives active in the establishment of the chapter included executives from Standard Oil, U.S. Steel, the Singer Sewing Machine Company, Otis Elevator, General Electric, National City Bank, and the New York Life Insurance Company.[3] Gottschalk procured a copy of Chamber of Commerce bylaws from Washington, and within a year, the Rio group had its own journal, the *Quarterly*. In the introductory issue, the editors summed up the purpose for creating a chapter and stated its goals:

> THE QUARTERLY, therefore, in making its initial bow to the public, takes pleasure in saying that it comes forward between covers of Brazilian-made domestic paper.
>
> Its inside is printed on paper from the United States.
>
> Its text is printed some of it in English and some of it in Portugese, the language of Brazil.
>
> Its typographic work is done by a Brazilian printing company; its illustrations are electrotypes done in Brazil.
>
> It has not, however, like Dr. Jekyll and Mr. Hyde, a dual personality.
>
> There is nothing "hyphenated" about it.
>
> But it is, as it should be, thoroughly Pan-American.[4]

In the eyes of the Rio group, Pan-Americanism meant the development of interlocking commercial and cultural ties between the United States and Brazil, and between the United States and all of Central and South America. However, the nations and regions of the Western Hemisphere did not enjoy hemispheric communications owned and operated by North and South American governments and corporations, but rather they remained an area dependent on, if not dominated by, European-controlled communication systems. Before World War I, various British cable corporations represented the major controlling force in communications matters.[5]

Great Britain had built an enviable position in Latin American commerce, including all major areas of Latin American economic activity: agriculture, finance, mining, railroads, public utilities, and communications (manufacturing remained underdeveloped). British finance capitalists, in close cooperation with British diplomats, had proven adept at developing industries abroad that then became dependent on British support for their continued growth. The establishment of British technology at a national scale for a newly developing industry, railroad, or utility had led to a lucrative (and noncompetitive) trade in the replacement and maintenance services.[6] However, new war priorities meant that Great Britain could no longer command its previous influence in Latin America, particularly in South American trade and commerce. British investment and influence did not simply vanish, but American interests began to fill a void that grew during the early stages of the war. In hindsight, observers can conclude that World War I coincided with a decline of British influence in South America, but history is written retrospectively—for American policymakers in 1915, the decline was not completely clear, and in some areas British dominance seemed to be increasing. Radio appeared to be a growing area of British influence. Various branches of the Marconi Company negotiated and secured several wireless concessions in South America just as the war began.[7]

While the aims and goals of the Marconi companies were alarmingly evident to American policymakers concerned with international communications, the aims and goals—much less the organization—of the American radio industry left much to be desired. A confusing patent situation had developed within the American radio manufacturing industry, and the confusion acted as a fetter on growth. It appeared that no single corporation could use all of the latest technology to produce a reliable radio system with transoceanic range through its own patents; however, ongoing research indicated that impressive breakthroughs took place when conflicting patents came together. The research laboratories at General Electric and American Telephone and Telegraph conducted much of this new research.[8]

The General Electric laboratory began its operations in 1900, and as early as 1901, Reginald Fessenden had requested assistance in constructing a high-speed alternator necessary for continuous-wave transmission. Although radio research did not seem to be an area for immediate industrial applications in 1901, the laboratory functioned with some autonomy (in fact, it was the first large-scale corporate research laboratory in the United States to enjoy such autonomy), and research did not always need to show immediate promise for manufacturing and sales. The early work with Fessenden's alternator further introduced some of the General Electric researchers to the vagaries of radio; they were, of course, already aware of theories and experiments in electromagnetism and wave transmission. By 1909, radio activities at the General Electric laboratory included work on high-speed alternators and on the properties of the vacuum tube, work that coincided with research on the fundamental aspects of the incandescent light bulb. Interest centered on two- and three-element vacuum tubes; three-element tubes had tremendous possibilities as amplification devices that could boost weak signals in a receiver as well as boost signal strength at transmission. Operating with adequate financial resources and support staff, General Electric researchers put the tubes through a rigorous testing beyond that Lee DeForest had been able to do.[9] By 1914, scientists at General Electric agreed that radio research in general, and the three-element vacuum tube in particular, had great commercial potential, but scientists and executives also ruefully recognized that for the moment General Electric did not hold all of the patents necessary to realize such potential.

Although executives, engineers, and scientists at General Electric became interested in radio earlier than the research laboratories of other corporations in the American electrical manufacturing industry, interest did not languish at those corporations, either. Like General Electric, American Telephone and Telegraph's initial interest in radio was piqued by Fessenden, who demonstrated his methods for engineers in 1906. From 1906 to 1912, American Telephone and Telegraph engineers conducted transoceanic experiments with voice equipment (wireless telephony, or radio telephony, the forerunner of radio broadcasting) but could not generate enough power with spark-gap apparatus.[10] In 1912, DeForest demonstrated his three-element vacuum tube for Bell Labs, and the laboratory subsequently investigated transcontinental and transoceanic wireless telegraphy and telephony using banks of vacuum tubes. In one experiment, a voice message sent by American Telephone and Telegraph from Washington, D.C. to the California coast was also heard by a wireless operator in Hawaii.[11] As a result of this activity, American Telephone and Telegraph had a strong research interest in radio by 1915, and even controlled a number of patents, but could not control the radio industry solely on the strength of its own patents. General Electric and American Telephone and Telegraph found themselves in similar patent stalemates.

While industrial giants such as General Electric and American Telephone and Telegraph had a growing interest in radio, policy-makers must have wondered if these companies, or if any American corporations, would ever play a prominent role in international communications or in developing the communications systems of Latin American nations. The organizational problems of the American radio industry, the growing presence of the Marconi companies, and the apparent desires of Latin American nations such as Brazil, Uruguay, and Mexico to control their own domestic wireless communications led American political leaders interested in the global growth of radio to consider a foreign policy that promoted government ownership of Latin American wireless communications. If Latin American governments at least owned their own wireless systems, then the spread of Marconi and other European communications corporations in the region might be slowed or even halted, which would eventually eradicate American business dependence on the European communications systems in hemispheric trade. Furthermore, governments would still need equipment suppliers and perhaps even assistance in systems operations, which the American radio industry might someday provide.

By 1915, Brazil had shown its desire to control internal wireless communications on several occasions, including its expropriation of Amazon Wireless in 1913. However, Brazil's position on trans-oceanic wireless remained ambiguous. On the one hand, concessions with foreign corporations such as the Marconi interests continued to be discussed as a possibility; on the other, the Brazilian Telegraph Administration achieved a number of remarkable breakthroughs in long-distance radio experiments. The Brazilian Telegraph Administration began installing wireless on Brazilian warships in 1910, and a station on the island of Fernando de Naronha established communications with Paris and with Dakar, Senegal in 1911.[12] In the aftermath of the *Titanic* disaster, Brazil (as did virtually all nations) adopted the recommendations of the London Conference on Wireless Communications held in 1912. This led to a rapid increase of shipboard and coastal stations in

Brazil and in all of Latin America. In 1913, Brazil's minister of foreign affairs, Dr. Lauro Muller, toured the United States and called for greater experimentation in wireless communication between Brazil and the United States.[13] Brazil even planned a station that would reach Cape Town, South Africa. By 1914, as war broke out in Europe, the Brazilian Telegraph Administration operated a dozen stations on the coast and an additional twenty in the interior.[14]

The conflict in Europe had an immediate effect on transatlantic communications: the transit time of a New York City-London round-trip message via undersea cables jumped from forty minutes to seven hours due to war censorship by British cable operators.[15] The one place where American policymakers moved swiftly concerning radio communications was in Panama, where the outbreak of war prompted Secretary of State William Jennings Bryan to tell the American legation in Panama that "it is of the greatest urgency that this [United States] Government secure immediate and exclusive control over wireless stations throughout Panama and its territorial waters."[16] The Panamanian government conceded to this situation and by the end of August 1914 authorized the complete control of all radio activities within Panama by the United States; the U.S. Navy exercised this control through the duration of the war.[17] In the Pacific, the new U.S. Navy wireless chain handled some commercial traffic, which partially relieved the situation in that part of the world,[18] but overall, the slowdowns once again drove home America's communication deficiencies. The British censorship exacerbated years of mounting frustration over the lack of American international communications capabilities. Now the recent gains by the Marconi interests in South America threatened to extend the old problem into the new field of radio.

In June 1915, Bryan received a letter from Secretary of the Navy Josephus Daniels discussing the radio problem in South America. Daniels suggested that European and Asiatic operation of South American wireless communications raised a host of problems, including whether the systems would follow the guidelines of neutrality. The time was propitious for advising the South American nations to consider "controlling their own radio stations completely and perfectly, so no good reason could be advanced that might lead to a suspected breach of neutrality" on their part.

"Further, it is thought desireable to bring to the attention of these countries the advantages to be derived from the installation of radio apparatus of the American make due to the very high state of the art" of American radio.[19] Of course, this could well lead to agreements about communications with the U.S. Navy and American commercial shipping, and with American stations in places like Panama. Daniels was one of the first to argue against European expansion in Latin American radio by combining economic nationalism, the "Old World-New World" metaphor, and American technological superiority. Over the next few years, this combination would become a widely shared ideology among American policymakers and be initially targeted at the various companies associated with Gugliemo Marconi.

Marconi had first incorporated around his radio patents in 1897, and the parent company in Great Britain—British Marconi—had genuine global reach. As Marconi interests expanded beyond England, they formed an associated or branch corporation in each nation. In theory, this international system promoted each company as a separate and distinct entity, and citizens of various nations held a portion of the stock in their national branch. In practice, the parent company in London restricted the autonomy of each branch, and despite attempts to convey the opposite, each branch was effectively mediatized by the home office. American Marconi was one of the biggest branches of the group. The parent company sent a representative to Argentina as early as 1910 to promote wireless telegraphy and to attempt to secure a concession for exclusive rights in Argentina. Although the Argentine government was interested in what Marconi had to offer, they made no initial committments.[20] Marconi had better success in Chile; the Chilean government had sent their director of wireless telegraph service on a European fact-finding tour in 1910. While traveling, he contacted Marconi and the Telefunken investors, and both corporations began installing equipment in Chile in 1911.[21] American Marconi interests secured a concession in August 1913 to construct and operate a wireless relay station in Brazil for completing a link between the United States and Argentina. However, Foreign Minister Muller blocked the signing of the concessions in the summer of 1915 because another American company, the Federal Telegraph Company (operating through its subsidiary, Federal Holdings) had visited Brazil in hope of securing a concession for communication with the United States.[22] Edwin Morgan pointed out that both companies had American financing, but he questioned whether his support of American Marconi truly followed the principle of American business expansion in light of American Marconi's ties to the parent company.[23] The interest shown by the Brazilian government in granting these concessions may seem somewhat contradictory in light of their earlier expropriation of Amazon Wireless and their unabashed suport of Brazilian experiments in radio. Despite the success of the Brazilian Telegraph Administration, Brazilian officials such as Muller considered it feasible for foreign interests to operate international wireless communications. Presumably this would allow the Brazilian Telegraph Administration to concentrate on developing domestic wireless communications (such as the 1913 plan) and later move into global communications.

The Brazilian Congress debated the relative merits of American Marconi and Federal Telegraph into November 1915. Marconi interests organized a Brazilian wireless company composed of leaders from the Brazilian Navy, Brazilian journalists, and Brazilian finance capitalists. British Marconi would provide technical support. Morgan advised Federal Telegraph to set up a similar structure.[24] In 1913, the intransigence of the Brazilian government had led to the demise of Amazon Wireless; two years later, the delay in unraveling the concessions for international communications worked in favor of American interests. American policymakers sharpened their opposition to the Marconi group, with Daniels pointing out that Gugliemo Marconi himself was a member of the board of directors on six different branch operations in addition to the parent company. Other connections between British Marconi and American Marconi made it "difficult to reconcile the statements of the various companies except under the assumption that to all intents and purposes they are but one company with two names, or that the American Marconi company is but a branch of the parent company." Diplomatic support of American Marconi in Brazil would actually undermine American interests and goals and support the "interests of foreign capital" rather than strengthen Pan-American bonds.[25] Daniels fully supported Federal Telegraph, noting they had no known foreign investment and also used equipment compatible with the U.S. Navy system. Alvey A. Adee of the State Department added that "Marconi is *It* everywhere" and the compatibility of Federal Telegraph encouraged technological uniformity throughout the Western Hemisphere. He recommended that the State Department support Federal Telegraph and also encouraged the Navy to develop a "paramount influence in the operation of the whole chain of North and South American wireless by a uniform system."[26] Perhaps Adee foresaw a longer conjuncture out of this series of events in which the Marconi interests would eventually be driven out of the Western Hemisphere altogether; in any case, he urged American diplomats to back Federal Telegraph exclusively, and later added that "it is not so long ago that the Marconi equipped vessels refused to take notice of S.O.S. calls from vessels using other systems."[27] American Marconi asked for further consideration, reminding the Navy that Marconi stations had provided free service during the American occupation of Veracruz in 1914 and arguing that "radio communication, because of its very nature, must be international in scope, for it is only in this way that its greatest opportunities for expansion and development can be taken advantage of."[28] Nevertheless, American policymakers in government organizations now officially frowned upon the international expansion of American Marconi. The company had become a paradox, at odds with the long-range ideology supporting the global expansion of American corporations.

The Navy continued to speak out against American Marconi. Assistant Secretary of the Navy Franklin D. Roosevelt suggested that American diplomats "lend their support to corporations which have no foreign connections, and which can furnish completely apparatus of purely American manufacture." The financial structure of American Marconi meant that "patent issues might tend to give the Engish Company too great a control over the American Company. . . ."[29] American corporations capable of participating in areas of radio activity, particularly manufacturing, stood to grow steadily and even to prosper under the shape of this forming policy. Federal Telegraph, using equipment compatible with Navy wireless, could clearly benefit through cooperation with American military interests.

Federal Telegraph had established a commercial wireless service in all the major West Coast cities of the United States by 1908 and had done well, handling many messages and "serving several thousand customers, among which are included all of the leading banks, corporations, and businesses in the cities that are served."[30] Service to Honolulu began in 1911, and by 1912, demand warranted expansion to day and night service between San Francisco and Honolulu. Hawaiian newspapers were the biggest clients. When naval tests in long-distance signaling bridged the gap between Washington, D.C. and Honolulu, the government awarded a contract to Federal Telegraph for the construction of a major naval station in Panama. The U.S. Navy had long held commanding influence over all uses of radio in Panama, as well as in the Canal Zone itself. An agreement between the United States and the Panamanian government concerning wireless telegraphy gave the Navy the right to name who could and could not install and use any kind of radio equipment in Panama. Such influence by the Navy was significant in view of the canal itself, as well as for the fact that the isthumus proper was the only landmass in the hemisphere where one wireless station (using the most advanced technology of its day) could simultaneously communicate with ships on both the Atlantic and Pacific oceans.[31] In addition, Federal Telegraph equipped forty-five warships and land installations. The Navy also outfitted a number of other land stations with equipment compatible with the Federal Telegraph system.

Although the equipment of Federal Telegraph did not have the ability to send a signal from one point to anywhere on the globe, the company led the way among American corporations in establishing a relay chain for international communications. Federal Telegraph also built a high-power American naval wireless station in the Philippines. The distance between the Manila station and the Honolulu station was about the same as from New York City to Buenos Aires. When Federal Telegraph reached the Navy station in Panama from its Honolulu station, the distance exceeded that of any regular previous transmission and was, in the eyes of the company, "probably a world's record. . . . These scientific and commercial developments of the company justify it in reaching out for a broader market and consequently South America had naturally been considered as one of the most attractive fields for this work."[32]

The Navy relationship with Federal Telegraph eventually led to policy problems concerning other American manufacturers using different wireless systems. In September 1916, new investors in the National Electric Signalling Company approached Secretary of the Treasury William McAdoo with plans for a radio system uniting North, Central, and South America. The company planned to build eight stations (four on each South American coast), but were "not ready to go any further in formulating the plans until we learn the attitude of our Government in reference to such a project," particularly desiring the opinion of a new interdepartmental advisory group investigating the options of government ownership of wireless communications in the Western Hemisphere.[33] McAdoo supported the plan, but the Navy disapproved, feeling convinced Latin American nations should

> own and operate their own radio stations and that no encouragement should be given to any firm in the United States or elsewhere to build stations in Central and South America for other than government ownership except when it is clear that the government concerned does not desire government ownership . . . we should be more concerned in government ownership and operation of stations on the American continents than in the interests of any radio concern in the United States.[34]

The State Department agreed and denied support for the proposal.

American Marconi and its investors, although set back by the policy in Brazil and Latin America, actively continued plans for expansion despite the closed view of government officials. The General Electric Company negotiated an exclusivity arrangement with the Marconi interests for the use of new equipment suitable for long-distance transmission and reception. The keystones of this arrangement were vacuum tube receivers (which Marconi interests could use in Europe, as they held European patent rights by virtue of their own research in tubes) and most important, a powerful new transmisson system based on a high-speed alternator developed at the General Electric laboratory (sometimes referred to as the Alexanderson alternator, so named for the project's principal researcher). Marconi corporations would operate, and General Electric would manufacture, the system.[35]

The first station completed by General Electric for American Marconi began operations in the United States in 1917; a second U.S. station was completed in 1918, and its transmissions could be heard throughout Europe. This second station, however, never became part of American Marconi but instead operated under the jurisdiction of the Navy. Upon American entry into World War I on

April 6, 1917, all radio stations in the United States and its territories were seized by the American government for national security measures as required by the Radio Act of 1912. The Navy took over station operations for the war's duration.[36]

The U.S. Navy, rather than any single corporation, played the leading role in American radio development during World War I. Naval activities in radio included the purchase of Federal Telegraph in early 1918. Acting through the powers of the United States Shipping Board, the Navy authorized the purchase of Federal Telegraph, ostensibly to block any possible purchase by Marconi interests. In addition to the purchase of Federal Telegraph, the Navy acquired the American rights to several German radio patents after they had been seized by Attorney General Alexander Mitchell Palmer, who used his wartime powers as alien enemy property custodian.[37]

The military demand for radio equipment led the American government to guarantee any manufacturer against patent infringement suits on radio equipment. This promotion of patent indemnity freed all manufacturers, including General Electric, American Telephone and Telegraph, and Westinghouse, to apply principles and methods from each other's research laboratories to their own commercial output. Naval shipboard installations, in great demand early in the war, used the newest advances in vacuum tube construction worked out by General Electric and American Telephone and Telegraph from 1908 to 1915. Throughout the war, the Navy operated high-power transmitting stations, and also operated receiving stations designed to listen in on all audible signals, no matter the source of transmission, as well as handle regular military and diplomatic traffic. The work of these receiving stations, although not as well known today as the high-power transmitting stations, was nevertheless extremely important. The Navy Department in Washington told Captain Allessandro Fabbri, the commander of one such receiving station, in September 1917 that the "daily log sheet as sent in from your station is becoming of more interest every day. . . ."[38] These receiving stations mark the rise of modern electronic surveillance and intelligence-gathering activities on a global scale by American military and intelligence forces. American expeditionary forces in Europe, as well as the fleet, also needed operators for wireless equipment. Training schools were established in several locations, usually at universities, to provide enlisted men with a background in radio. Such training would affect postwar growth in radio, as a pool of qualified individuals returned from the war and applied their radio experience in areas such as the broadcasting industry. These individuals also swelled the postwar ranks of amateur radio enthusiasts.

Soon after the Armistice, the Creel Committee on Public Information outlined the Navy radio record to the American public.[39] The Navy had rescued radio from the various "wildcat schemes such as United Wireless" and had eliminated the interference in a number of metropolitan areas such as New York City by reducing the number of stations in each area. Navy transmitting and receiving stations had lowered the round-trip message time between New York City and London to ten minutes, even lower than the prewar standard. Although a number of undersea cables had been cut during the war, the scope of the naval radio system was so vast that at no time was it necessary for its transatlantic system to be run at full capacity. The Navy also supplied American merchant vessels with communication officers to assist in radio operations. The expeditionary forces in Europe were not neglected by radio; the Navy and the Creel Committee regularly transmitted everyday news items from home that were printed quickly and posted in areas where American enlisted men congregated.[40] Finally, the Navy and the Creel Committee cooperated in the establishment of an international press service that supplied newspapers throughout the Western Hemisphere and as far away as China with the Allied response to German propaganda, including Germany's influence on Latin American communications.

The German international communications system posed a problem for Allied nations throughout the war. Although the Zimmermann telegram (which proposed an alliance between Germany and Mexico) was among the most sensational examples of German influence, it was not an isolated incident.[41] German radio corporations worked alone and also with the revolutionary Mexican government to build several wireless stations throughout Latin America before the war. For example, in El Salvador, a German-built station had supplied so much propaganda and pro-German information to the region by 1918 that American Minister Boaz Long suggested that American policymakers move directly against Germany by "taking the steps necessary to enable some

American company to acquire the German Telefunken station at San Salvador, so as to break the flow of propaganda and then replace that plant with an American radio station."[42]

In some cases these German stations had been built before the war by private German corporations using wireless telegraphy as an adjunct to their primary activities (such as the systems in Honduras operated by German mining companies and the system in Brazil operated by the Truxilla Railroad Company).[43] The Mexican government also sought out leading amateur radio enthusiasts in Central America, and on occasion gave them gifts of new radio equipment; this equipment was usually capable of receiving powerful Mexican and German stations.[44] Some of the German engineers who installed equipment in Central America had been associated with the Atlantic Communications Company, the German-based radio system on the northeast coast of the United States. Most of these engineers left the United States at the outbreak of war in 1914.[45] The American radio situation in Mexico was chaotic; the debts incurred by the revolutionary government had led Westinghouse and General Electric to refuse to sell radio-related equipment and replacement parts anywhere in Mexico, and so the government had turned completely to German manufacturers.[46] During the war, Mexican stations communicated with German ships and tried to reach the high-power station at Nauen outside of Berlin. The U.S. Navy station in Port Isabel, Texas, reported in March 1917 that "a [Mexican] arc station was heard very distinctly calling POZ [the Nauen call letters] for five minutes . . . the call was very strong, gruff and broken and could be heard at fifteen feet away from the receivers."[47] A few German coffee plantation owners in Mexico also used powerful receiving sets to pick up German news of the war, which they subsequently disseminated by word of mouth in their local communities.[48] Although in general the Caribbean remained free from German wireless installations, Germans did operate a station in the Danish West Indies. This station set up a regular relay between the Danish West Indies and Mexico City in the middle of the night, when no Mexican operators were on call in Mexico City and the station was completely staffed by German engineers. This station may well have been one of the factors that contributed to the American decision to purchase the Danish West Indies in 1917.[49]

German radio interests were also active in South America during World War I. Telefunken engineers built a powerful station in Peru, which brought in pro-German news during the early stages of the war.[50] In 1917, German engineers began constructing a station in Argentina, which they hoped would communicate on a regular basis with Nauen. The installation was hidden on a large, German-owned cattle ranch in the hope that Americans would not find it. Americans did locate the station, however, and arranged for pro-American Argentine military officers to oversee its operations.[51] The Seimens-Schukert Company, another German wireless company, received a concession to construct and operate a station that could communicate with Germany.[52] Siemens-Schukert later tried to import wireless equipment to Argentina via Spain in the hope that this indirect route would escape the eyes of Allied forces.[53] In Brazil, a high-power station supposedly capable of directly reaching Germany had been built in 1912 nearly three thousand miles upriver from the mouth of the Amazon, as an ancillary operation to the Rio Mamore railroad, a German line in northern Brazil. The Brazilian Telegraph Administration used Telefunken equipment extensively in the northern regions of Brazil, and although these stations were government owned and operated, communication with German stations certainly seemed plausible. The emigrant German population in areas such as Pernambuco regularly received German war news via a wireless relay that reached Buenos Aires and passed through Rio de Janeiro. It is unclear whether Germans actually operated their own station in Pernambuco, or whether the information passed through Brazilian stations or reached Pernambuco through shipboard installations.[54] Salesmen and exporters of American radio equipment who had worked the Brazilian market during the preceding ten years attested to Telefunken's exceptional activities in Brazil during the war.[55] In any case, German influence in Latin American communications eventually proved to be no less of a threat to American aims and goals than British interests, although the threat posed by each nation differed.

Thus, the period from 1914–18 held incredible changes for the American radio industry. To call these four years confusing is an understatement, and chaotic is perhaps an exaggeration; an accurate assessment lies somewhere in between. Policymakers during these four years had great difficulty in shaping the growth of the radio industry in harmony with broader American goals and interests. This difficulty stemmed in part from the fact that significantly more policymakers became involved with radio during the war. The Wireless Ship Act of 1910 and the more comprehensive Radio Act of 1912 placed administrative and licensing duties within the Department of Commerce, bringing many individuals from that department into the radio dialogue. Growing military concerns before the war involved policymakers from the Army and Navy. Of course, the beginnings of hostilities in Europe added to the urgency of military voices, and American entry into the war put military concerns in a dominant position for the war's duration. Senators, congressmen, and other government officials added to the cacaphony of opinions on what to do with radio.

New policymakers also came from the private sector, particularly from the larger corporations whose research laboratories had explored the physical properties and technologies of radio. This rising interest in radio research was, on occasion, shared with policymakers from the military branches. American Telephone and Telegraph and General Electric both demonstrated new techniques and approaches in radio to the Navy on several occasions.[56] Although these regular demonstrations are not in themselves indicative of new policy formation, they demonstrate the inception of close ties between the American military and the American radio industry in the area of technological invention and innovation. Military and private policymakers began to realize that their respective views covered a significant amount of common ground. The development and control of international radio communications in Latin America and elsewhere represented one common interest. New private-sector policymakers also emerged from the investors in growing companies such as American Marconi and Federal Telegraph. Again, military ties to these investors appear, especially to Federal Telegraph; even though the Navy opposed American Marconi more often than not, they also appreciated the company's support during the American occupation of Veracruz in 1914. American entry into World War I meant that these new private policymakers had to put military views to the forefront. However, the shift within the American political economy to an institutionalized wartime system provided many opportunities for direct interaction between the public and private sectors through agencies such as the U.S. Shipping Board and the War Industries Board. The voices grew in number and diversity before and during the war, but the political economic structure also grew, encompassed the voices, promoted the discourse, and enveloped the entire system within the ideology of economic nationalism and American technological superiority. True, the growth of the structure during this period often was highly uneven, but capitalism is always marked by uneven development.

Whether uneven or stable, these developments undeniably point to the genesis of a continual and lasting discourse between the participants of what is now identified as the American military-industrial complex. Radio in Latin America was one of the issues—and in fact an important issue—that brought the federal government, the armed forces, and corporate capital together into a common language of global power through economic nationalism and American technological superiority. The control of the means of communication at a global level has been an important component of military-industrial discourse since that discourse's inception, and the proclaiming of social benefits through increased access to information has long been a part of the rationalization process that legitimates the military-industrial complex. This rationalization of course continues; for example, Secretary of State George Schultz commented in 1986 that the Strategic Defense Initiative "is one dramatic example of the impact of intellectual and scientific change in our ways of dealing with the world. SDI can well be described, in fact, as a gigantic information processing system."[57] Schultz's statement demonstrates the power of this discourse, as instruments of death and destruction are disguised within a benign imagery associated with computers and everyday commerce. Susan Douglas, discussing the same time period but using a somewhat different set of questions and almost completely different evidence than I have, has drawn similar conclusions about the relationship between radio, World War I, and the emergence of the modern military-industrial discourse.[58]

Wartime measures for the American radio industry did not in fact impede the industry, but actually allowed radio to coalesce into a viable field of corporate economic activity, largely through the guarantee of patent indemnity that allowed the legal combination of unlicensed patents for commercial production. Of course, American armed forces were the only customers. Under the direction preferred by the military, the only new markets for the American radio industry after the war would be the governments of Latin America and other nations. In anticipation of this direction, the State Department instructed its Latin American officers in May 1918 to prepare a comprehensive report on the status of radio in each Latin American nation.[59] Despite these prospects, the American radio industry might have wondered whether this strategy presented the best opportunity for industrial growth.

Above and beyond the confusion resulting from rapid growth, new policymakers, and war tensions, one aspect of the connection between U.S.-Latin American foreign relations and the emerging American radio industry was abundantly clear by 1918: the shortcomings in American expansion into Latin America and the world at large caused by deficiencies in American-influenced international communications systems. American capital needed its own complete communications system for maximization of the global economy, because such a communications system could solidify the power of the American public sector and could also allow American businesses eventually to transcend economic nationalism and join the leading players on the global stage of capitalism. In order to realize this, and also to advance to a new ideology of international control of capitalism, the American radio industry needed new markets, new directions for growth, and new and innovative uses of radio equipment. Military officials favored government ownership; the Department of Commerce stressed private ownership by American firms; the State Department, for the time being, concentrated on promoting American equipment suppliers regardless of ownership issues.[60] Although an American radio industry had indeed risen during the war, how best to encourage industrial growth, both at home and abroad in the years ahead, loomed as an immediate problem for postwar policymakers.

Notes

1. U.S. Ambassador to Brazil Edwin Morgan to State Department, 19 March 1913, Record Group (RG) 59, 832.74/3, Department of State, National Archives, Washington (DSNA).

2. American Consul Albert Gottschalk to State Department, 20 October 1913, RG 59, 632.11171/1, DSNA.

3. Gottschalk to State Department, 29 May 1915, RG 59, 632.11171/2; Gottschalk to State Department, 26 June 1915, RG 59, 632.11171/4; Gottschalk to State Department, 8 August 1915, RG 59, 632.11171/6; all DSNA. In the report of August 8, Gottschalk said that it seemed assured that a local chamber of commerce would be established: "I have declined thus far to hold any office in the new Chamber—this because I believe the Consulate-General can wield a better and stronger influence by remaining in the background." He reaffirmed one year later that "I should be departing from the truth were I to say that I have not had an intense satisfaction in creating and launching this Chamber. It has seemed to give proof positive to this community, as well as to the Chamber of Commerce of the U.S., that our Consular service was able to do real and lasting work other than merely assisting individuals to buy and sell" (Gottschalk to State Department, 10 August 1916, RG 59, 632.11171/12, DSNA).

4. A copy of the first issue of the *Quarterly* is in Gottschalk to State Department, 29 May 1916, RG 59, 632.11171/11, DSNA.

5. Joseph Tulchin, *The Aftermath of War: World War 1 and U.S. Policy Toward Latin America* (New York: New York University Press, 1971); Michael Hogan, *Informal Entente: The Private Structure of Cooperation in Anglo-American Economic Diplomacy, 1918–1928* (Columbia: University of Missouri Press, 1977); Brady A. Hughes, "Owen D. Young and American Foreign Policy 1919–1929," Ph.D. diss., University of Wisconsin, Madison, 1969; Emily S. Rosenberg, *Spreading the American Dream: American Economic and Cultural Expansion 1890–1945* (New York: Hill and Wang, 1982).

6. Carl Perrini, *Heir to Empire: United States Economic Diplomacy, 1916–1923* (Pittsburgh: University of Pittsburgh Press, 1969), p. 26.

7. George A. Schreiner, *Cables and Wireless and Their Role in the Foreign Relations of the United States* (Boston: Stratford, 1924), pp. 153–54; Josephine Young Case and Everett Needham Case, *Owen D. Young and American Enterprise* (Boston: Godine, 1982), pp. 237–42. After the war, these concessions became part of an American-English-French-German (AEFG) radio consortium that operated in South America. The consortium is discussed in later chapters herein.

8. Most of what follows concerning radio and industrial research comes from Hugh G. J. Aitken, *The Continuous Wave: Technology and American Radio, 1900–1932* (Princeton: Princeton University Press, 1985), chaps. 2, 3, 4; Rupert Maclaurin, *Invention and Innovation in the Radio Industry* (New York: Macmillian, 1949); John G. Glover and William B. Cornell, eds., *The Development of American Industries* (New York: Prentice-Hall, 1941); Leonard S. Reich, *The Making of American Industrial Research: Science and Business at G.E. and Bell, 1876–1926* (Cambridge: Cambridge University Press, 1985); and National Resources Committee, *Technological Trends and National Policy* (Washington: Government Printing Office, 1937), pp. 3–23, 210–88, 315–28. Westinghouse instituted

a laboratory in 1916. Federal Telegraph Company (discussed later in this chapter) was the first American radio manufacturing corporation to develop a wireless system with transoceanic range; Aitken examines this company in detail.

9. Aitken, *The Continuous Wave*, chap. 4, and Maclaurin, *Invention and Innovation in the Radio Industry*, both have excellent discussions of DeForest's research with the three-element tube (his Audion) and the later work of General Electric. Improvements by General Electric included construction of a special furnace that produced a glass shell of increased strength that was virtually free of impurities and had a much higher vacuum level than DeForest had attempted.

10. N. R. Danielian, *ATT: Story of Industrial Conquest* (New York: Vanguard, 1939) is a comprehensive account of the company's early years. Frank C. Waldrop and Joseph Borkin, *Television: The Struggle for Control* (New York: William Morrow, 1938) analyzes the involvement of American Telephone and Telegraph in film and broadcasting. Aitken, *The Continuous Wave*, chap. 2, explains the limits of spark-gap transmission, a method that produced vast interference and made inefficient use of the spectrum. Continuous-wave transmission replaced spark-gap methods during and just after World War I.

11. Douglas, *Inventing American Broadcasting*, p. 241.

12. J. C. Oakenfull, *Brazil in 1911* (London: Butler and Tanner, 1912), p. 134. Fernando de Naronha is in the Atlantic about 250 miles southeast of the mouth of the Amazon River.

13. *New York Journal of Commerce*, 17 July 1913.

14. Pan American Union, *Descriptive Data: Brazil, 1914* (Washington: Government Printing Office, 1914), p. 14.

15. *New York Journal of Commerce*, 24 September 1914.

16. Secretary of State William Jennings Bryan to American legation, Panama City, 13 August 1914, RG 59, 819.74/5a, DSNA.

17. Bryan to Secretary of the Navy Josephus Daniels, 31 August 1914, RG 59, 819.74/59, DSNA. Also see "History of Wireless Telegraph Agreements Between Panama and the United States," memo, Division of Latin American Affairs, 15 May 1914, RG 59, 819.74/46; A. R. Alfaro, Panamanian legation to United States, to Secretary of State Charles Evans Hughes, 19 December 1922, RG 59, 819.74/106; both DSNA.

18. Paul Schubert, *The Electric Word: The Rise of Radio* (New York: Macmillian, 1928), pp. 100–01. The Navy had a station as far as Samoa by 1915; see *New York Journal of Commerce*, 26 April 1915.

19. Daniels to Bryan, 16 June 1915, RG 59, 810.74/-, DSNA.

20. Robert W. Bliss, American chargé d'affaires, Buenos Aires, to State Department, 11 October 1910, RG 59, 835.74/-, DSNA.

21. American Consul to Valparaiso Alfred A. Winslow to State Department, 1 November 1910, RG 59, 825.74/-; Winslow to State Department, 1 May 1911, RG 59, 825.74/1; Winslow to State Department, 24 October 1911, RG 59, 825.74/3; all DSNA.

22. Gottschalk to State Department, 20 August 1913, RG 59, 832.74/4; Morgan to State Department, 24 August 1915, RG 59, 832.74/6; Chauncey Eldridge, Federal Telegraph Company, to Secretary of State Robert Lansing, 6 November 1915, RG 59, 832.74/13; all DSNA.

23. Morgan to State Department, 24 August 1915, RG 59, 832.74/6, DSNA.

24. Morgan to State Department, 9 November 1915, RG 59, 832.74/12; Morgan to State Department, 10 November 1915, RG 59, 832.74/17; both DSNA. Marconi investors also spread a false rumor that Federal Telegraph did not hold Brazilian patent rights for its radio equipment.

25. Daniels to Lansing, 18 November 1915, RG 59, 832.74/14, DSNA. Daniels's phrase "interests of foreign capital" is illuminating. Clearly, he saw a distinction between the relative powers of foreign currencies. The fact that Brazilian capital was involved no matter the outcome was incidential; British capital was, of course, another issue. Such statements from policymakers indicate that they saw the United States as an equal in the ranks of European economic powers rather than as a symbol of the rise of all the New World nations in their economic relationships with Europe; like all ideologies, the "Old World-New World" metaphor proved flexible enough to accommodate a broad range of ruling-class interests. For a discussion of the metaphor, see David W. Noble, *The End of American History: Democracy, Capitalism, and the Metaphor of Two Worlds in Anglo-American Historical Writing, 1880–1980* (Minneapolis: University of Minnesota Press, 1984); for a study of economic competition with European interests, see Emily S. Rosenberg, "Anglo-American Economic Rivalry in Brazil During World War 1," *Diplomatic History* 2 (Spring 1978): 131–52.

26. J. B. Butler-Wright, Divison of Latin American Affairs, to Second Assistant Secretary of State Alvey A. Adee, 23 November 1915, RG 59, 832.74/13memo; Adee to Butler-Wright, 29 November 1915, RG 59, 832.74/13a; both DSNA. Emphasis in original.

27. Adee to Butler-Wright, 3 December 1915, RG 59, 832.74/13b, DSNA. Of course, Adee meant "C.Q.D." instead of "S.O.S.," but the warning is clear.

28. Edward Nally, president, Marconi Wireless Telegraph Company of America, to Lansing, 21 December 1915, RG 59, 832.74/19, DSNA.

29. Roosevelt to Lansing, 14 January 1916, RG 59, 832.74/20, DSNA.

30. Eldridge to Lansing, 11 May 1916, RG 59, 832.74/32, DSNA. This long document (on which the next few paragraphs of this study are based) is a narrative of the historical development of Federal Telegraph, and a projection for future work by the company in Brazil. For more on Federal Telegraph, also see Aitken, *The Continuous Wave*, chap. 3; and Douglas, *Inventing American Broadcasting*, pp. 243–83.

31. "History of Wireless Telegraph Agreement between Panama and the United States," memo, Division of Latin American Affairs, 15 May 1914, RG 59, 819.74/46, DSNA, discusses this arrangement in detail.

32. Eldridge to Lansing, 11 May 1916, RG 59, 832.74/32, DSNA. The Honolulu-Panama circuit approximated the distance Marconi achieved in 1910 between the British Isles and his yacht while sailing in the South Atlantic. See *Year Book of Wireless Telegraphy and Telephony 1915* (London: The Wireless Press, 1915), p. 28.

33. Secretary of the Treasury William McAdoo to Lansing, 11 September 1916, RG 59, 810.74.79, DSNA. In January 1916, the State Department had hosted a conference for delegates to the Pan American Scientific Conference and proposed a Pan American radio system, based on government ownership, to handle all military, governmental, and commercial traffic within the hemisphere. Although Latin American delegates insisted they were not empowered to commit their nations to such a plan, the momentum continued through 1916 under the guise of hemispheric military cooperation. See Hogan, *Informal Entente*, p. 145; and Fred Fejes, "Imperialism, Media and the Good Neighbor: New Deal Foreign Policy and United States Shortwave Broadcasting to Latin America," Ph.D. diss., University of Illinois, Urbana, 1982, pub. Norwood: Ablex, 1986 (all citations from dissertation), pp. 20–21. Also see Lansing to American Minister to Cuba William Gonzales, 20 April 1916, RG 59, 837.74/36, DNSA, in which Lansing points out that such a plan does not necessarily militate against "the granting of concessions to reputable American firms for the erection and operation" of wireless stations. This protective attitude of American private corporations would be put on a back burner during the war but would never disappear from policy discourse. The Navy-State advisory group eventually coalesced into the Interdepartmental Radio Advisory Committee (IRAC), a committee still in existence and of major importance in managing government and military uses of telecommunications.

34. Lansing to McAdoo, 11 November 1916, RG 59, 810.74/79, DSNA.

35. This agreement is reviewed by a number of scholars, including Aitken, *The Continuous Wave*, chaps. 5, 6; and Maclaurin, *Invention and Innovation in the Radio Industry*. Owen Young later told radio and magazine interviewer Mary Margaret McBride that these negotiations were the impetus for eventually forming the Radio Corporation of America (RCA); see "Freedom of the Air," *Saturday Evening Post*, 16 November 1929. Concurrent with the General Electric-Marconi negotiations, American Telephone and Telegraph granted large war loans to the Bank of England through the financial network of J. P. Morgan. Although the loans are not directly related to the Marconi arrangement, the close relationship between two of the largest American communications corporations and British financial institutions is striking. Perhaps these two incidents deserve to be considered as purely private American initiatives toward the same general values of American economic expansion shared with government officials; on the other hand, these conditions could suggest attempted control of the American communications industry by British finance capitalists. Both hypotheses represent intriguing approaches for further research. On the loans, see Danielian, *ATT*; and Horace Coon, *American Tel and Tel* (New York: Longman, Greens, 1939).

36. A very few experimental and university stations were allowed to continue their work unimpeded by the Navy. The Navy's involvement in radio during this period is detailed in L. S. Howeth, *History of Communications—Electronics in the United States Navy* (Washington: Government Printing Office, 1963); "History of the Bureau of Engineering—Navy Department—During World War" (Washington: Government Printing Office, 1922); and Susan Douglas, "The Navy Adopts the Radio, 1899–1919" in *Military Enterprise and Technological Change*, ed. Merrit Roe Smith (Cambridge: MIT Press, 1985).

37. These patents had been held in the United States by the Atlantic Communications Company, organized in 1909 by Telefunken as an American subsidiary. Glover and Cornell, *The Development of American Industries*, p. 826.

38. Navy Department to Allessandro Fabbri, Bar Harbor, Maine, 8 September 1917, in Box 1, Allessandro Fabbri Papers, Library of Congress Manuscript Division, Washington (hereafter Fabbri Papers). This interesting collection demonstrates the point of view of a rank-and-file naval officer who commanded a receiving station. Fabbri's brother, Egisto Fabbri, was an original backer of Thomas Edison when Edison began providing electric current to New York City consumers. David F. Noble, *America by Design* (New York: Alfred E. Knopf, 1979), p. 9.

39. "Permanent Control of Radio in U.S. by Navy Urged by Secretary Daniels at Hearing Before House Committee," *Official U.S. Bulletin*, 13 December 1918. My appreciation to Mark Tolstedt for bringing this document to my attention.

40. Douglas, *Inventing American Broadcasting*, p. 280.

41. P. Edward Haley, *Revolution and Intervention: The Diplomacy of Taft and Wilson with Mexico, 1910–1917* (Cambridge: MIT Press, 1970), pp. 247–59; Barbara Tuchman, *The Zimmermann Telegram* (1958; repr., New York: Ballantine, 1979).

42. "Summary of Important Events Relating to Radio Communications in This Hemisphere," U.S. Minister to El Salvador Boaz Long to State Department, 10 April 1918, RG 59, 816.74/42, DSNA. Long added that "should it be necessary, the American government could buy the radio plants outright but the expediency of such a step is questionable, for an American Company could do many things in these countries that the American government could not. . . ." This long memo, which discussed the need for American investment in Latin American communications facilitites, received considerable attention in the State Department immediately after the war. On German stations in El Salvador, also see Tulchin, *The Aftermath of War*, pp. 229–30; Douglas, *Inventing American Broadcasting*, pp. 269–76; and Hughes, "Owen D. Young and American Foreign Policy," p. 72.

43. Secretary of the Navy Edwin Denby to Hughes, 28 November 1922, RG 59, 813.74/1, DSNA. This is one of a number of State Department documents scattered through the various decimal files on internal affairs in Central America that discuss German wireless and the role of the

Mexican government in promoting wireless (invariably German equipment) in Central America. The Mexican government usually financed the construction of these stations, but the projects had trouble getting off the ground for a number of reasons, including the defeat of Germany, as well as the fact that the equipment was spark-gap rather than continuous wave; even by 1918, governments had begun to agree on the abandonment of spark-gap apparatus due to the massive interference these stations caused and the incredible bandwidth these transmissions required. Through international agreement, spark-gap was banned by 1930.

44. "Memorandum in Connection with the Activities of the Mexican Government in Costa Rica during the World War and up to the Present Time," George Davis, Tropical Radio Telegraph Company [owned by United Fruit] to Assistant Secretary of State Leland Harrison, 19 November 1923, RG 59, 813.74/2, DSNA. Davis explained that

> in 1917, an amateur was operating a small set in San Jose, the only one of its kind in the country. About this time he received a summons from the Mexican Minister in San Jose to call and see him. He called on the Mexican Minister who—after confirming the fact that the amateur was operating a receiving set there— asked him if he would be glad to have a new receiving set and the Minister promised that he would get it. . . . The set was brought ashore without papers of any kind . . . it was delivered to the Minister of War in Costa Rica, who in turn delivered it to the amateur. The instrument was of Telefunken design and was capable of copying [receiving] Chapultepec [Mexico's largest station] easily, and the amateur states that he could copy Europe with it.

Also see Walter Thurston, American legation to Costa Rica, to State Department, 23 September 1921, RG 59, 818.74/42; George Summerlin, chargé d'affaires, Mexico City, to State Department, 9 March 1922, RG 59, 817.74/55; both DSNA.

45. Roy Davis, American legation to Costa Rica, to State Department, 30 August 1923, RG 59, DSNA. It is indeed a small world; when I learned Portugese in 1981–82 as a graduate student at Northwestern University, in part so I could conduct research on this topic, my instructor, Vera Muller-Bergh, told me that one of her distant relatives had emigrated from Germany to Brazil during World War I to build German wireless stations in South America.

46. American Ambassador to Mexico Henry Fletcher to Lansing, 14 March 1917, RG 59, 812.74/60, DSNA.

47. Lansing to Fletcher, 2 April 1917, RG 59, 812.74/63a, DSNA. The odd description of the signal ("gruff, broken and could be heard at fifteen feet") is a typical account of spark-gap transmissions and receptions.

48. Thomas Berman, American consul to Tabasco, to Lansing, 28 May 1917, RG 59, 812.74/93.

49. Fletcher to Lansing, 22 August 1917, RG 59, 812.74/104, DSNA.

50. William W. Handley, American consul-general, Lima, to Lansing, 2 June 1917, RG 59, 823.74/8; memo, U.S. Navy, 12 July 1917, RG 59,

823.74/9; Benson MacMillian, American legation, to Lansing, 21 July 1917, RG 59, 823.74/10; all DSNA.

51. F. J. Stimson, American legation, to Lansing, 27 April 1917, RG 59, 835.74/10; Stimson to Lansing, 15 May 1917, RG 59, 835.74/12; Stimson to Lansing, 16 May 1917, RG 59, 835.74/14; Stimson to Lansing, 17 July 1917, RG 59, 835.74/18; Stimson to Lansing, 19 September 1917, RG 59, 835.74/20; all DSNA.

52. Pan American Union, *Memorandum Concerning Cable and Radio-telegraphic Communication with Mexico, Central and South America, and the West Indies, Second Pan American Financial Conference, 19–24 January 1920* (Washington: Government Printing Office, 1920), located in file 11–14-10, Box 99, Owen D. Young Papers, Van Hornesville, N.Y. (hereafter, Young Papers).

53. E. Robbins, American legation, to Lansing, 24 July 1918, RG 59, 835.74/24, DSNA.

54. A. B. Bielander, Bureau of Investigation, Department of Justice, to Leland Harrison, State Department, 7 May 1917, RG 59, 832.74/25; American Consul to Para William Pickerell to State Department, 31 July 1917, RG 59, 832.74/33; A. T. Hacherle, American legation to Brazil, to State Department, 30 August 1917, RG 59, 832.74/36; all DSNA.

55. Memo of 26 May 1920 on Walter Schare, file 11–14-10, Box 99, Young Papers. Schare was a salesman for DeForest equipment and traveled to Brazil around 1910. He stayed after the collapse of United Wireless, importing and selling whatever radio equipment he could muster.

56. See Box 2, Fabbri Papers, for correspondence reporting on regular visits to this station by General Electric and American Telephone and Telegraph engineers and representatives.

57. "The Shape, Scope and Consequences of the Age of Information," address by George P. Schultz to the Stanford Alumni Association's First International Conference, Paris, 21 March 1986. My appreciation to the Annenberg Program on Telecommunications Policy, Washington, for this document. Schultz's equation of the Strategic Defense Initiative (SDI) with a benign if gigantic computer program is elegantly disarming.

58. Douglas, *Inventing American Broadcasting*, chap. 8.

59. Lansing, circular to all American Legations and Embassies in Latin America, 9 May 1918, RG 59, 810.74/95a, DSNA.

60. Long to State Department, 3 April 1919, RG 59, 810.74/97; State Department report for President Woodrow Wilson (but never presented), undated, with explanatory memo of 27 July 1920, RG 59, 810.74/108 (summarizes some wartime communications problems); both DSNA; Glenn Stewart, Department of Commerce, to State Department, 16 June 1919, RG 151, file 544—Radio—Latin America, Box 2371, Department of Commerce, National Archives, Washington.

3

International Communications Conferences, 1919–39

As the end of World War I approached, American armed forces had shown that the radio equipment produced for military use was durable, reliable for long-distance communications, and a viable competitor (often of superior quality) to European systems. American business and government representatives recognized the American radio industry's potential to present American visions of the postwar world. These visions included a dominating role for the United States as an economic and diplomatic leader, as well as a protector of peace. A commanding American presence in international communications was an absolute necessity to realize these visions.[1] The war had fully revealed the strategic value of a worldwide cable and radio system, and consequently American military leaders advocated a commanding role for themselves in communications policy and a high level of international cooperation with other governments in communications technology. Business leaders, both from within the communications industry and from businesses such as banking and manufacturing, which participated in the global economy, were convinced that control over communications was essential to overseas trade expansion and productivity. In addition, postwar policymakers from all nations held the sincere belief that improved international communications represented one of the lasting keys to world peace—a belief that deserves credit for its foresight, as time has shown it to be somewhat true.

Although American policymakers agreed on the need for expansion into international communications, as well as for the United States to assume a commanding role in international diplomacy governing electrical communications in order to meet commercial, strategic, diplomatic, and cultural goals, the actual methods of achieving these goals remained in flux after the

Armistice. A consensus was needed to determine whether the government or private firms would lead in shaping an American system of international communications. Further, policymakers had to address a host of new radio uses discovered during the war, as well as the certainty that more uses would be discovered in the future. The relationship between radio communications and undersea cables communications raised still another round of questions. Not only did these issues have to be reconciled within the United States, but they also had to be faced with respect to the rest of the world.

In order to reconcile these issues in a way that would protect and promote the American radio industry in the global economy, the development of negotiating positions and strategies for international communications conferences became a vital component in the growth of the American radio industry during the 1920s. As a part of this development, the relationship between the American radio industry and the American government needed further definition as well as a leadership consensus. Initially, the relations between American public and private policymakers were spurred by three international communications conferences: the Washington Conference of 1920, the Mexico City Conference of 1924, and the Washington Conference of 1927. It was after these three conferences that American principles concerning international radio communications were elaborated and enunciated at a number of conferences throughout the 1930s. This chapter will discuss how the need for an international policy in radio encouraged the formation of an industry-government consensus on the future of the American radio industry, how the mantle of leadership in the formation of foreign and domestic radio policy was assumed by the private rather than the public sector, and the implications of that leadership for the American radio industry, for U.S.-Latin American relations, and for the rest of the world.

The radio situation in Latin America demanded immediate attention after the Armistice. Of the nearly hundred wireless stations in Latin America by 1918, only six were known to have been exclusively supplied and constructed with American equipment. More than seventy stations had either been built by European companies or by Latin American governments using European equipment.[2] Boaz Long pointed out that the American radio industry's increased involvement in Latin American communications was the only sure way to prevent the continuing advances by British and German interests; he also questioned whether the policy of government ownership adopted during the war actually proved the best method for protection and promotion of long-term American interests:

> an American Company could do many things in these countries that the American Government could not . . . the principle of Government ownership in the plan of 1915 was not to militate against the granting of concessions to reputable American firms. Let us consider what might be done toward a unification of wireless communications in this Hemisphere by aiding sympathetic and efficient American companies to secure concessions and erect the radio plants needed to protect the interests of our Government.[3]

Communication matters were among the many topics planned for discussion at the Paris Peace Conferences; the need for a strong American presence in Latin American communications undoubtedly concerned the American delegations to the conferences.

The Paris Peace Conferences to end World War I opened in January 1919, and a conference devoted to communications issues convened during the first month of proceedings. The Inter-Allied Wireless Telegraphy and Signal Corps Conference primarily brought together delegates from the military branches of the various nations. The group studied frequency needs and technical progress, then drafted a rough proposal on wireless designed to foster further discussion by the delegation leaders of the United States, France, England, Japan, and Italy.[4] Despite this activity, communications issues remained difficult topics throughout the conferences. Although the Allied nations signed the proposal drafted by military conferees, they also agreed that a continuation of communications negotiations after Paris was in the best interests of all nations. Accordingly, the nations agreed to call for a worldwide radio conference, to be held at an indefinite date, and also scheduled a preliminary communications conference—involving the United States, England, France, Italy, and Japan—to convene in Washington sometime in 1920.[5]

During the Paris meetings, the American delegates eventually concluded that the lack of an established American industrial concern with a significant investment in international radio was a disadvantage at conference negotiations and would be a disadvantage in the future. Even the staunchest proponents of a government-owned system, for example, Secretary of the Navy Josephus Daniels, finally began to consider the arguments in favor of significant participation and even leadership from the private sector. Executives such as Owen Young of General Electric and David Sarnoff of American Marconi convincingly debated the merits of private initiative and whether government ownership would stifle growth, innovation, and development in the radio field.[6] If government ownership had to be forsaken, then the diplomatic support of a major American corporation in radio was the next best alternative in the view of military leaders such as Daniels. The rank-and-file officers in the Navy generally echoed the same viewpoint.[7] As the Paris Peace Conferences ended in June 1919, the likeliest candidate among American corporations to fill this role appeared to be the General Electric Company.

While the Paris Peace Conferences were in session, naval officers had met with General Electric officials to discuss the specific use of the company's transmitting system (the Alexanderson alternator), as well as the role of American corporations in postwar radio. The communications strategies of the European nations, as evidenced at the conferences, were built upon a growing practice of public-private cooperation between national governments and European communications corporations. In exchange for de facto monopoly privileges in radio communications, European concerns such as the Marconi interests and Telefunken of Germany acquiesed in a variant of public-private cooperation cast along the lines of corporatism.[8] Within the communications industry, this European variant followed a pattern of government officials generally leading in policy decision making (especially on relations between capital and the state), whereas military and diplomatic officials had particular emphasis on policy formation. Business concerns were not left out in this statist model, but neither did they dominate.

In the United States, however, certain interests had spoken out against the rising statist model. Although policymakers did not explicitly enunciate a corporatist alternative to the European variant, the need for some sort of public-private cooperation had become evident. The problem for policymakers was the shape and direction of that variant. Should the European pattern be followed, or should international communications (and domestic communications in radio) be developed along a different line, one cast with more input from societal entities such as private enterprise and less input from the government? These were the issues that led to the meetings between General Electric and Navy officials.

An early agreement between General Electric and the Navy led to the temporary suspension of ongoing negotiations with the Marconi interests for the use of the Alexanderson alternator. After suspending these negotiations, General Electric organized its radio holdings into a subsidiary, the American Trans-Oceanic Radio Corporation—later renamed the Radio Corporation of America (RCA)—in order to enter the radio field.[9] The pieces used in building RCA came from both the Navy and from the parent company. The Navy, still holding the American Marconi stations as well as virtually all other American radio stations under the wartime provisions of the Radio Act of 1912, kept the Marconi stations until General Electric purchased them from Marconi investors. The parent company retained control over manufacturing, gave responsibility for operation and equipment sales to RCA, cross-licensed patents, and incorporated RCA in October 1919. The same year, General Electric launched a new global subsidiary, the International General Electric Company.[10] RCA quickly turned its attention to the international sphere. One of its first actions was an agreement with Marconi interests outlining spheres of influence in radio development. In November 1919, the two parties cross-licensed certain patents and also generally divided world markets. Marconi interests received the British Empire outside the Western Hemisphere, RCA received the Western Hemisphere, and most of Asia was designated an area for free competition.[11]

In the aftermath of the Paris Peace Conferences, RCA and American military officials at first enjoyed a high degree of cooperation. In a short time, however, the relationship began to deteriorate. As RCA grew and subsequently entered into cross-licensing agreements with other American corporations involved in radio—for example, American Telephone and Telegraph, United Fruit Company, and Westinghouse—corporate concerns at RCA moved in a variety of directions while military officials retained a narrower view of the uses of radio. However, the immediate concern for American policymakers was the pending Washington conference on electrical communications.[12]

The 1920 Washington Conference sparked the interest of many American businessmen, who hoped for improved overseas communications services. Exporters, overseas traders, salesmen, and executives regularly complained about poor service offered to Americans in international communications. The National Foreign Trade Council (NFTC) wrote to the State Department in November 1919 about the conference. The NFTC had heard many complaints about poor communications service, and added that it knew of other trade associations receiving similar complaints. Their letter advised that problems could be alleviated by the businessmen themselves, noting that "the inclusion of competent business representatives in the American delegation at the proposed conference would assist in leading to the adoption of measures tending to provide the entire world with adequate facilities."[13]

In order to assimilate the broad and divergent views of communications interests outside the federal government, a series of meetings between government and industry leaders began in 1920 to discuss the scope of the industry, the role of international communications in world policy, and radio's potential for the future. One remarkable series of meetings began in the spring under the direction of Secretary of Commerce J. W. Alexander, who called together various radio manufacturing and commercial interests, as well as representatives of government departments vitally concerned with radio.[14] At the meetings, Alexander led the group through an examination of a document that had been signed by American delegates in Paris.[15] By the end of May, the group had substantially rewritten the text of the protocol. When they concluded their meetings, they presented their revisions to the American delegation of the 1920 Washington Conference and encouraged its use as a negotiating position.[16]

This group, known as the 1920 Department of Commerce Radio Conference Committee, produced interesting modifications in the Paris Protocol. The committee structured a system of wave allocation tied to technological capability. Rather than strict, inflexible allocations, the new system relaxed its controls as research progressed upward into the higher portions of the electromagnetic spectrum. Therefore, utilization of these higher frequencies would mean control of more spectrum space, a principle that continues today. RCA executives were vitally concerned with occupying the

maximum amount of spectrum space possible at this time.[17] A
mandate requiring the consideration of rights of way already
established during the allocation of new frequencies promoted the
principle of first-come, first-served in spectrum use and perpetu-
ated the rewards inherent in technological progress.[18] Yet another
new provision allowed for the multiple use of a wave length by a
nation, an application necessary for the American-style broadcasting model which would spread through North and South
America in the 1920s. Other changes included a clause prohibiting the combination of radio and cable conferences and conventions. Business interests believed this combination would give
Europeans, with their established cable corporations, a greater
advantage in radio matters. Committee members agreed that international technical cooperation was necessary, but proposed that
technical groups at the international level be purely advisory and
have no formal or binding powers.[19] The Commerce Department
and Secretary Alexander fully supported the opinions of the
business leaders on the committee. Alexander deserves credit for
instituting the close ties between his department and the American radio industry, credit usually given his successor, Herbert
Clark Hoover. Undeniably, Hoover did an outstanding job of continuing and expanding this friendship, but the relationship clearly began with Alexander.[20]

Other meetings of different groups continued throughout the
summer and fall of 1920, providing industry leaders the opportunity to formulate and share opinions on the development of
international communications. One important meeting was the
India House Conference (so named for the hotel in New York City
where the meetings were held) on cable communications. A dozen
of the leading American trade associations, including the National
Foreign Trade Council, the American Manufacturing Export Association, the Merchants Association of New York, the National
Association of Manufacturers, and the U.S. Chamber of Commerce, met to develop a unified position in international communications policy. Conferees suggested that American delegations
to international communications conferences view cable and radio as essentially separate fields of activity and therefore press for
separate conferences and agreements to cover cable and radio.
American dominance in communications was an underlying theme
of the report. The India House group concluded that

the Government of the United States should encourage the development of cable and radio facilities in this country, so that the United States may become a focal point for such communications. . . . Earnest consideration should be given at once to the matter of developing, at every desirable point throughout the world, whatever facilities may be necessary to [place cable and radio] under direct control of citizens of the United States.[21]

The State Department met with cable and radio businessmen in September 1920 to receive their views on the conference. The businessmen explained their opposition to both the principles of the 1919 Paris Radio Protocol and the Universal Electrical Communications Union (a topic scheduled for discussion at the upcoming 1920 Washington Conference) through their spokesman, former Secretary of State Elihu Root. The Universal Electrical Communications Union was a European proposal to create a single global governing agency for radio activities. Root argued that the "companies feel that the service in America and for America has been successful and efficient as conducted by private enterprise and that joining the Union could only handicap it . . . adherence could result in European domination."[22] The Universal Electrical Communications Union could enforce a combined convention of cable and radio, which in turn could promote the statist models of European communications into the international area. This specter of government control haunted American business interests. Despite their opposition to adherence, the companies saw wisdom in cooperation. Cooperation with Europe would be necessary to ensure that worldwide communications could be conducted by American corporations. Strict adherence to principles such as union enforcement of international communications could erode business leadership in communications policy, however.

In the month preceding the 1920 Washington Conference, the American delegation finalized its plans for negotiations. Delegation chairman Norman Davis saw a variety of factors increasing the importance of international communications, including the rise of global democracy, the growing connections between foreign and domestic policy (and between foreign and domestic economic spheres), and the fact that international commercial and political relations had become more intimate. Cable and radio communications were trade forerunners, but the structure and performance of the world communications system as it stood in September 1920 found the United States not at the core of international communications activity, but "as a part of the general contributing field to be reached and exploited. . . . This must be changed and this country be made a focal point of a world system of electrical communications." Davis also believed that the admirable success of the European statist models deserved credit, and that greater effort should be made to apply these methods at home. "Some method must be sought for reconciling the interests of the American private communications interests, and the larger national interests. Guaranteed relations between the government and business are common in England, France, Japan, and Germany."[23] Davis shared these views with other delegates. The unity within the delegation resulted in part from the lack of private representation within the delegation; all of the delegates came from government departments.[24]

After two short delays, the preliminary conference called for in Paris opened in Washington on October 8, 1920. Undersea cables issues dominated most of the proceedings, as the disposition of captured German cables had been agreed upon in Paris as the major conference topic. The regular proceedings proved complex and tedious. Although relatively little concerning international radio was discussed and finalized, each nation did begin to enunciate its own viewpoint of postwar international communications. American delegates favored separate agreements for cables and radio, but European nations pressed for combined conventions and Americans eventually conceded this combination for the duration of this one conference. The American delegation felt that acquiescence in the European plans for combined conventions did not have to result in complete adherence, but at least negotiating under such conditions demonstrated that Americans believed international agreements were important in the orderly development of global communications. Of course, as Walter Rogers, an American delegate, noted, this implied a willingness on the part of the American government to impose adherence on American companies. American business interests, excluded from the actual proceedings, rankled at these developments and expressed displeasure in the negotiating ability of the American delegation. The conference adjourned for several months before it reconvened in 1921, and finally reached agreement only on the disposition of German cables that had been captured during the war. Delegates also suggested that the League of Nations call a worldwide radio conference sometime during the decade.[25]

The change in administrations from the Wilson to the Harding presidencies in March 1921 saw the roles and influence of several government policymakers, including Norman Davis and Walter Rogers, begin to diminish. Although Davis and Rogers continued as communications advisers through much of 1921, their ideas — which had increasingly been at odds with business interests — no longer coincided with the new government policymakers.[26] The most prominent new government policymaker in radio, Secretary of Commerce Herbert Hoover, continued and expanded the harmonious relationship Alexander instituted between the department and the radio industry. Hoover's contemporaries at the State Department who were interested in radio included Undersecretary of State Henry Fletcher and Foreign Trade Adviser Prentiss Gilbert. Gilbert drafted a proposal for radio policy guidelines on April 2, 1921, suggesting that a worldwide communications system in radio would offset and neutralize British advantages in cable communications. In order to create such a radio system, policymakers needed to choose among supporting a government-owned system, a few large companies, or a combination of both. Gilbert also noted that radio communication might be viewed as a natural monopoly because of spectrum scarcity and that policymakers should not fear such a monopoly because the resultant worldwide system would further the political, economic, and strategic interests of the United States. He also advocated a national communications commission with duties and powers strikingly similar to those assumed by the Federal Radio Commission (forerunner of the current Federal Communications Commission) in the late 1920s.[27]

Five days later, representatives from the State Department, Commerce Department, and RCA drafted a memo to Hoover on enunciation of American radio policy. Hoover then directed the memo to President Warren Harding as a recommendation for the text of Harding's upcoming speech to a joint session of Congress.[28] In the speech, delivered April 12, 1921, the president labeled international communications as one of many national problems too pressing for lawmakers to neglect. Harding called for active encouragement of the extension of American owned and operated radio services around the world and stressed that radio connections between the United States and other nations should be free of foreign intermediation. The continued growth of the American press and other news agencies was tied intimately to communications growth, a trend Harding found particularly desirable. This trend could eventually foster a climate in which "the American reader may receive a wide range of news and the foreign reader receive a full account of American activities. The daily press of all countries may well be put in position to contribute to international understandings by the publication of interesting foreign news."[29] Harding's comments on international communications followed the text of the Hoover memo virtually word for word, and his statement represents a further reversal by government leaders toward advocating government ownership.

As the proceedings of the 1920 conference negotiations became known within the American business community, more and more businessmen voiced strident opposition to American adherence to international communications treaties and European models of government-directed communications systems. They continued to question the methods, tactics, and motivation of government officials such as Davis and Rogers and felt that government representatives had failed to create a sense of mutual trust and understanding in radio. In order to alleviate these tensions, government and industry officials scheduled a meeting for the end of May at the Hotel Commodore in New York City.[30]

One week before the Hotel Commodore meetings, RCA published a pamphlet on the Universal Electrical Communications Union, which RCA felt would subordinate corporate decision making to the whims of European nations. The pamphlet was a no-holds-barred attack on the union concept and an indictment of the American delegation to the 1920 Washington Conference. RCA felt that American delegates had often taken a step backward for business interests throughout the proceedings. "If the principle of entrusting governmental functions to a Commission, if the principle of the League of Nations, if the complete subordination of American communications interests to those of foreign governments and the abandonment of any attempt to create a distinctively American world-wide communications system for use in peace and in war, and if the hampering of American radio development are desired," noted RCA, "this proposed Union should be adopted. Otherwise, it should not be." RCA reasoned that the union ran counter to the American political economic system: "Governments which own or operate their own communications facilities can make up deficits by taxation, but it is useless to attempt to force private enterprises to embark on uneconomic, losing projects *for they could not obtain their capital and operating requirements from investors*." If the United States entered the union, foreign governments would exercise control over American communications and discourage new technological developments. The American delegation had to believe faithfully and desire fully that the United States "shall become the center of a world system of communication, and not continue to be an outlying link" in order to promote industrial growth and to "afford the American merchants direct communications not dependent on the courtesy and whims of other nations. . . ." To meet this goal, RCA asked the federal government to throw its total and unquestioning support to the American radio industry. Foreign interests were too strongly entrenched in the undersea cables industry for Americans to dominate that field of activity immediately, but radio was a different matter. RCA implored the American delegation and the federal government to work toward a completely separate radio convention in all international negotiations. *"In a Radio Convention, the United States would be in the dominant position, measured by past and present accomplishments in the radio field*, and the smaller nations, wishing more and more to communicate direct with the United States, should be entirely helpful to the aims of the United States."[31] A similar pamphlet prepared by United Fruit's subsidiary, the Tropical Radio Telegraph Company, added that "the Union was the outgrowth of war time conditions when the Allied Governments were operating all means of communication and was not the result of demands of commerce under peace conditions . . . it is in fact a 'League of Nations' both in thought and in principle and was designed to function as a League of Nations. As such it subordinates our national interests to the interests of foreign governments who are in the majority . . . this would result in entangling alliances which, as was so clearly indicated by the last Presidential election, is not the desire of the people of this country."[32]

The Hotel Commodore meetings convened May 26 and 27, 1921, with the first day devoted to cable issues and the second to radio issues. Walter Rogers opened the first day by assuring participants that the meetings were not designed to promote a government viewpoint, but were merely an exchange of ideas.[33] Some businessmen felt that Rogers pushed for the union; he replied that he simply wanted to be helpful to American users and American companies.[34] J. J. Carty of American Telephone and Telegraph saw many similarities between the union and the League of Nations, joining in the line of thought advanced by Tropical Radio Telegraph Company. Participants agreed on keeping cable and radio agreements separate. However, delegates needed to use caution even if a radio conference could be dominated; Charles Neave felt that adherence to radio provisions was too general an adherence for RCA and the American radio industry.[35] Continual technological advancements and new uses of radio made policy difficult to formulate, noted C. B. Cooper of the Ship Owners Radio Service. "I do not think anybody wants to say that they know just what the end of the radio communication is going to be. It is a subject that has to be handled with gloves and possibly in a stalling manner . . . but at the same time commercial companies want to know they will have a certain band of wave lengths they can use."[36]

Businessmen often referred to specific sections of the 1920 Department of Commerce Radio Conference Committee report that modified the 1919 Paris Protocol in areas such as frequency allocation. Many wondered why that report was not more evident in the preliminary report of the American delegation to the 1920 Washington Conference and were convinced that business views did not get complete support. Some felt that American delegations had been consistently outmaneuvered at international communicatons conferences and negotiations. Alfred Goldsmith of RCA summed up this sentiment by calling the "present draft of regulations a hollow shell—here and there a trifle of the language of the 1920 conference committee remains, but with the spirit and soul withdrawn and the vital intent and purpose that gave it force and meaning left out." Goldsmith reiterated that spirit and soul: "Present its provisions repeatedly and energetically . . . insist upon it and prefer rather to withdraw from the convention than accept anything such as this proposed draft."[37] Others backed Goldsmith with suggestions that commercial interests be directly appointed to future delegations in order to prevent such problems.

Businessmen were also concerned by negotiations between the United States and smaller nations. Many objected to the idea of negotiating first with the "Big Five" and subsequently moving on to the smaller nations after a five-power agreement. To do so, said Carty, was tantamount to the American government implying that five federal governments run the world: "If that is to be the basis of it, why it is a very important announcement to make for the American government, at any rate."[38] Carty succinctly expressed the growing opposition within the American communications industry to government interests leading the rest of the United States into a global concert of powers. If such an activity should be desired, its impetus, according to Carty and others representing business interests, should be the decision and responsibility of the private rather than the public sector.

The Hotel Commodore meetings represent a watershed in achieving an early industry-government consensus on radio policy—a consensus shaped by the leadership of the private sector. After these meetings, the fundamental tenets of American foreign policy concerning radio—that is, private ownership and management of facilities, nonadherence to international agreements, separate radio and cable agreements, representation of American business interests in delegations, government support of American commercial users and operators, and a drive to obtain and use as much of the spectrum as possible—were enunciated more and more often by American radio interests until such tenets became stated consistently in a chorus by government and industry leaders. Private interests took the lead in formation of radio policy at the Hotel Commodore meetings and still continue in that leadership. By the end of the year, a committee on radio communications, chaired by Goldsmith and staffed completely by members from the private sector, pledged to "present a concrete and acceptable program for international treaties and national legislation covering the regulation of radio communications" and proclaimed that "wise and proper international regulations and national legislation can be drawn up only by conference at which the commercial and private interests of the United States have adequate representation."[39]

Soon after the Hotel Commodore meetings, a private agreement among the major radio interests of the United States, Great Britain, France, and Germany finally tied up the many loose ends of transcoceanic wireless telegraphy with South America. The American-English-French-German (AEFG) Consortium was created in September 1921, when Owen Young concluded negotiations to provide service along with Marconi investors from England and France and Telefunken in Germany. In order to provide immediate service to South America and also rectify long-standing difficulties and obstacles toward an understanding of respective rights in South America, RCA agreed to operate long-distance wireless telegraphy through a consortium. This sorted out the concessions conflicts—so vexing to E. C. Benedict and Amazon Wireless—that had existed since the early 1900s, opened new services for American merchants, and granted American and European merchants better access with South American businesses and markets.

The arrangement conserved valuable spectrum space that RCA felt would have been otherwise wasted. The State Department and Commerce Department both approved of this private initiative and, at Hoover's urging, the Navy added its approval.[40] The war had shown that radio's broad potential could be generated by discoveries, innovations, and growth. These engines of industrial change had to be harnessed after the war and sustained as long as possible for continued economic development. Now, with the old problems in wireless telegraphy largely alleviated, business interests had been fully opened to participate in the most lucrative areas of industrial development, for example, the rapidly rising worldwide fascination with broadcasting. The consortium Young and RCA shaped kept private ownership intact, did not entangle itself with undersea cable corporations and issues, and conserved valuable spectrum space for future use. American business interests had led the formation of American radio policy in South America (in part through a privately conducted concert of powers, which must have pleased J. J. Carty) to the appreciative support of the public sector. In order to continue this momentum, the notion of private leadership in policymaking had to be introduced into diplomatic negotiations concerning international communications. The Inter-American Committee of Electrical Communications scheduled for 1924 in Mexico City provided the first opportunity to voice the new leadership in a diplomatic setting.

The 1924 Mexico City Conference began in response to a general resolution adopted at the Fifth International Conference of American States held in Santiago in 1923. RCA met with the

Commerce Department's Bureau of Foreign and Domestic Commerce to discuss the upcoming conference, and asked the bureau to state its case on frequency allocations as strongly as possible. J. G. Harbord said that the company appreciated that commercial interests were no longer excluded from participation in radio matters, and looked forward to adequate industry representation in Mexico City. He also suggested an "open declaration of American policy, no matter what convention may be concluded . . . this would leave us unhampered and in a position to take advantage of our radio development during the next decade, which promises to be more rapid than in any other country. At the end of that time, America's position in the radio field will be so assured that we can more clearly dictate a new convention along lines which we regard as acceptable."[41]

American Telephone and Telegraph voiced similar opinions, especially on adequate industry representation among the American delegation. J. J. Carty contacted RCA, International Telephone and Telegraph, General Electric, and the United States Independent Telephone Association. He told the last group that "the gathering in Mexico of so many South American communications representatives would furnish us an opportunity to show the delegates whatever we cared to in the way of machinery or devices . . . and bring to their attention any new American ideas."[42] Fifteen nations attended the conference, which opened on May 27 and closed on July 22, 1924. U.S. Ambassador to Mexico Charles Warren headed the delegation, and representatives from RCA, International Telephone and Telegraph, All American Cables, American Telephone and Telegraph, and Westinghouse attended.

Upon their arrival, the American delegates told local reporters that their only plans were for cooperation. Mexico City's *El Excelsior* reported that "none of them have prepared ideas or projects to present at the assembly; but, if they can, they plan many opportunities to cooperate with the various delegations to resolve in the end all of the problems of international communications that are presented in the discussion."[43] In fact, local reporters seem to have either been in a fog or a smokescreen. American delegates did in fact arrive with a conviction to press for the principle of private ownership and the separation of cable and radio agreements.[44] This conviction grew from the consensus first reached at the Hotel Commodore meetings. The 1924 Mexico City Conference was the first international diplomatic conference since those meetings to address radio issues specifically, and private and public policymakers saw the opportunity in Mexico to begin enunciating their philosophy to the rest of the world. In 1924, this philosophy included the separation of cable and radio agreements at international conferences and conventions. Industry leaders undoubtedly had their own international business concerns at the forefront, because circumstances within the American radio industry suggested that the United States was on the verge of dominating world radio development. Government leaders had been convinced of the need for American supremacy in radio. In addition, all government leaders, especially military and diplomatic officers who had served since World War I, doubtless remembered the frustrating cable censorship practices of Great Britain ten years earlier. Even the government representatives, who still might have been less enthusiastic about radio leadership coming from the private sector, nevertheless shared a broad enough range of interests with that private sector to see eye to eye on developing policy that would hold out for a division of radio and cable and thereby encourage private radio enterprise. This spectrum of agreement that existed from businessmen to military officers is another indication of the growth of what is now identified as the military-industrial complex;[45] it is also an excellent example of the power of consensus to promote the interests of industry, state, and—theoretically—society.

However, a major problem surfaced at the start of the Mexico City Conference. The head of the Brazilian delegation, Tobias Moscoso, pushed for a single convention to cover cable and radio. The American delegation saw Moscoso as hostile to the program of the American delegation and attempted to have him replaced within his delegation by Brazilian delegate Mario de Barros Barreto, a delegate whom, unlike Moscoso, the Americans found friendly.[46] A vote of all nations in a plenary session favored a single convention for cable and radio, which placed American delegates in a quandry. Although they could not adhere to the vote for a single convention, neither could they risk appearing uncooperative. To alleviate the problem, the American delegates continued to attend and to participate actively in subcommittee meetings while they made plans to oppose the vote for a single convention by means of appropriate reservations at the proper time.[47]

Within the subcommittees, American delegates pressed their views on the principles of private ownership. Questions arose concerning the new AEFG consortium operating in South America, and American delegates responded that the consortium really was no concern of the conference; it was simply an example of the American principle of private enterprise in practice.[48] By the final days of the conference, Americans realized that the extension of electrical communications through government ownership versus the principles of private ownership had become the fundamental philosophic issue. Delegates drafted a final agreement that called for the permanent establishment of a union designed to promote government ownership; American delegate William Vallance noted that the plan embodied principles contrary to the national policy of the United States. The American delegation opposed the final convention of the 1924 Mexico City Conference and voiced their opposition through an open declaration of American policy delivered by delegate Allen Babcock. The value of private enterprise, the need for protection of commercial interests willing to invest in hemispheric communications, and the danger of regulation "in a manner that interferes with the rights of management inherent in the private ownership of communications services" emerged as major themes. Babcock concluded by recommending against ratification of the convention.[49]

In general, Pan American nations did ignore the recommendations of the 1924 Mexico City Conference; only four nations ratified the convention. Most nations may have refused to ratify the convention in part because of the early announcement of the 1927 Washington Conference. This global conference was announced by the League of Nations in 1925, and had probably been discussed informally in Mexico City, because diplomats had agreed as early as 1920 that a worldwide radio conference should be held sometime during the decade. Perhaps Latin American nations took a "wait and see" attitude in expectation of the 1927 Washington Conference rather than ratify a convention that could quickly be obsolete. American diplomats may have argued this very point to Latin American governments. In any event, the 1924 Mexico City Conference agreements remained outside the mainstream of communications development in the Western Hemisphere. The failure of the conference to have a lasting impact on hemispheric communications helped U.S. interests, because the

convention clearly deviated from American policy for international communications. Some nations voiced cynicism at the
conference's failure, and some delegates saw their failures as
typical of Pan Americanism. These delegates saw the entire Pan
American movement as little more than a vehicle for the aims and
goals of the United States. Vallance sensed this growing cynicism
while the conference was in session.

> There has been some manifestation of objection to the Pan
> American Union as an intermediary for sending the Convention
> to the Governments concerned on the ground that it is an
> instrumentality used by the United States to further its politi-
> cal ambitions in Central and South America. . . . The Latin
> Americans feel that the United States is becoming so powerful
> that it is endeavoring through peaceful penetration and eco-
> nomic domination to control the affairs of these countries.
> Moscoso, appreciating this sentiment, has made the most of it.
> The United States has been charged with having in mind nearly
> complete control of communications facilities in this hemi-
> sphere, so that in case of difficulties it could stop the cable and
> radio stations and isolate any unruly country.[50]

Despite these opinions, American interests generally received the
levels of support they desired from the Pan American nations in
the aftermath of the 1924 Mexico City Conference. In 1924, Canada, Mexico, and Cuba received invitations to the annual national
radio conference called by Herbert Hoover to discuss domestic
issues in radio, particularly broadcasting.[51] The three nations
attended with observer status and took part in discussions concerning spectrum management in North America. This meeting
set an important precedent for the establishment of regional
conferences as a legitimate venue for spectrum decisions within
the Western Hemisphere during the 1930s.

Despite previous announcements, a worldwide radio conference still had not convened by 1925. The conference envisioned at
the 1920 Washington Conference had yet to meet, and the guidelines of the last worldwide conference, the 1912 London Conference, were hopelessly outdated in many areas of radio communications. The global radio conference call for 1927 in Washington
was not unexpected and had been proposed in 1920. American
policymakers initially greeted the call with little if any enthusiasm. Secretary of the Navy Curtis Wilbur had grave doubts whether

the United States had anything to gain from the conference, but saw no choice but to participate. Under the circumstances, Wilbur felt it best that the United States serve as host because "we would be less in danger of losing anything material if it were held in the United States rather than elsewhere."[52] Policymakers probably wondered if yet another government-controlled union plan would emerge as in 1920 and 1924. They also worried that the call for combined radio and cable conventions might be repeated. William Vallance warned Wallace White, who had been in Mexico City and was also to be an American delegate in 1927, that Mexico or other nations might attempt to undermine the American position on private ownership, and asked White to discuss the issue privately with individual Latin American representatives whenever appropriate. John Warren of the Tropical Radio Telegraph Company voiced similar concerns to 1927 delegate Stephen Davis.[53]

The private sector developed dual pursuits in preparation for the 1927 Washington Conference. First, they continued to meet with government officials and reiterated the importance of maintaining the American position on private initiative and sticking to previously expressed principles such as the Babcock declaration. Second, the large American corporations centrally concerned with radio, including American Telephone and Telegraph, General Electric, RCA, and Westinghouse, worked in tandem to develop a broad range of plans and proposals for the American delegation to present during the conference. These proposals generally dealt with global frequency allocations (further elaborating the ideas first set forth by the 1920 Radio Conference Committee at the Commerce Department meetings) and with the rights of private management of radio systems in global communications. RCA and American Telephone and Telegraph began co-authoring a number of proposals in 1925. The State Department arranged for a meeting of radio firms in 1926 to examine the progress on drafting proposals for the 1927 conference.[54] American firms expected to be a part of the American delegation and also to have representatives at the conference. By the time the conference opened, firms either part of the official American delegation or that had their own representatives present included RCA, Independent Wireless Telegraph Company, Tropical Radio Telegraph Company, Federal Telegraph Company, American Telephone and Telegraph, United States and Haiti Telegraph Company, International Telephone and

Telegraph, All American Cables, Western Union, Commercial Cable, and the Mexican Telegraph Company. Other American radio institutions in attendance included the National Association of Broadcasters, the Institute of Radio Engineers, and the American Radio Relay League.[55]

One other factor must be considered in the private sector's attitude concerning the 1927 Washington Conference: the newly enacted Radio Act of 1927. This legislation, signed by President Calvin Coolidge on February 23, affirmed the supremacy of private initiative in the domestic radio activities of the United States. Although the legislation certainly provided some regulatory framework and even some restrictions, the law did not in any way threaten the rights of private ownership of radio and broadcasting communications; on the contrary, it upheld those rights to the fullest. This legislation, which settled once and for all any lingering doubts about private leadership in the internal development of the American radio industry, must have been a relief to American broadcasters and the American radio industry as a whole. In addition, it quelled any potential accusations of the United States forcing a set of principles on the rest of the world that were not upheld in American domestic radio legislation.

Early in 1927, the American delegation began extensive preparations for the conference, scheduled for later that year. The American foreign service provided policymakers and delegates with background information on radio development around the world, updated market trends and statistics, and forecast investment climate in global radio. This information also influenced the drafting of American proposals for the conference.[56] In their call for the 1927 Washington Conference, the League of Nations had also recommended which nations should receive chairmanships of committees within the conference. The American delegation, following the advice of industry representatives such as J. J. Carty, drew up a list of alternative chairmanships. William Vallance believed that the presence of private communications companies in Canada would ensure a similarity of views with American positions. Vallance also thought that a Pan American nation would be a good selection for a chair in order to help gain support from the Pan American nations as a whole for American proposals. Brazil seemed a likely candidate because the American embassy in Rio de Janeiro had recently reported that a member of the American naval mission currently in Brazil had developed an influential position in the selection of the Brazilian delegation.[57]

The Washington Conference convened on October 8, 1927, with Coolidge giving the welcoming address. He repeated what Harding had said before Congress in 1921 and appealed for wider communications as a key to world understanding and lasting peace. Herbert Hoover, serving as conference chairman, continued the theme begun by Coolidge in calling for the worldwide expansion of radio. Hoover also pointed out the urgent need for a broad agreement on the global allocation of frequencies. The industry representatives within the American delegation had prepared a comprehensive and visionary frequency allocation proposal designed to reward technological innovations with larger portions of the spectrum, and also suggested that spectrum space be allocated on the basis of services rather than nations. In practice, the American system meant that the spectrum would be allocated into portions for each useful application, or service, achieveable through radio technology and not on a basis of a certain section of the spectrum set aside for each nation, regardless of how a nation used their section. (Europeans favored the allocation of spectrum space to individual nations regardless of service applications.) The American delegation also pressed for the principle of regional agreements not subject to European or Asian approval for spectrum management in the Western Hemisphere. Both of these issues carried the conference and were major achievements for American interests. American corporations were free to maximize certain lucrative aspects of radio without having to work around frequencies assigned to other nations, and American policymakers could determine the most advantageous spectrum uses within the Western Hemisphere without the interference of European concerns. This freedom over spectrum decisions within the Western Hemisphere would be exercised by Americans at a number of regional radio conferences in the 1930s. Perhaps most important of all, the adoption of the American system of frequency allocation placed future control of the spectrum firmly in the hands of the technological research and development laboratories of the major radio corporations of the world and only on the fingertips of national governments. (The underdeveloped nations of the world are still struggling to get a grip on the process of global frequency allocations.) Thus, private interests came to determine the uses of a single shared global resource. The United States also defeated a European proposal for the global licensing of receiving sets, diluted the power of an international technical advisory group, and forestalled the impetus for combining cable and radio agreements.

In addition to their role as delegates, the American radio industry also used the 1927 Washington Conference as a lyceum for the full-scale introduction of American philosophies on global communications. Private interests organized tours of American radio manufacturing plants and hosted dinners and banquets for visiting delegates. J. J. Carty invited all delegates to a dinner at the Willard Hotel in Washington during the first week of the conference. American Telephone and Telegraph promised to treat guests to a display of international telephonic communications augmented by loudspeakers and a lighted map of interconnected cities that, Carty assured, "when carefully carried out is most impressive."[58] Radio plants on the tour included those of General Electric, Westinghouse, American Telephone and Telegraph, and RCA. All demonstrated the American methods and principles of private industrial management and the latest in technological innovation; the pedagogy was not offered in vain, as delegates were consistently enthusiastic over what they heard and saw.[59]

The 1927 Washington Conference was an unqualified success for the American government, the American radio industry, and the principle of private leadership. Ten years earlier, a confusing, if not chaotic, situation had existed in American radio. By 1927, policymakers had put the American radio industry at the forefront of global communications development. The impetus, as well as the methods, for achieving this goal came from the private rather than the public sector on most occasions. By the end of the decade, the American radio industry had succeeded in shaping international radio policy in its own image. Continued prosperity and growth in radio now seemed assured in foreign markets; maximizing trade opportunities became a major goal of American broadcasters and manufacturers. Among the most lucrative opportunities, spurred by public enthusiasm at a global scale, lay the spread of American-style broadcasting. In the 1920s, the nations of Latin America proved most receptive to assimilating the American model of broadcasting; by the 1980s, this model would be present throughout the world — augmenting, if not replacing, other models of radio broadcasting.

Each of the three international radio conferences held from 1920–27 mark the progress of consensus as public and private sectors worked together to build the American radio industry on a global scale. During the 1920 Washington Conference, which in a broad sense occupied policymakers from the 1919 Paris Peace Conferences to the 1921 Hotel Commodore meetings, policymakers reached a tentative consensus concerning radio, which was then subjected to an initial testing and enunciation. If the 1920 Washington Conference marked the time of consensual experimentation and formation, then the 1924 Mexico City Conference marked the solidification and promotion of that consensus, particularly through the attitude of the American delegates as evidenced by the Babcock declaration. The 1924 Mexico City Conference was extremely important in the growth and progression of the radio consensus, because it allowed the first opportunity to argue the new radio policy in an international forum. American policymakers were probably concerned about international reaction to their views in the period between the 1924 and 1927 conferences. This concern may be in part responsible for policymakers' somewhat bleak and pessimistic attitude during preparations for the 1927 Washington Conference, especially in 1925 and 1926 when no one could really be sure of the success achieved at the 1924 Mexico City Conference — in a sense, the 1927 Washington Conference hopefully would affirm that success. In retrospect, observers of the past can recognize that the 1927 Washington Conference affirmed that success completely.

Along with the affirmation of success, American radio policymakers of the 1920s came to realize that international communications conferences concerning radio and electrical communications were no longer likely to be occasional affairs with ten-to-fifteen-year lapses between global meetings but, because of the widespread and rapid worldwide adoption of a number of radio technologies, should instead meet every few years to allocate new frequencies and discuss new technologies. The 1930s are indicative of this new global attitude toward worldwide communications conferences, which were held in Madrid in 1932 and again in Cairo in 1938. In addition, conferences were held within the Western

Hemisphere in 1929, 1931, 1933, 1937, and 1939.[60] A number of conferences also convened at regional levels in Europe and Africa (considered the same region according to agreements reached in 1927) and Asia.

American strategies at the global and Western Hemisphere conferences were built around the confidence and convictions of U.S. superiority in radio matters realized with the 1927 Washington Conference. For example, the American policymakers planning for the 1932 Madrid Conference recognized that the familar call for combined radio and telegraph conferences would doubtless reappear. However, they also felt confident enough that such a combination would no longer threaten American radio corporations — as long as certain safeguards and careful planning were built into negotiating strategies and subcommittee personnel appointments at Madrid.[61] American preparations for Madrid included consultations with many of the familiar faces who had worked out American negotiating positions for various 1920s' conferences, and also regular meetings with American corporations, radio trade associations, and radio amateurs. More than fifty American corporations and organizations were invited to Madrid as either official representatives or invited associates of the American delegation.[62]

The conference proceedings were dominated by the combination of radio and telegraph agreements, to which the American delegates only gave token opposition. Of greater concern for the American delegation was the beginning of heated debates on frequency allocations for individual nations. Observers of contemporary international communications conferences such as the World Administrative Radio Conferences (WARC) and other International Telecommunications Union (ITU) proceedings[63] would find themselves on familar ground as they reviewed the speeches, strategies, and unusual alliances as individual nations (particularly those outside the mainstream of technological research and development) scrambled for a share of the spectrum. Certain interested parties in Canada found themselves in similar positions with the Union of Soviet Socialist Republics when it came to philosophies on spectrum allocations. Just before the opening of the conference, the Canadian Parliament had been audience to a long diatribe from Graham Spry, head of the Canadian Radio League (an organization similar to the American Radio Relay

League).[64] Spry called on Canada to send a delegation that would vote with the Europeans against whatever the United States proposed. He saw American corporations as holding a de facto monopoly over Canadian radio in all fields, including programming, advertising, and manufacturing. This monopoly power had the result of defusing any Canadian proposals for more Canadian broadcast bands. Spry also suggested that giving support to Europe could open the way for European radio interests to come to Canada and compete against the American monopoly; Spry felt such a scenario might in the long run be in the best interests of the Canadian people, and in any event would not make things any worse than conditions at the time. In practice, Spry's recommendations were not endorsed fully by the Canadian delegation at Madrid, which preferred to negotiate privately with the Americans, Mexicans, and Cubans as a way to find a more efficient assignment of North American broadcast frequencies.[65] The Soviet delegation, interested in propagandistic uses of radio broadcasting to Western Europe,[66] saw European nations as "the problem," and argued for more broadcast bands for itself and for other nations that seemed to be excluded or underrepresented in the spectrum allocations process.[67]

American policymakers accepted the expected combination of radio and telegraph agreements at Madrid; they did not accept the dialogue of nations that argued vehemently against American proposals for uses and allocations of the spectrum. The regional conferences held within the Western Hemisphere during the 1930s became important venues for all the nations in the New World to follow U.S. leadership and develop a consensus about international radio matters. Such a consensus would go a long way toward protecting American interests at future global conferences, in part because—excluding Europe—the rest of the world (especially the underdeveloped world) had begun to view Latin nations in a leadership role in regard to relations with industrialized nations. A consensus fostered by the U.S. was also more of a realistic goal than in the 1920s because American private radio interests had begun to secure close ties with Latin American private radio interests. These ties ranged from the executives and industrialists of the large broadcasters and manufacturing organizations down through the thousands of amateur radio enthusiasts who were springing up throughout the hemisphere.[68]

The best opportunity for reaching a regional agreement on radio in general, and broadcast frequencies in particular, appeared to be a conference called in Havana in November 1937. Certain South American nations had held small, regional conferences earlier in the decade, but the Havana Conference held the potential for attendance by virtually all of the nations of North and South America and presented a timely opportunity to meet just before the global conference in Cairo in 1938. Cuban radio offficals had visited the United States in 1936 to meet with American policy-makers to sketch out plans for the conference.[69] The American chargé d'affaires in Havana believed that the choice of Cuba was a good one because Cubans enjoyed a reputation as "honest bro-kers" among other Latin American nations. He added that the most important objective of the conference would be for the American countries to reach an agreement over a broad range of views so that a united front might be presented in Cairo. Amling Prall of the Federal Communications Commission (FCC)—beginning to take on a significant role as an international as well as domestic policymaking agency—saw the 1937 Havana Conference as of "the utmost importance since it allows for the American nations to coordinate a plan which may possibly counter at Cairo the Euro-pean plans . . .," especially in areas such as new allocations for shortwave frequencies.[70] Secretary of State Cordell Hull prepared a long report for President Franklin Roosevelt on the upcoming conference and echoed the advice of his predecessor twenty years previously, Robert Lansing, when Hull concluded that the prob-lems that needed resolution in Havana were of the utmost impor-tance to the United States government and to American corpora-tions.[71]

The desired united front was realized at Havana, and the momentum of success carried forward into plans for the Cairo Conference. For the first time, the FCC took the leading role in preparing American plans and negotiating strategies, although the agency received considerable assistance from the State Depart-ment.[72] Although a number of complex issues would face Ameri-cans at Cairo, including shortwave and the beginnings of concerns about "visual broadcasting" or television, probably the greatest obstacle stemmed from the incredible global growth of all radio uses, and of broadcasting in particular. Conference planners estimated that the number of receiving sets in the world had doubled between 1932 and 1936; the radio industry had become a major global entity. In ten years, shortwave alone had gone from an experiment to an established service with more than two hundred stations around the world.[73]

The spirit of friendship and goodwill that emerged from Havana was also evident at Cairo among the various delegations from North and South America. The contention among nations and regions for sections of the spectrum continued from Madrid. The United States succeeded in acquiring large sections of the spectrum in higher frequencies, which would be used for new military applications of radio technology and also for such new consumer services as television. In part, these frequencies were gained through the advocacy of regional agreements and inter-American cooperation.[74] The 1938 Cairo Conference confirmed that regional agreements concerning the Western Hemisphere would be accepted with little if any opposition from the rest of the world; when the American delegates filed their final reports on the Cairo proceedings, they singled out the success of the 1937 Havana Conference — and the subsequent acceptance of that conference by the rest of the world — as one of their most significant accomplishments.[75] In fewer than than twenty years, American public and private policymakers concerned with international communications conferences had moved from mutual misunderstandings (and even occasional mistrust) to a broad and visionary consensus that first absorbed the mindset of American policymakers and later set the stage for consensus and goodwill on radio matters among virtually all public and private policymakers in the Western Hemisphere.

For the next four decades, any opposition that did surface was marginalized. For example, the American legation in Costa Rica reported in 1937 that a letter recently published in a local paper argued a global tendency was emerging for small countries with weak broadcasting facilities to form defensive groups against the larger nations whose powerful stations dominated the broadcast bands. The writer went on to predict that powerful American broadcasters would push their complaints of interference from other stations in other nations to the furthest conceiveable limit in an attempt to control their channel on the spectrum and increase their audiences. The writer concluded that the future held "a defensive bloc of relatively small countries in radio communications confronting the United States . . . a similar bloc will exist in Europe against England, France, Germany, and even Russia, which holds itself unbound outside of conventions, with incalculable potencies."[76] American policymakers invariably viewed such arguments with contempt. The underdeveloped world would have to wait forty years for these issues to become vocalized globally in the debate for a New International Information Order; in the interim, the American radio industry would carve out a hegemonic position in global radio affairs.

One marvels at how much was accomplished by American policymakers at international communications conferences in such a relatively short time, especially when the beginnings of the American dialogue on international radio policy had to first answer the question of whether public or private concerns should take the lead in owning, operating, and directing the future of radio. The question loomed large in 1919; by 1939, evidence that such a question had ever been raised no longer exists among the various documents left behind by the subjects whose past lives are now our lived past. What led the U.S. government to agree to support the primacy of private industry in the radio field? The answer to what is, frankly, a major question can only begin to emerge when one steps out of the two decades of relations between capital and the state summarized in the preceding pages and into a long-term analysis of the nature of the American political economy and international capitalism. As Thomas McCormick argues, the 1920s cannot be isolated from the Progressive Era that preceded it nor the New Deal that followed; neither can the period from 1900–1939 be analyzed without attention to the events of the century that preceded it, as well as to events as the century draws to a close.[77] What is the pace and direction of change in the past hundred years? Few would argue against the evidence that capitalism—as represented by the multinational corporations—has continued to be a dominant force in world affairs by increasing their influence on the formation of public policy issues. In the 1920s and 1930s, radio provides evidence of that rise, particularly in the influence that corporations were able to gain and keep to this day over the development of a shared global resource—the electromagnetic spectrum.

Finally, questions concerning the relations between the public and private sectors must be asked against the pace and direction of change over what Fernand Braudel called "world time."[78] Braudel suggested world time as part of a method of analysis of the long-term development of European capitalism on a global scale for the past five hundred years. In world time, the historical relationship between state and capital suggests that private leadership in society ultimately remains paramount through historical change. Thus it is to to be expected that the nation whose corporations held a leading role in developing radio into an industry should be led by representatives of that industry in the promotion of private leadership in domestic and global radio development. A historical analysis of the relationship between state and capital concerning American radio and international communications conferences from 1919 to 1939 bears out Braudel's conclusion that it is capitalism that dominates: the state either struggles to survive, or more often—as in the case of twentieth-century global radio policy—accommodates to prosper.

Notes

1. Michael Hogan, *Informal Entente: The Private Structure of Cooperation in Anglo-American Economic Diplomacy, 1918–1928* (Columbia: University of Missouri Press, 1977); Joseph Tulchin, *The Aftermath of War: World War 1 and U.S. Policy Toward Latin America* (New York: New York University Press, 1971); George A. Schreiner, *Cables and Wireless and Their Role in the Foreign Relations of the United States* (Boston: Stratford, 1924); Emily S. Rosenberg, *Spreading the American Dream: American Economic and Cultural Expansion 1890–1945* (New York: Hill and Wang, 1982); Brady A. Hughes, "Owen D. Young and American Foreign Policy, 1919–1929," Ph.D. diss., University of Wisconsin, Madison, 1969; Philip T. Rosen, *The Modern Stentors: Radio Broadcasters and the Federal Government 1920–1934*, (Westport: Greenwood Press, 1980); James Schwoch, "The American Radio Industry and International Communications Conferences, 1919–1927," *Historical Journal of Film, Radio and Television* 7 (October 1987): 289–309.

2. State Department report for President Woodrow Wilson (but never presented), undated, with explanatory memo of 27 July 1920, Record Group (RG) 59, 810.74/108, Department of State, National Archives, Washington (DSNA). This memo summarizes some wartime communications problems.

3. U.S. Minister to El Salvador Boaz Long to Secretary of State Robert Lansing, 30 April 1918, RG 59, 816.74/42, DSNA.

4. Hughes, "Owen D. Young and American Foreign Policy," pp. 73–84; Hugh G. J. Aitken, *The Continuous Wave: Technology and American*

Radio, 1900–1932 (Princeton: Princeton University Press, 1985), p. 331; Mildred Feldman, *The United States in the International Telecommunications Union and Pre-ITU Conferences* (Published privately, 1975).

5. Tulchin, *The Aftermath of War*, p. 210; Feldman, *The United States and the International Telecommunications Union*, p. 34; Long to Lansing, 30 June 1919, RG 59, 574.D1/3; Long to Admiral William H. G. Bullard, Navy Department, 30 July 1919, RG 59, 574.D1/3a; both DSNA.

6. Hogan, *Informal Entente*, pp. 132–34; Aitken, *The Continuous Wave*, pp. 354–86; Josephine Young Case and Everett Needham Case, *Owen D. Young and American Enterprise* (Boston: Godine, 1982), pp. 174–80; Kenneth Bilby, *The General: David Sarnoff and the Rise of the Communications Industry* (New York: Harper and Row, 1986), pp. 35–45; Long to Division of Latin American Affairs, 3 April 1919, RG 59, 810.74/97, DSNA; Glenn Stewart, Division of Latin American Affairs, memo, 16 June 1919, RG 151, file 544 — Radio — Latin America, Box 2371, Department of Commerce, National Archives, Washington (DCNA). Sarnoff, an executive at American Marconi, transferred over when the Marconi stations were purchased by General Electric for RCA.

7. The Allessandro Fabbri Papers, Library of Congress Manuscript Division, Washington, contain several documents on this topic, including the following letters to Fabbri from other officers: 28 October 1918, 29 November 1918, 4 December 1918 (all Box 2); and 20 January 1919, 26 January 1919, and especially 29 July 1919 (all Box 3), which discusses the pivotal role of General Electric. This letter from Commander Stanley C. Hooper explains how in the absence of government ownership "the G.E. Company will undoubtedly get into the radio compass game and swallow up all the rest which will be a God-send and give us a high power radio system, strictly American, which will be on equal terms with British Marconi." The radio compass was one of many important navigational and aeronautical radio applications discovered during the war. Also see Susan Douglas, "The Navy Adopts the Radio, 1899–1919," in *Military Enterprise and Technological Change*, ed. Merritt Roe Smith (Cambridge: MIT Press, 1985); and Dallas Smythe, "The Structure and Policy of Electronic Communication," *University of Illinois Bulletin* 54 (1957): 48–53.

8. An excellent introductory essay on corporatism is Phillipe Schmitter, "Still the Century of Corporatism?" in *The New Corporatism*, ed. Frederick Pike and Thomas Stritch (Notre Dame: University of Notre Dame Press, 1974), pp. 85–131. Corporatism, once perjoratively associated with fascism, has come under reexamination as a theoretical framework for describing and analyzing the relationships between representative interest groups such as business, labor, or the farm bloc, and the decision-making process of federal governments. Schmitter distinguishes between two variants of corporatism, a statist model whereby the public sector is likely to dominate policy formation, and a societal system in which private interests assume the mantle of leadership. A narrower theoretical focus somewhat at odds with Schmitter's dual model is developed in Peter

J. Williamson, *Varieties of Corporatism: A Conceptual Discussion* (Cambridge: Cambridge University Press, 1985); also see Thomas McCormick, "Drift or Mastery? A Corporatist Synthesis for American Diplomatic History," *Reviews in American History* 10 (1982): 318–30; Leo Panitch, "The Development of Corporatism in Liberal Democracies," *Comparative Political Studies* 10 (1977): 61–90; James Schwoch, "The Information Age, the AT&T Settlement: Corporatism-in-the-Making?," *Media Culture and Society* 6 (1984): 273–88; J. T. Winkler, "Corporatism," *European Journal of Sociology* 17 (1976): 100–36; John P. Rossi, "A 'Silent Partnership'?: The U.S. Government, RCA, and Radio Communications with East Asia, 1919–1928," *Radical History Review* 33 (1985): 32–52; and Thomas McCormick, "Corporatism: A Reply to Rossi," *Radical History Review* 33 (1985): 53–59.

9. In an early agreement between General Electric and the Navy, plans were drawn up for the creation of the American Trans-Oceanic Radio Corporation; the same basic agreement was used when the name of the new corporation changed to the Radio Corporation of America. See Three Party Agreement between the General Electric Company, the International General Electric Company, and the American Trans-Oceanic Radio Corporation, 21 May 1919, file 2–113, Box 42, Owen D. Young Papers, Van Hornesville, N.Y. (hereafter Young Papers).

10. Hogan, *Informal Entente*, pp. 132–37; Aitken, *The Continuous Wave*, pp. 332–36, 355–419; Case and Case, *Owen D. Young*, pp. 181–87; Smythe, "Structure of Electronic Communication," pp. 48–53; Fred Fejes, "Imperialism, Media and the Good Neighbor: New Deal Foreign Policy and United States Shortwave Broadcasting to Latin America," Ph.D. diss., University of Illinois, Urbana, 1982, p. 22; Hughes, "Owen D. Young and American Foreign Policy," pp. 52–83; James G. Harbord, RCA, to Secretary of State Charles Evans Hughes, 10 March 1923, RG 59, 810.74/118; Owen D. Young to Stephen Davis, State Department, 30 September 1920, RG 59, 811.74/206; both DSNA. On the International General Electric Company, see Theodore Geiger, "The General Electric Company in Brazil," *National Planning Association Studies of United States Business Performance Abroad* (Washington: National Planning Association, 1961). Charles Neave, chairman of the board of International General Electric, regularly met with government officials in the early 1920s to discuss international communications policy; for example, see Young to Undersecretary of State Norman Davis, 20 September 1920, RG 59, 574.D1/161, DSNA.

11. For three interesting studies of free competition in Asia, see Rossi, "A Silent Partnership?"; Thomas Nutter, "American Telegraphy and the Open Door Policy in China," Ph.D. diss., University of Missouri, Columbia, 1974; and Harry Kirwin, "The Federal Telegraph Company: A Testing of the Open Door," *Pacific Historical Review* 22 (1953): 271–86.

12. Lansing to (President) Wilson, 23 September 1919, RG 59, 574.D1/13, DSNA. Lansing felt that preparation and delegate selection was a matter of great importance and that a clarification of the government's relationship to the nascent radio industry loomed as "one of the most important questions the Government now has to consider."

13. O. K. Davis, National Foreign Trade Council, to Assistant Secretary of State William Phillips, 26 November 1919, RG 59, 574.D1/12, DSNA. The American Manufacturers Association, the Merchants Association of New York, and the Illinois Manufacturers Association sent similar letters.

14. This group met several times between March 30 and May 31, 1920. See Commerce Secretary J. W. Alexander to Lansing, 19 May 1920, RG 59, 574.D1/47, DSNA. The minutes for the first meeting are in RG 28, folder 19.52, Box 1, Records of the Post Office Department, Bureau of the Second Assistant Postmaster General, Division of Air Mail Service, National Archives, Washington. Those present included John J. Carty and Frank B. Jewett, American Telephone and Telegraph; John Hogan, International Radio Telegraph Company (a Westinghouse subsidiary); Michael Pupin of Columbia University; and Charles Stewart of the American Radio Relay League. My appreciation to Jerry Clark of the National Archives for showing me the Post Office records.

15. This was the report of the military conference signed with France, England, and Italy on August 25, 1919. For a discussion, see Feldman, *The United States in the International Telecommunications Union*, p. 61, note 57. Some sources abbreviate this protocol as follows: EU-F-GB-I Protocol. Also see W. H. Bullard, "History of the EU-F-GB-I Protocol of August 25, 1919," no date, file 11–14-46, Box 123, Young Papers.

16. *EU-F-GB-I Radio Protocol (of August 25, 1919) as Modified and Commented upon by a Committee Appointed by the Secretary of Commerce* (Washington: Government Printing Office, 1920) (hereafter *Modified Protocol*). The committee was composed of representatives from the Departments of War, Navy, Post Office, and Commerce; the U.S. Shipping Board; the Institute of Radio Engineers; and various commercial and manufacturing interests, scientists, and amateurs. Although this is a published government report, it is difficult to locate; the copy I read is in Box 29, Papers of Norman Davis, Library of Congress Manuscript Division, Washington (hereafter Davis Papers).

17. This is one reason why Owen Young favored international agreements and cooperation (negotiated by the operating companies themselves) in transoceanic wireless telegraphy. The spectrum space saved through such private management could be used by RCA and American interests for future discoveries and applications.

18. *Modified Protocol*, p. 97. This argument continues today as Americans advocate that nations most capable of using satellite space should maximize the space while less industrialized nations should wait until their progress warrants satellite space, which will then be found for them. Two government publications that discuss American views on different aspects of spectrum allocation and satellite use are the International Communication Agency's *The United States and the Debate on the World 'Information Order'* (1979) and the Department of Commerce's *Direct Broadcast Satellites: Policies, Prospects, and Potential Competition* (1981) (both Washington: Government Printing Office).

19. *Modified Protocol*, pp. 71–74.

20. Even the best accounts of the relationship between the Department of Commerce and the American radio industry, such as Rosen, *The Modern Stentors*, fail to credit Alexander. Some of the correspondence on Alexander's support of these meetings is in RG 40, file 67032/3, Box 130, DCNA. Also see Alexander to Secretary of State Bainbridge Colby, 19 May 1920, RG 59, 574.D1/47, DSNA. In July 1920, Alexander headed one of the first committees of the Pan American Union to examine radio, the Inter-American High Commission of Communications. See Secretary of the Treasury David F. Houston to Colby, 16 July 1920, RG 59, 574.D1/180, DSNA.

21. "Recommendations of the India House Conference," no date, Box 29, Davis Papers; also see Feldman, *The United States in the International Communications Union*, p. 11.

22. Memo on conference with cable and radio interests, Third Assistant Secretary of State Van S. Merle-Smith, 4 November 1920, RG 59, 574.D1/238, DSNA.

23. Memo of 18 September 1920, Box 28, Davis Papers.

24. Postmaster General Albert S. Burleson joined Davis with four State Department delegates, three Navy and two Army delegates, and one Commerce delegate. Feldman, *The United States in the International Telecommunications Union*, p. 34.

25. The British and French delegations had carefully prepared a negotiating strategy that would force combination of radio and cable issues. American delegate Walter Rogers to Hughes, 26 July 1921, RG 59, 574.D1/463, DSNA. Also see memo of 18 September 1920, Box 29, Davis Papers; Rogers to State Department, 8 June 1921, RG 59, 574.D1/511, DSNA; Charles Neave, RCA and International General Electric, to Davis, 30 November 1920, RG 59, 574.D1/291, DSNA; and Feldman, *The United States in the International Telecommunications Union*, pp. 14–15.

26. In a memo Davis wrote for his successor on March 3, 1921, he remarked that international communications remained among the five most important problems for the State Department. He recommended strong support for American corporations attempting to develop radio services in China. Box 9, Davis Papers.

27. Memo by Foreign Trade Adviser Prentiss Gilbert, 2 April 1921, RG 59, 574.D1/618, DSNA.

28. Arthur Kennelly, Institute of Radio Engineers, to Secretary of Commerce Herbert Hoover, 7 April 1921, RG 40, file 67032/3, Box 130, DCNA. Fletcher and Rogers were among those who drafted this memo.

29. Philip Moran, ed., *Warren G. Harding, 1865–1923* (Dobbs Ferry: Oceana, 1970), p. 40. This support of the American press echoed the findings of the American Newspaper Publishers Committee on Cable and Radio Communications, which had called for expansion of American interests in international communications services for the American press. Members included the *New York Times*, *New York Herald*, *New York Tribune*, *Chicago Tribune*, *Chicago Daily News*, *Philadelphia Public Ledger*, the International News Service, and United Press. See the letter of

this committee to Assistant Secretary of Commerce Stephen Davis, 29 October 1920, Box 30, Davis Papers. Also see J. L. Renaud, "U.S. Government Assistance to Associated Press's World-Wide Expansion," *Journalism Quarterly* 62 (1985): 10.

30. *Conference Between the American Delegates to the International Conference on Electrical Communication and Various Representatives of the American Telegraph, Cable and Radio Companies* held in the Hotel Commodore, New York NY, 26–27 May 1921, in RG 59, 574.D1/minutes, commodore hotel, DSNA (hereafter *Hotel Commodore minutes*).

31. All quotes from RCA pamphlet on the Universal Electrical Communications Union, 23 May 1921, in RG 40, file 67032/3, Box 130, DCNA; all emphases in original. Several businessmen brought this pamphlet to the Hotel Commodore meetings and cited passages during the discussions.

32. Pamphlet, 23 May 1921, "Memorandum of Tropical Radio Telegraph Company Respecting the Proposed Universal Electrical Communications Union," printed by Tropical Radio Telegraph Company, in folder "Universal Electrical Communications Union 1920–1921," Box 677, Commerce Papers of Herbert Hoover, Herbert Hoover Presidential Library, West Branch, Iowa (hereafter HHPL—Commerce).

33. *Hotel Commodore minutes*, p. 3.

34. Ibid., p. 12.

35. Ibid., p. 57.

36. Ibid., p. 106.

37. Ibid., pp. 271–73.

38. Ibid., p. 273 1/2.

39. Alfred Goldsmith, RCA, to Hoover, 16 December 1921, RG 40, file 67032/3, Box 130, DCNA. Perhaps Hoover and other government officials interpreted reports such as this as a mandate for the first national broadcast communcations conference, held in February 1922. See Rosen, *The Modern Stentors*, pp. 39–41.

40. Aitken, *The Continuous Wave*, pp. 464, 490–92; Case and Case, *Owen D. Young*, pp. 237–42; Fejes, "Imperialism, Media and the Good Neighbor," pp. 22–24; Schreiner, *Cables and Wireless*, pp. 153–54; Hogan, *Informal Entente*, pp. 143–45; Hughes, "Owen D. Young and American Foreign Policy," pp. 94–102; Gleason Archer, *History of Radio to 1926* (New York: American Historical Society, 1939), pp. 227–39; James Herring and Gerald Gross, *Telecommunications: Economics and Regulations* (New York: McGraw-Hill, 1936), pp. 82–85; Leslie Tribolet, *The International Aspects of Electrical Communications in the Pacific Area* (Baltimore: Johns Hopkins University Press, 1924), pp. 57–59; Sir Osborne Mance, *International Telecommunications* (London: Oxford University Press, 1944), p. 64. Mance suggests that a Spanish company was also in the consortium. Most of these accounts extensively discuss the relationship between the consortium and the Monroe Doctrine, as Young had structured a system that gave RCA decison-making power over and above the other members. The consortium was not the only important agreement

Owen Young negotiated with Europe during the 1920s. He is best remembered for arranging the Dawes Plan in 1924 and the Young Plan in 1929, both of which offered solutions to the nagging problems of Allied war debts and German reparations. The unofficial American observer to the negotiations of the Reparations Commission, Roland W. Boyden, worked closely with Young on drafting the Dawes Plan. See Hughes, "Owen D. Young," p. 166. Boyden was the arbitrator of a 1924 patent dispute between RCA and American Telephone and Telegraph. Perhaps his admiration of Young influenced the final decision, which surprisingly went in favor of RCA. Young and Boyden both received honorary degrees from Harvard University during the same commencement ceremony on June 20, 1924. See Case and Case, *Owen D. Young*, pp. 278, 296.

41. Harbord to Stephen Davis, 19 October 1923, RG 151, Box 2731, DCNA.

42. State Department memo on conversation with J. J. Carty, American Telephone and Telegraph, 25 October 1923, RG 59, 574.D4/17 1/2; Carty to William R. Vallance, Solicitor's Office, 14 May 1924, RG 59, 574.D4/74; Carty to Vallance, 15 May 1924, RG 59, 574.D4/75; and American delegation, 1924 Mexico City Conference (hereafter Mexico City delegation) to State Department, 2 July 1924, RG 59, 574.D4/136; all DSNA.

43. Clipping from *El Excelsior*, Mexico City, 27 May 1924, in Mexico City delgation to State Department, no date, RG 59, 574.D492/-, DSNA (my translation).

44. Undated proposal written by delegate Wallace White in preparation for 1924 Mexico City conference, RG 59, 574.D4/179, DSNA. White believed that a successful conference would be "most speedily and completely realized through the enactment in each country of legislation recognizing and conferring the right of private ownership and operations of these communications enterprises. . . . Owners may make the rules for management and adminstration of their properties. . . . The power of government to supervise these activities should not be based on the ownership of them."

45. See the preceding chapter of this study for a discussion of the American radio industry's role in the emergence of a discourse on the military-industrial complex; also see Douglas, *Inventing American Broadcasting*, chap. 8.

46. Mexico City delegation to State Department, 17 June 1924, RG 59, 574.D4/98; Hughes to U.S. Ambassador to Brazil Edwin Morgan, 23 June 1924, RG 59, 574.D4/108a; both DSNA. Morgan inquired in Rio whether Barreto could replace Moscoso, but Moscoso retained the chairmanship. After the conference, Barreto called on Morgan and asked for his assistance in securing employment in RCA's Rio office. I have been unable to determine whether Barreto ever worked for RCA. See Morgan to State Department, 14 January 1925, RG 59, 574.D4/166, DSNA.

47. Mexico City delegation to State Department, 17 June 1924, RG 59, 574.D4/102; Mexico City delegation to State Department, 27 June 1924, RG 59, 574.D4/111; both DSNA.

48. State Department to Mexico City delegation, 7 July 1924, RG 59, 574.D41b/-, DSNA.

49. Vallance to Hughes, 17 July 1924, RG 59, 574.d41b/1, DSNA; Feldman, *The United States in the International Telecommunications Union*, pp. 111–12. The Babcock statement formally introduced the philosophy of private leadership in radio policy into the realm of international diplomacy. In 1926, J. G. Harbord of RCA (who had wished for an open declaration by American delegates at the Mexico City Conference) reiterated the Babcock statement in full (as well as offering suggestions for the upcoming 1927 Washington conference) in "America's Position in Radio Communication," *Foreign Affairs* 4 (April 1926): 465–74.

50. Vallance to State Department, 18 July 1924, RG 59, 574.D4/141, DSNA.

51. See RG 59, 811.74C731/-, DSNA on attendance of Canada, Mexico, and Cuba at the 1924 National Radio Conference.

52. Secretary of the Navy Curtis Wilbur to Hughes, 3 March 1925, RG 59, 574.D7/15, DSNA.

53. Vallance to White, 27 July 1927, RG 59, 574.D7/749 1/2; John Warren, Tropical Radio Telegraph Company, to Stephen Davis, 27 July 1927, RG 574.D7/775; both DSNA.

54. W. E. Lowry, Interdepartmental Radio Advisory Committee (IRAC), to Vallance, 28 March 1925, RG 59, 574.D71a/-; L. E. Whittemore, American Telephone and Telegraph, to Vallance, 17 March 1925, RG 59, 574.D7/20; memo, IRAC, 26 July 1926, RG 59, 574.D7/331 1/2; all DSNA.

55. Feldman, *The United States in the International Telecommunications Union*, pp. 40–47; Hogan, *Informal Entente*, p. 157; Commerce Department memo on businesses to be invited to conference, 16 March 1926, RG 59, 574.D7/246; Wittemore to Vallance, 28 September 1927, RG 59, 574.D7/927; both DSNA. Although international worker solidarity was in theory represented by the attendance of delegates from the Union of Soviet Socialist Republics (a nation with an intense interest in radio broadcasting during the 1920s and 1930s), one of the only labor owned and operated stations in the United States, WCFL Chicago, was denied participation—perhaps because it partly financed its operations through regular payments from labor unions, a system at odds with the advertising revenue for American commercial broadcasters. See William Green, American Federation of Labor, to Vallance, 16 August 1927, RG 59, 574.D7/774; and Nathan Godfried, "The Origins of Labor Radio: WCFL, the 'Voice of Labor,' 1925–1928," *Historical Journal of Film, Radio and Television* 7 (June 1987): 143–159. On early uses of broadcasting by the Soviets, see Thomas Guback and Stephen Hill, "The Beginnings of Soviet Broadcasting and the Role of V. I. Lenin," *Journalism Monographs* 26 (December 1972); and Leon Trotsky, "Radio Science, Technology and Society" (1926) in *Communications and Class Struggle*, vol. 2, ed. Armand Mattelart and Seth Siegelaub (New York: International General, 1983), pp. 252–59.

56. For typical examples of background information, see Edgar Bancroft, U.S. minister to Japan, to State Department, 30 June 1925, RG 59,

574.D7/36; American consul to Riga, Latvia, to State Department, 25 July 1927, RG 59, 574.D7/771; both DSNA. For examples of market statistics and investment climate, see Joseph Freed, Freed-Eisemann Radio Company, to State Department, 4 January 1926, RG 59, 574.D7/203, DSNA; George Lewis, Croseley Radio Manufacturing Company, to R. A. Lundquist, Department of Commerce, 15 December 1924, RG 151, file 544 — radio — Brazil, Box 2727, DCNA.

57. Vallance to Assistant Secretary of State William Castle, 21 June 1927, RG 59, 574.D7/686, DSNA.

58. Memo by Vallance on conversation with Carty, 28 May 1927, RG 59, 574.D7/643; Carty to Vallance, 1 June 1927, RG 59, 574.D7/649; both DSNA. A similar lighted map also appeared in the background of a 1987 AT&T television commercial featuring spokesperson Cliff Robertson.

59. "As visitors in the operating departments of AT&T and RCA, they forgot the precise language of the council chamber and reveled wholeheartedly in the marvels revealed in breathtaking number and variety. There was more than articulate surprise in the exclamation, 'This conference must end soon, for we shall never be able to explain all these uncanny things.' There was more than an epigram in the admiring tribute, 'Governments continue, but private enterprise improves.'" Raymond C. Willoughby, "Radio, a Test of Democracy," *Nation's Business*, January 1928, p. 36.

60. Feldman, *The United States in the International Telecommunications Union*, pp. 114–17.

61. U.S. Ambassador to Switzerland Hugh Wilson to State Department, 31 May 1930, RG 59, 574.G1/17; Vallance to Castle, 2 October 1930, RG 59, 574.G1/77; both DSNA.

62. The invitees included nine government agencies (including the Federal Radio Commission, attending its first global radio conference); American Telephone and Telegraph; the American Radio Relay League; Columbia Broadcasting System (CBS); International Telephone and Telegraph; National Broadcasting Company (NBC); RCA; Pan American Airways; Tropical Radio Telegraph Company; Westinghouse; the National Association of Broadcasters (NAB); the *New York Times*; the American Newspaper Publishers Association; and the U.S. Chamber of Commerce. See memo for Castle by Treaty Division, 4 December 1930, RG 59, 574.G1/137; and E. F. Morgan, Commerce, to State Department, 16 December 1931, RG 59, 574.G1/520; both DSNA.

63. A study of the International Telecommunications Union is J.L. Renaud, "The Changing Dynamics of the International Telecommunications Union: An Historical Analysis of Development Assistance," Ph.D. diss., Michigan State University, East Lansing, 1986.

64. After seven years of research on American foreign policy and the radio industry I am convinced that the riveting topic of radio and American-Canadian relations deserves a book of its own. In order to complete my research for this book, I have turned away from what would most likely be a long and fabulous journey through a number of archives and

manuscript collections in Washington, Ottawa, and elsewhere. Dallas Smythe has cleared some of the way for such historical research with his *Dependency Road: Communications, Capitalism, Consciousness, and Canada* (Norwood: Ablex, 1981). Graham Spry delivered his speech in April 1932; see Hanford McNider, American ambassador to Canada, to State Department, 5 April 1932, RG 59, 574.G1/609. The information in this chapter is based largely on this document. Also see Spry's "A Case for Nationalized Broadcasting," *Queen's Quarterly* 38 (Winter 1931): 151–69. My appreciation to Manjunath Pendakur for this article, and for alerting me to collect information on Spry as I visited various archives. On the American Radio Relay League, see Clinton DeSoto, *Two Hundred Meters and Down: The Story of Amateur Radio* (West Hartford: American Radio Relay League, 1936).

65. Feldman, *The United States in the International Telecommunications Union*, pp. 74–82, 114.

66. Mattelart and Siegelaub, *Communications and Class Struggle*, vol. 2, pp. 252–59.

67. J. Briggs, American delegation to 1932 Madrid Conference, to Castle, 23 November 1932, RG 59, 574.G1/1123, DSNA.

68. See chapter 5 for an examination of ties between private commercial broadcasters through North and South America. The American Radio Relay League (ARRL) had long argued the significance and importance of international amateur radio; for example, their presentation to the FCC in preparation for the 1938 Cairo Conference points out how international amateur radio fosters world understanding:

> It is impossible to have tens of thousands of citizens of the various nations of the world in constant communication with each other without making some contribution to better relations. The average American amateur makes scores of contacts every year with amateurs in other lands, and friendship follows communication . . . it must be conceded that this general atmosphere of "hands across the sea" makes for better understanding and more amicable relations between nations. Of particular importance does this aspect become when it is realized that, in other countries, the licensed transmitting amateur is usually the highest type of individual, often mature, and almost inevitably of a certain economic independence. This type of international intercourse is of the highest type, for it eliminates all selfishness, all credos, all materialistic or propagandistic motives, and aims only at the cultivation of international unity based on direct human friendship.

This pipeline to such individuals in other nations is one of the most enduring qualities of the global reach of the American radio industry, from popular reception through popular transmission. For the ARRL report, see "Presentation for the Amateur Service made by the American Radio Relay League," June 1936, FCC Docket no. 3929, filed in RG 59, 574.G2/26, DSNA.

69. "Visit of Cuban Radio Officials to United States," State Department memo, 4 December 1936, RG 59, 576.K1/3, DSNA.

70. H. Freeman Matthews to State Department, 1 February 1937, RG 59, 576.K1/11, DSNA; Federal Communications Commission (FCC) Chairman Amling Prall to Secretary of State Cordell Hull, 6 February 1937, RG 59, 576.K1/17, DSNA. The years examined in this book generally preclude the FCC's history of global influence.

71. Hull to President Franklin D. Roosevelt, 30 July 1937, RG 59, 576.K1/167, DSNA.

72. Prall to Hull, 17 March 1937, RG 59, 574.G2/178, DSNA. Prall assured Hull that everyone could depend on the FCC, and promised "from now on there is going to be in Washington a body to keep tabs on the international situation."

73. Memo, State Department Treaty Division, 13 November 1936, RG 59, 574.G2/41, DSNA; proposals of International Broadcasting Union for 1938 Cairo Conference, 8 February 1937, RG 59, 574.G2/134 ½, DSNA.

74. Feldman, *The United States in the International Telecommunications Union*, pp. 82–87; report by chair of American delegation Wallace White to Hull, 16 June 1938, RG 59, 574.G2/491, DSNA.

75. Department of State Publication 1286, Conference Series no. 39, *International Telecommunications Conference Cairo 1938, Report to the Secretary of State by the Chairman of the American Delegation, with Appended Documents* (Washington: Government Printing Office, 1939), filed in RG 59, 574.G2/736, DSNA.

76. Clipping from *Listin Diario*, San Jose, Costa Rica, 13 October 1937, in Franklin Atwood, American legation, to Hull, 13 October 1937, RG 59, 576.K1/274, DSNA.

77. McCormick, "Corporatism: A Reply to Rossi," pp. 54–55.

78. Braudel introduces this concept in *Civilization and Capitalism, 15th-18th Centuries*, vol. 3: *The Perspective of the World*, trans. Sian Reynolds (New York: Harper and Row, 1984), pp. 17–18.

4

Broadcasting Growth in
Latin America

As discussed in the previous three chapters, the American radio industry and American government policymakers developed a foreign policy for the radio industry designed to maximize its spread into the global economy and also allow American leaders a large measure of control over the direction of hemispheric communications. This chapter will examine the day-to-day spread of broadcasting in Latin America (primarily during the 1920s) as its growth was encouraged by the cooperation of the American radio industry and the American government. This examination begins with a detailed study of activities in Brazil, followed by a nation-by-nation account of the rest of Latin America. Brazil is used for a opening case study because it is a large country, and many different American individuals worked in Brazil toward promoting radio broadcasting. The initiation and early growth of broadcast activities in other nations, accounts of which follow the discussion of Brazil, were in many ways similar to the Brazilian experience.

The day-to-day cooperation by American individuals in promoting Latin American radio broadcasting growth that entailed was not brought about by the "architects" of radio policy so much as by the "carpenters." In other words, the individuals who worked out the cooperation between capital and the state on an everyday basis were not so much the leading executives and investors in the radio industry and the highest echelon of government representatives in the Commerce and State Departments. Instead, this chapter is the story of State Department consular representatives, Commerce Department commercial attaches, mid-level government workers in such branches as the Electrical Equipment Division of the Bureau of Foreign and Domestic Commerce or the Division of Latin American Affairs at the Department of State, traveling salesmen drumming up business for American radio equipment throughout the Western Hemisphere, operators of import-export houses in both the United States and Latin America, and a worldwide radio broadcasting audience whose enthusiasm for the product was unprecedented in modern history.

Brazil

Little, if any, radio broadcasting of any nature existed in Brazil in 1922. No Brazilian entities had begun any sort of regular indigenous broadcasting, and various government restrictions effectively prohibited the ownership of a receiving set without permission from the executive branch. However, Commerce Department officials did not feel that the lack of broadcasting, nor governmental restrictions on set ownership, prevented the eventual introduction of broadcasting throughout Brazil. In April, R. A. Lundquist of the Bureau of Foreign and Domestic Commerce wrote Commerce Attache to Rio de Janeiro William R. Schurz about the future of broadcasting in Brazil. Radio broadcasting was growing rapidly in the United States, and Lundquist expected that public interest would soon begin in other nations. He asked Schurz for a report on any restrictions that would prevent the sale of American radio equipment in Brazil.[1]

The major Brazilian cultural event in 1922 was the celebration of the national centennial, scheduled to run through 1922 and part of 1923. The focal point of the centennial celebration was a full-scale exposition hosted in Rio de Janeiro. The exposition featured exhibits, pavillions, and presentations from nations around the world.[2] American firms and organizations built several elaborate displays showing the broad range of American manufacturing and agriculture, as well as the latest advances in consumer products and cultural pastimes. American film distributors shipped hundreds of hours of recent productions to the exposition and helped finance the construction of several theaters.[3] Although films probably represented the highlight of American displays of cultural entertainment, the new broadcasting medium also had displays built and sponsored by American radio manufacturing corporations. Westinghouse mounted a major presentation depicting the pleasureable entertainment and enjoyment available through the radio.[4] The display featured a listener comfortably seated in a wicker chair, with Westinghouse radio apparatus placed on a long table. The listener used headphones, although a loudspeaker took up one corner of the table. He leaned back, smoked a pipe, and enjoyed the radio fare along with a breeze from a small electric fan. Various radio tubes and a phonograph also occupied the table. The entire display was surrounded by a low fence behind which fair-goers viewed the proceedings.[5]

Westinghouse had not merely simulated broadcasting; they actually set up a broadcasting system for the centennial exposition. A transmitter had been installed on Mount Corovado (now the site of a well-known statue of Jesus), and daily transmissions were received at the exposition grounds. Although the sale of receiving sets had not been legalized, Westinghouse cicumvented the problem by installing several loudspeakers throughout the fairgrounds and giving the president of Brazil a high-quality Westinghouse receiver. The Westinghouse radio exhibit so impressed Brazilian officials that the company received an exposition grand prize; Western Electric also received an exposition grand prize for its radio exhibit.[6] Best of all for the enthusiastic Cariocans, Westinghouse had no plans to dismantle its broadcasting system after the centennial. Within a few months of the exposition opening, the *New York Times* reported that the "radiophone craze" had hit Rio de Janeiro with the same kind of fervor that had become an old story in the United States. Despite official regulations preventing set ownership, several homes and buildings had quickly installed receivers, and listeners as far away as Sao Paulo tuned in for the daily programming of concerts, news reports, and lectures. The *New York Times* believed this was the first big broadcasting station to operate in South America.[7]

The availability of receiving sets in the face of official prohibition at first appears somewhat of a mystery. However, American radio manufacturers began exporting sets to Brazil in 1922 despite the ownership prohibitions. Exporters hoped for an easing of martial law during the exposition, but a decree in 1922 postponed relaxation of radio regulations. In view of these developments, importing houses apparently kept their sets under cover, primarily stockpiling them, but also distributing them surreptitiously, in expectation of a future relaxing of regulations.[8] A relaxation had not come about as the centennial wound down in 1923, but the American consul to Sao Paulo still was convinced that broadcasting would someday be widespread in Brazil. E. M. Larvion reported that

> Conditions are apparently favorable for radio broadcasting . . . a local telephone company has erected a broadcasting station with the understanding that it has to be demolished as soon as the centennial exposition is closed and that for the present the Brazilian government has made no plans for radio stations in Brazil . . . it appears that it is unlawful for one to own a radio set or in any way to establish a radio station. If this is correct, there will be no market . . . until some legislation is enacted for recognizing this industry.[9]

The impasse on receiver set ownership finally began to break about eighteen months after the opening of the centennial exposition. In February 1924, the Brazilian minister of public works authorized the establishment of four broadcasting stations.[10] Although it did not completely address the nationwide concerns of broadcasting growth, the authorization did create an important opening for the spread of broadcasting. In December 1923, the Bureau of Foreign and Domestic Commerce had forecast radio progress and market potential in northeast Brazil. A radio club had been founded in Pernambuco, and the club members operated a small transmitter and a few receiving sets. The bureau thought this club represented one of the first indications of a promising future market.[11] The Brazilian Ministry of Communications granted club members authorization to own and operate receiving sets upon proof of citizenship.[12] The formation of several such radio clubs would play a major role in introducing radio broadcasting to much of Brazil.

Radio fever soon spread down the coast to Bahia. Three local businessmen—Oscar Carrascosa, Agenor Miranda, and Archimedos Gonclaves—formed a radio club there and had attracted about a hundred members by March 1924.[13] In addition, several neighboring towns contacted the Bahia club about their operations. In October 1924, the radio club ordered transmitting equipment from the United States. Homer Brett, the local American consul, welcomed these developments.

> Hitherto there has been no possibility of selling any considerable number of radio receiving sets, as the nearest broadcasting station was at Rio, a distance of 700 miles. . . . Nothing resem-

bling the market in American states of similar population can be developed as the individual purchasing power does not exist, but it is probable that every small village and town, of which there are hundreds, will purchase at least one receiving set in the next year or two.[14]

The situation in northeast Brazil was not unique; radio broadcasting had quickly captured the imagination of people around the world. By 1924, the Bureau of Foreign and Domestic Commerce had received so many requests from its attaches for radio literature that the bureau initiated a regular series of reports and mailings detailing radio broadcasting's latest advances.[15] Commerce officials reported that a great deal of interest in radio had been displayed in Brazil since the centennial exposition. The department recommended that American radio manufacturers establish local agencies for radio sales throughout Brazil, and also back up radio exports with advertising campaigns. One saleman who had recently returned from Rio de Janeiro described the city as "radio mad!" and reported that Brazilians quickly read any and all literature on radio.[16]

The Brazilian broadcasting boom continued in 1924 with the establishment of a radio electrical school in Pernambuco. The school was one of the first Brazilian institutions designed to train radio technicians.[17] During 1924, the Brazilian government adopted an informal policy of granting citizens permission to own a set if they paid an inexpensive registration fee. Brazilians began to install sets in their homes at an increased rate, even in the interior of the nation. Listeners in Para and in the Amazon valley heard stations as far away as Rio de Janeiro, Buenos Aires, New York City, Pittsburgh, and Schenectady.[18] Finally, an executive decree issued in November 1924 eliminated virtually all restrictions on set ownership, and also provided guidelines for the construction and operation of transmitters. Most of the regulations remaining after the decree attempted, by limiting transmission hours slightly, to alleviate problems of static and interference caused by the relationship between tropical conditions and the electromagnetic spectrum. In addition, the decree approved commercial advertising, program sponsorship, and private ownership of broadcast stations.[19] The American radio industry applauded these events. George Lewis of the Croseley Radio Manufacturing Company told

Commerce Department officials that his company had not been able to devote much attention to foreign demand because of the initial surge of the domestic market. However, Lewis felt that the initial domestic demand had been met by the end of 1924, and he saw great promise in Brazil.[20] The momentum toward broadcast growth carried into 1925, and American consulates increasingly received requests from Brazilians for American radio catalogues and magazines. Consuls also informed American radio manufacturers and exporters of new Brazilian radio clubs as they formed.[21]

American foreign service representatives in Brazil prepared a comprehensive report on broadcasting as it stood in 1925. Alphonse Gaulin reported that considerable progress had been made in broadcasting development and that the use of radio as an entertainment medium was common. Gaulin pointed to the introduction of agricultural programming and the daily reporting of coffee exchange quotations as important trends for the future. He concluded by citing the proliferation of radio clubs, the printing of broadcast schedules in local newspapers, and the popularity of new broadcast-oriented magazines such as *RADIO* as strong indicators of the potential of the Brazilian market.

> There is potentially, a very important market for radio equipment in Brazil. Although little has been done in the past towards development of radio activities, radio devotees have within the past two years become quite active. Radio receiving sets will probably never be distributed in Brazil as in the United States, because of the poverty of the working classes. . . . In spite of the obstacles, a number of American manufacturers have found this market to be a profitable one, and it is believed that others may do likewise.[22]

Among the obstacles American radio manufacturers and exporters faced were the nature of the Brazilian market (including its climate) and the temperament of the local consumer. Commerce Department attaches found that

> sets which will give reasonable uniform reception of Buenos Aires will satisfy the Brazilian market. Such sets must be well constructed, foolproof, and require a minimum of servicing. The average Brazilian set owner is easily discouraged and disposed to abandon radio if his receiving set does not fully meet the claims of the dealer in the matter of range. Brazilians

are not generally inclined to acquaint themselves with the
technical operations of their sets, and there are few radio
mechanics or engineers to assist them. . . .[23]

This disdain for technical operations and lack of trained engineers and mechanics was endemic in Latin America during the
1920s and 1930s. Concurrent with the lack of major technological
research centers in Latin America was the lack of "Yankee ingenuity" among the consuming publics of the Latin nations; the
widespread American fascination with inventors, inventions, and
inventing that was a core attribute of American society during the
rise of radio never materialized in Latin American societies.
Manufacturers had to make their sets easier to operate, which also
had an impact on the domestic market; by the late 1920s, sets were
appearing in the United States that could be operated easily with
few controls.[24] Manufacturers also had to compensate for high
humidity and other variables of the tropical climate by using more
brass and copper parts in wiring and set construction. However,
sets built to withstand tropical conditions could be exported to
other tropical areas such as Cuba, the Philippines, and certain
parts of Africa. Exporters faced some foreign competition in the
Brazilian market, but by the latter part of the decade American
sets and parts dominated sales to the point where they represented nearly 90 percent of the market. Two small domestic
manufacturing plants operated in Brazil and assembled imported
parts, but they accounted for a very small market share.

Brazilian radio listeners demonstrated enthusiasm similar to
that of American listeners in the 1920s. Along with the publication of *RADIO*, local newspapers regularly listed broadcast schedules. In Rio de Janeiro, most editions of the morning daily *O Jornal*
published a radio section that included program listings, articles
on new developments in broadcasting, and occasionally schema-
tic diagrams of simple radio circuits. Brazilians enjoyed their own
stations, and also regularly tuned in to stations from abroad, such
as the many stations of Buenos Aires. Listeners in Pernambuco in
1925 also began to listen regularly to experimental shortwave
broadcasts from KDKA in Pittsburgh (owned by Westinghouse).
American consul Fred Eastin believed this proved that broadcasting, particularly as it was conducted in the United States, could be
"an important factor in the closer approximation of Brazil and the

United States in a friendly relationship."[25] KDKA suspended some of its shortwave broadcasts in the summer, which led to protests from Pernambuco listeners. The *Diario do Pernambuco* went so far as to speculate that a frustrated American radio salesman had "obtained the cessation by KDKA of its irradiation on shortwave" in revenge for a poor sales trip to the Pernambuco area earlier that year.[26] In fact, the halt of transmissions was no more than an evaluation of experiments at KDKA. Westinghouse engineer C. W. Horn assured Pernambuco residents that transmissions would resume soon.

> I have known for quite a while that KDKA's Shortwave reached such distant points as Brazil. . . . We have never considered the Shortwave transmitter as a broadcasting station, and, therefore, do not hold ourselves responsible to any audience. . . . Any interruptions such as are necessary in experimental work which have caused disappointment and annoyance are entirely unintentional on our part . . . the summer season is upon us and transmission is more difficult. . . . I assure you that we are very much interested in having Brazilian people listen to our station and I shall make every effort to see that our operations are interrupted as little as possible.[27]

The transmissions did in fact resume in the fall, and over the next few years KDKA was joined on Latin American radio dials by a number of other American shortwave broadcasters.

By the end of 1925, Brazil ranked sixth of all export markets for American radio equipment.[28] As the decade passed, more and more Brazilians perceived the American-style broadcasting permeating their everyday lives as an indispensible source of entertainment, information, culture, and their own national consciousness. The introduction of broadcasting at the centennial exposition—the celebration of a century of political independence—probably helped to link the production and consumption of broadcasting with the social progress believed to be inherent in a hundred years of nationhood. Broadcasting moved inward with the construction of a thousand-watt station in Manaus in 1926.[29] Later that same year, the radio club of Pernambuco hosted a radio convention and exposition. Club members welcomed any displays of catalogues, illustrated books, magazines, or advertising leaflets that American radio manufacturers and exporters could provide.[30] By 1927, twelve stations with daily broadcast schedules served Brazilian cities. Five had been built exclusively with American equipment. A new station opened in Porto Alegre in 1927. This station, run by the Societade Gaucho de Porto Alegre, was the first to operate in the southern section of Brazil between Sao Paulo and Buenos Aires and opened another region of the country to the broad range of possibilities of broadcasting.[31]

Brazil climbed to the fifth spot in American exports of radio equipment by 1928, trailing only Argentina (which imported three times the volume of Brazil) in South American markets. U. S. Ambassador Edwin Morgan reported that Brazilian radio regulations had begun to follow the guidelines of the 1927 Washington Conference held the previous year. Brazil instituted a systematic organization of radio frequencies by service, which opened far greater areas of the spectrum for shortwave transmission into Brazil from abroad.[32] Although exports to Brazil in 1929 increased more than $100,000, to a yearly total of $550,037, Brazil ranked only ninth in American radio equipment export markets that year as Argentina and Mexico both surpassed $1 million and Cuba exceeded $650,000. By 1929, Sao Paulo had reached the same level of broadcasting development as Rio de Janeiro. While the centennial exposition had led to the permanent establishment of broadcasting two years earlier in Rio, radio proved just as popular among the Paulistas, and when given the opportunity, it grew just as quickly. A thousand-watt station opened in Sao Paulo in 1927 and led to a shortage of receivers, parts, and headsets in the city, as well as increasing demand for American receiving sets.[33] Another station opened in Sao Paulo in February 1929, and from its inception supported itself with advertising revenue. This station, as well as two other new stations in Sao Paulo, used American equipment exclusively in their construction.[34]

The roots of the American radio industry had firmly taken hold in Brazil by 1930, a hold cemented through the introduction of broadcasting. As an export market, Brazil steadily absorbed increases in American exports of radio equipment throughout the 1920s. Broadcasting stations first appeared in major cities along the coast in the earlier part of the decade. As the decade closed, broadcasting stations opened in the interior and in medium-sized cities such as Porto Alegre and Cruziero do Sul, while the number of stations in large cities such as Rio and Sao Paulo increased.

Finally, as an advertising vehicle, radio broadcasting in Brazil also followed the general trends of American-style broadcasting. Radio advertising became more and more common in 1928, 1929, and 1930. Broadcasting proved to be an effective medium to reach a population wealthy enough to afford receiving sets and other goods priced beyond the reach of mass buying power, although more and more everyday products also came to be advertised in the 1930s as the radio set became a more common possession among Brazilian citizens.[35] Products advertised through Brazilian broadcasting included automobiles, phonograph records, radio sets, motion pictures, cigarettes, clothing, and furniture. American advertising agencies began to open their first branch offices in South America to coincide with this rise in radio advertising in the late 1920s.

American consular representatives from the State Department and commercial attaches from the Commerce Department played important roles in the introduction of broadcasting in Brazil. Both departments cooperated with the various American exhibitors at the centennial exposition in 1922, including the radio exhibits. During the rest of the decade, consular and attache assistance followed a general pattern, with some specialization in each department. A general concern of both departments was the penetration, protection, and promotion of the American radio industry. In practice, the commercial attaches often concentrated on the establishment of a radio equipment market. The Commerce Department believed that radio manufacturing could grow more effectively both at home and abroad with departmental assistance and a greater awareness of global consumption patterns in radio equipment.

Although State Department consuls certainly promoted exports and sales of American radio equipment in Brazil, they also devoted their energies to the overall establishment of the American broadcasting model. This included American programming patterns, the growth of advertising, the guidelines of the 1927 Washington Conference, assistance for radio clubs in securing American radio literature, training and technical workshops for Brazilians, availability of American music in the form of sheet music and recordings, and radio fairs and exhibits. In a sense, the State Department consular service moved beyond the promotion of American radio equipment into the broader area of promotion of the entire American broadcasting style. Both promotion of American radio equipment and promotion of the American broadcasting style proved determinant in transplanting the American radio industry and American mass culture into Brazil. In other Latin American nations during the 1920s, similar patterns of cooperation were evident between state and capital: the American government, as represented by consuls and attaches; and the American radio industry, as represented by manufacturers, exporters, salesmen, and traders, protected and promoted the growth of the American radio industry and American-style broadcasting throughout Latin America.

Mexico

Mexico in the 1920s was second only to Canada in the volume of American radio equipment imported; annual exports to Mexico topped $250,000 in 1925 and surpassed $1 million by 1929.[36] American public and private radio policymakers all agreed that Mexico held great potential as a market for American radio equipment and for American-style broadcasting. George Sweet, who had been involved with radio in the U.S. Navy during the war, believed that the reception of American broadcasts in Mexico would go a long way toward better relations between Mexicans and Americans of all classes.[37] In 1921, Constanto de Tarnara, an electrician with American training, established in Mexico City one of the first Latin American stations based on the American model of broadcasting. Others in Mexico City quickly followed his lead. Although these broadcasters had begun experiments in Mexico City in 1921, radio was still not well known outside of the Federal District two years later. The American consul in San Luis Potosi thought that many residents in his area would not be able to afford a receiving set in the forseeable future, yet the selling of sets to miners and others in remote locations could nevertheless begin immediately; further, sales would likely increase if American suppliers could offer generous credit terms to local merchants who stocked American radio sets and parts.[38]

During the middle part of the decade, broadcasting stations began operations in the other large and medium-sized cities of Mexico. By 1925, stations were on the air in Guadalajara, Veracruz, Mazatlan, and Chihuahua.[39] By 1930, at least twelve broadcasting stations, privately owned and supported by advertising, operated in Mexico City alone, and more than 90 percent of the hundred thousand receiving sets throughout Mexico were American models. Mexico had a small indigenous manufacturing industry but consumers preferred American sets, especially after the introduction in 1925 of AC-operated sets (alternating current—or household current rather than battery-operated). This important innovation eliminated large, cumbersome storage batteries similar in size to today's automobile battery. Demand for powerful American sets employing three to six tubes grew during the decade because these sets could receive distant signals from all of Mexico and much of the United States.

Advertising also proved a successful component of radio broadcasting in Mexico. By 1930, more than thirty stations in Mexico regularly accepted commercials and program sponsorship from large and small businesses. These commercials and programs reinforced the same kinds of consumer habits and consumption patterns associated with consumer ideology in the United States.[40]

The Caribbean and Central America

In the Caribbean, two patterns of radio development emerged in the 1920s.[41] The politically independent island nations such as Cuba tended to follow American trends in radio broadcasting growth, whereas the island colonies such as Jamaica tended to show inhibited growth, a lack of local broadcasting (although not of receiving sets), and a greater measure of control over radio enforced by the colonial power. In the 1930s, these island colonies did begin to develop radio broadcasting somewhat dependent on European models of broadcasting.

Of the islands that followed American trends, Cuba showed the most rapid growth. Radio broadcasting had been introduced by International Telephone and Telegraph, which built stations in Havana and San Juan in the early 1920s. Although they began to withdraw from broadcasting in 1922 in order to concentrate exclusively on telephone service, the stations continued to operate twice a week.[42] Cubans quickly embraced the radio habit, and Havana alone had at least thirty-one broadcasting stations by 1930, although some operated at irregular hours. After the 1927 Washington Conference, Cuba instituted a frequency realignment so listeners could receive more American stations. Virtually all sets in use were American models. American exports of radio equipment to Cuba climbed from about $85,000 in 1925 to more than $650,000 in 1929, a remarkable growth rate for a four-year period. American broadcasters showed an early interest in the Cuban radio situation. American Telephone and Telegraph set up a link between its flagship station, WEAF New York, and Havana station PWX in February 1924 for an experimental chain broadcast.[43] Rates for commercial time on Cuban stations remained extremely low throughout the 1920s. Havana was one of the first Latin American cities penetrated by branches of American advertising agencies, which often used radio as a medium for product campaigns. Commercials covered a range of products, including women's clothes, soap, fruit drinks, cameras, phonographs, and various Havana shops.

In the Dominican Republic, radio did not grow as it did in Cuba. However, one broadcasting station operated on a regular basis throughout the decade, and although the number of sets in use was small, American shortwave receivers proved popular. The local station accepted advertising, and products promoted included food, mattresses, cigarettes, American radios and phonographs, and local hotels and theaters. Although the local American consul believed in 1930 that Dominican listeners did not want another station of their own because they preferred tuning in American stations, by 1934 seven stations broadcast in Santo Domingo and an additional four broadcast in other cities, suggesting that Dominicans and other Latin American audiences did enjoy several of their own stations as well as several stations from the United States.[44]

In Haiti, one station, owned by the Haitian government and supervised by a U.S. naval officer, supplied regular programming and accepted advertising. However, most sets in use belonged to the families of the American troops who occupied Haiti. American phonograph records, when broadcast locally, were popular among the few native Haitians who had receiving sets. The station also cooperated with the Haitian government in broadcasting a number of educational programs and lectures in Creole.[45]

An extremely low standard of living and the lack of disposable income for consumer products among all but a very few residents impeded the growth of radio in Central America. Despite the obstacles, Honduras, Guatemala, El Salvador, Nicaragua, Costa Rica, and Panama all showed signs of assimilating American patterns of radio broadcasting. Of all Central American nations, Costa Rica showed the most promise and the greatest development. A station operated in San Jose, and Costa Rica quickly implemented the recommendations of the 1927 Washington Conference in frequency allocations. Although advertising was still somewhat uncommon even by 1930, two stations in Costa Rica accepted commercials and charged low rates to sponsors. American sets remained popular throughout the decade with Central American listeners. However, sets were expensive and reception subject to static. The *Diario de Central America*, a Guatemalan newspaper, estimated in January 1925 that there were only about sixty receiving sets in and around Guatemala City.[46] Honduras also had one station that accepted advertising. The owners claimed that although the number of sets owned by Hondurans remained small, the installation of several loudspeakers throughout Tegucigalpa enhanced listenership and increased the effectiveness of radio advertising.

The U.S. Navy's special involvement with Panama had delayed the development of broadcasting and the ability of Panamanians interested in radio to enjoy the latest radio advances. For example, the chair of a local radio club in Panama complained in 1922 that local amateur radio enthusiasts did not enjoy the pleasure of regular radio contacts with other amateurs in North and Central America and that the Navy was to blame.[47] American policymakers were sympathetic to concerns, and early in 1923 the American government relaxed its radio policy for Panama so radio broadcasting could grow quickly. Panamanians were given permission in 1923 to own and operate receiving sets without prior approval of American or Panamanian authorities; in addition, the Navy began a broadcast schedule from the Canal Zone.[48] The actions satisfied Panamanian broadcast enthusiasts briefly, but by 1925 they had successfully lobbied for their own broadcast station free of direct American control.[49]

Argentina

Along with Brazil, Mexico, and Cuba, Argentina represented a major market for the spread of the American radio industry in

Latin America.[50] During the 1920s, Argentina had radio growth and development equal to, if not greater than, Brazil and Mexico. Buenos Aires had twenty broadcasting stations by 1930, and Argentine broadcasters enjoyed a free hand from any extensive government restrictions. Regulations primarily covered frequency allocation; no exceptional restrictions prohibited importing, manufacturing, or merchandising equipment.

Interest in broadcasting was evident in Buenos Aires even before 1920, and by 1923 three major stations provided a regular broadcast schedule. In addition, a weekly magazine, *Radio Cultura*, reported on the latest developments in equipment and programming.[51] The Buenos Aires stations were received through much of Argentina, especially in the plains areas where no mountains blocked their signals. Radio quickly proved so popular that an RCA executive commented in 1923 that "The vogue of radio down here surpasses anything that can be imagined . . . entire operas are broadcast every night . . . the roofs of the buildings are loaded with antenna wires . . . last year, the number of amateurs amounted to a few hundred; this year, there are more than 25,000."[52] Program fare included general news of the day, weather reports, market reports, music, lectures, and performances by visiting classical musicians. Program content was unrestricted (or restricted only by the proper sensibilities of the broadcasters themselves), and advertising was permitted; sponsors included local banks, the local distributor of Victor records, radio equipment, foodstuffs, and "La Voz del Aire," the newest Westinghouse radio set on the Argentine market. American sets were popular and represented the majority of those in use. One powerful Buenos Aires station was operated by Radio Sud America, a branch of RCA originally established to sell RCA equipment, and which subsequently began radio broadcasting as an adjunct to equipment sales. In 1924, Radio Sud America began to pick up the signal of KDKA Pittsburgh occasionally and rebroadcast KDKA in Buenos Aires, which proved popular with Argentine audiences.[53] British and German sets were also available, and Argentina had a moderately sized indigenous radio manufacturing industry. The major Argentine receiver—the Pekam—was found throughout Argentina and to a lesser extent in Brazil, Uruguay, Paraguay, Bolivia, and Chile.

Argentine broadcasters generally structured their program content similar to that of American broadcasters, offering popular music and entertainment with occasional news reports and lectures supported by advertising revenue. The major Argentine broadcasters each owned several stations. One such broadcaster, Jaime Yankelevich, occasionally offered simultaneous sponsored programs over his eight stations—an early form of chain broadcasting or network distribution of programs. By the early 1930s, nearly fifty stations broadcast in Argentina, about thirty of which operated daily. All of these stations gained their operating revenue through the sale of advertising, although commercial announcements rather than sponsored programs had become the rule. These stations also began broadcasting prerecorded electrical transcriptions on a regular basis in the early 1930s. A new network, the "Primera Cadena Argentina de Broadcasting," linked stations in Buenos Aires, Rosario, Bahia Blanca, Cordoba, and Mendoza.[54]

Uruguay

Uruguay's proximity to many of the major urban areas of Brazil and Argentina, especially Buenos Aires, provided a multitude of stations for Uruguayan listeners, and thus radio development and growth nearly paralleled the Brazilian and Argentine experiences.[55] Montevideo had nineteen broadcasting stations by 1930, and, as in Brazil and Argentina, national regulations supported private ownership and advertising revenue. The American radio industry enjoyed an extremely receptive national market in Uruguay. Both General Electric and Westinghouse had associations with stations in Montevideo. The General Electric station was one of only two stations with sufficient power to be heard throughout Uruguay and, by extension, Buenos Aires and the southern section of Brazil. The local American consul noted in 1925 that "homemade sets are now being supplanted by the newer and more attractive sets from both Uruguayan and foreign factories. Almost all the parts used in local manufacture are American . . . the buyers seem to have more confidence in the American product, owing to the fact that the United States is, to them, the home of radio development, and the place from which emanates the most radio information. . . ."[56] This view of the United States as the home of radio development surely must have been gratifying to American public and to private officials involved with the radio industry. Uruguayan stations also kept pace with the latest American technological innovations and were among the first in South America to convert to long-playing transcription discs.[57]

Bolivia and Paraguay

American radio equipment entered both Bolivia and Paraguay through direct imports, which were small in volume, and also through an informal or undocumented manner.[58] For example, a number of sets in Paraguay entered through Argentine importers of American radio equipment, who subsequently exported the equipment to Paraguay. Neither nation showed the extent of development as an export market as did most other nations such as Brazil, Mexico, or Cuba. Neither country showed promise as a market for steady growth. A few Bolivians did operate powerful receiving sets capable of picking up stations in Buenos Aires, Santiago, and the United States.[59] Both Bolivia and Paraguay had one broadcasting station in its capital. Although the station in Asunción did not always accept advertising, perhaps due to its irregular hours of operation, the station in La Paz regularly aired commercial messages. Various sponsors included auto dealers, soft drinks, local jewelers, clothing stores, and merchants. Local Bolivian newspapers also sponsored short news reports on the La Paz station. The Asunción station operated with a very low-power transmitter; the highlight of each week was a concert broadcast every Friday night at 9. These concerts helped develop what interest there was among Paraguayans in the possibilities of owning a radio set.[60]

Chile

In Chile, German exports posed the major alternative to American equipment, although American receiving sets accounted for about two-thirds of the Chilean market.[61] The penetration of American radio equipment and American-style broadcasting resembled that of other major South American export markets. However, the disparity of purchasing power between the upper and the lower classes in Chile tended to stymie growth. Because of the Andes Mountains, Chilean listeners also had difficulty picking up foreign stations, which also slowed growth. Reception from the six stations in Santiago and Valparaiso remained relatively clear throughout the nation all year. These six stations accepted commercial advertising, and all met their operating expenses through advertising revenue.

Peru and Ecuador

The radio development in Peru and Ecuador somewhat resembled the relationship between Argentina and Paraguay.[62] Although Peru became a strong export market and also had stations that accepted advertising by the end of the decade, Ecuador did not show any significant signs of radio growth. As late as 1930, no broadcasting stations operated in Ecuador, and the few citizens with receiving sets primarily listened to stations in Lima. The introduction of shortwave receivers led to a few sales, but overall growth was small.

The Peruvian government took a more active role than most Latin American governments in the introduction of broadcasting within its borders. The government originally authorized a broadcasting monopoly to Marconi interests early in the 1920s.[63] This monopoly included an agreement that the Marconi interests would provide 50 percent of all receiving sets in Peru. However, this agreement eventually broke down, in part due to the brisk sales that exhausted the quota of American equipment while the Marconi equipment (according to a local American consul) could not be moved from the shelves. In addition, Americans—as well as some Peruvians—argued that the Marconi agreements did not specifically address commercial radio broadcasting, and therefore broadcasting in Peru was open to all comers.[64] The government dissolved the monopoly in 1926 by revoking the import quota system. Two broadcasting stations operated in Lima, and one of these accepted advertising. The government continued to involve itself in radio matters more directly than did other Latin American nations and oversaw the operations of the commercial station, although the programming content tended to follow American patterns of radio programming.

Colombia, Venezuela, and the Guianas

A lack of purchasing power among all but a very few wealthy citizens, coupled with severe interference and static from tropical conditions, at first inhibited radio development in Colombia, Venezuela, British and French Guiana, and Surinam.[65] In the Guianas and Surinam, one station operated at very irregular hours in Georgetown. A very few shortwave listeners were scattered about the Guianas and Surinam, occasionally picking up distant signals from Mexico, the United States, the Caribbean, and northeast Brazil.

Colombia and Venezuela also had reception problems, particularly in trying to pick up foreign stations. Two stations began operations in Bogota in 1929 and 1930, while one station opened in Caracas in 1924. Venezuela, like Peru, also had attempted to make broadcasting a monopoly, but the action was later revoked and regulations changed to favor private ownership and advertising support. Government officials in Venezuela had at first been dubious about the mass ownership of receiving sets; they worried that government communications via wireless would be received by all the public. By 1924, however, American consuls and radio representatives had allayed that fear, and Venezuela began to be developed as an export market for American radio equipment.[66] The Bogota stations also accepted advertising. The owner of the Caracas station also owned a radio and phonograph distribution firm specializing in American sets and recordings. The Caracas station occasionally picked up the shortwave broadcasts of WGY (owned by General Electric) in Schenectady and rebroadcast the signal over its frequency in Caracas.

Latin America was the American radio industry's biggest success story, but the carpenters of radio expansion were at work around the world. Asia and Africa also had radio encouraged by the activities of the American radio industry. Africa and most of the Middle East never reached the level of broadcasting that was the norm in Latin America by 1930, but certain African nations, such as the Union of South Africa, became important markets for American radio equipment.[67] Few Africans showed an initial interest in radio broadcasting, but by the 1930s it had become popular in North Africa where European stations were easy to receive.

In Asia, some nations became important export markets for American radio equipment, especially Japan, Australia, and New Zealand.[68] In addition, the American radio industry enjoyed a closed export market in the Philippine colonies. Although Japan in the early 1920s was a major American radio export market, by 1930 a successful radio set sub-assembly industry controlled by Japanese investors and protected by legislation had changed the nature of the Japanese export market from one based primarily on receiving sets to one based primarily on radio parts, especially tubes and loudspeakers. Japan also controlled the Korean market. In China, radio was more popular with the large foreign population than with native Chinese.

Radio in India remained, as might be expected, in the domain of British influence. Australians, on the other hand, proved very receptive to American equipment and American-style broadcasting, as did New Zealanders. Radio receiving equipment also made its way into the island nations of the South Pacific. Pacific island listeners heard broadcasts from Australia, New Zealand, Japan, Hawaii, and American cities on the Pacific Coast. A Fijian newspaper summed up the island's enthusiasm for broadcasting in 1925 by noting "when conditions are favorable, the air is literally crowded with American stations . . . the joys of a good receiving set far out-weigh the ownership of a motor car."[69]

Along with the protection and promotion of the American radio industry, the carpenters of radio expansion also played a role in promoting at a global level the modern American culture of consumption.[70] The new wave of prosperity that the American-controlled world communications system helped deliver provided a step forward in the standard of living for American consumers, and in the 1920s that step forward often included the purchase of a radio set and the regular reception of broadcast programming.

The new consumer culture, although centered in American society, was not confined to domestic events. In the case of radio broadcasting, the carpenters of capital and the state spread not only an industry but also the culture that spawned that industry. However, the maturation and subsequent global expansion of a culture of consumption not only stems from the joint activities of capital and the state, but also from the historical process of capitalism on its own terms, that of capitalism working alone in a global context to advance the culture of a world system. An examination of capitalism working on its own in the global spread of radio broadcasting involves reworking some of the same issues examined previously, but asking different sets of questions and examining different bodies of evidence. The results of capitalism on its own terms for the American radio industry and Latin American broadcasting are discussed in the next chapter.

Notes

1. R. A. Lundquist to William R. Schurz, 1 April 1922, Record Group (RG) 151, file 544—radio—Brazil, Box 2727, Department of Commerce, National Archives, Washington (DCNA).

2. Introduction, Final Report, United States Commission to the Brazil Centennial Exposition, Library of Congress Manuscript Division, Washington (hereafter Exposition Report). For a first-hand account of the exposition as seen by an American official, see D. C. Collier, letter to unknown recipient (Herbert Hoover?), 25 July 1923, folder "Conferences—Brazil Exposition 1923 and undated," Box 152, Commerce Papers, Herbert Hoover Presidential Library, West Branch, Iowa (hereafter HHPL—Commerce). Collier discusses the scheduling of American films and points out how attendance increased after government propaganda films were replaced with Hollywood comedies and dramas; the distribution of 1,500 corncob pipes at a smoker; and a lottery that gave away a Singer sewing machine, a Congoleum rug, a Beeman garden tractor, an Underwood typewriter, twelve Gem safety razors, and two cases of bicarbonate of soda. He also gives a tally of awards and prizes garnered by Americans during the exposition.

3. Exposition Report, pp. 115–39.

4. Exposition Report, pp. 303–29; American Consul-General to Brazil Alphonse Gaulin to State Department, 7 October 1922, RG 59, 832.74/54, Department of State, National Archives, Washington (DSNA).

5. Exposition Report, photographs, pp. 305, 308.

6. Exposition Report, pp. 305, 329; "Broadcasting Above the Clouds in Brazil," *Current Opinion* 74 (May 1923): 605.

7. *New York Times*, 27 August 1922. They were wrong.

8. Gaulin told his superiors in Washington that "certain firms who have imported receiving sets are reported to be keeping them under cover, and while stocks are on hand no attempt is being made to make sales. It is hoped that by the beginning of next year something more definite will have been accomplished. At any event the preliminary steps have been taken in introducing broadcasting here and indications seem to point to a promising future market," 7 October 1922, RG 59, 832.74/54, DSNA. On the introduction of broadcasting in Brazil, also see Maria Elvira Bonavita Federico, *Historia da Comunicacao Radio e Television no Brasil* (Petropolis: Vozes, 1982); Luiz Carlos Saroldi and Sonia Virginia Moreira, *Radio Nacional O Brasil em Sintonia* (Brasilia: FUNARTE, 1984).

9. American Consul E. M. Larvion to State Department, 16 April 1923, RG 59, 832.74/55, DSNA.

10. American Ambassador to Brazil Edwin Morgan to State Department, 5 February 1924, RG 59, 832.74/60, DSNA.

11. Bureau of Foreign and Domestic Commerce, Electrical Equipment Division, Special Circular no. 149, "Radio Progress in North Eastern Brazil," 18 December 1923, RG 151, file 544—radio—Brazil, Box 2727, DCNA.

12. American Consul to Pernambuco Verne Richardson to State Department, 31 March 1924, RG 59, 832.741/-, DSNA.

13. American Consul to Bahia Homer Brett to State Department, 11 March 1924, RG 59, 832.76/-, DSNA.

14. Brett to State Department, 20 October 1924, RG 59, 832.74/65, DSNA.

15. For examples, see Bureau of Foreign and Domestic Commerce to Schurz, 18 April 1924, RG 151, file 544—radio—Brazil, Box 2727; C. E. Heaton, Stromberg-Carlson Telephone Manufacturing Company, to Lundquist, 20 May 1924, RG 151, file 544—radio—general, Box 2723; Klien-Schweitzer import-export house to Lundquist, 21 May 1924, RG 151, file 544—radio—general, Box 2723; all DCNA.

16. Bureau of Foreign and Domestic Commerce, Electrical Equipment Division, Special Circular no. 210, 1 May 1924, RG 151, file 544—radio—Brazil, Box 2727, DCNA.

17. American Consul to Pernambuco Fred Eastin to State Department, 22 November 1924, RG 59, 832.74/66, DSNA.

18. American Consul to Sao Paulo A. T. Haeberle to State Department, 16 March 1924, RG 59, 832.74/62; American Consul to Para John Hickerson to State Department, 8 November 1924, RG 59, 832.74/67; both DSNA. Reports of long-distance reception (which seems unthinkable now) are common during this period, largely because the electromagnetic spectrum was so uncrowded compared to current conditions that radio transmissions could often travel much greater distances because they did not suffer attrition due to interference. In addition, today's precise engineering of bandwidth, frequency, and transmitter power was not so much a concern of broadcasters in the early 1920s.

19. Bureau of Foreign and Domestic Commerce, Electrical Equipment Division, Special Circular no. 377, 30 June 1925, RG 151, file 544—radio—Brazil, Box 2727, DCNA.

20. George Lewis, Croseley Company, to Lundquist, 15 December 1924, RG 151, file 544—radio—Brazil, Box 2727, DCNA. The Croseley Company also owned one of the most influential radio stations in the history of American broadcasting: WLW Cincinnati. See Lawrence Wilson Lichty, "The Nation's Station: A History of Radio Station WLW," Ph.D. diss., Ohio State University, Columbus, 1964.

21. For examples, see Eastin to State Department, 31 January 1925, RG 59, 832.74/68; Hickerson to State Department, 10 March 1925, RG 59, 832.74/69; Eastin to State Department, 13 June 1925, RG 59, 832.74/70; all DSNA; for a discussion of what the bureau could do for the American radio industry, see P. E. D. Nagle, Department of Commerce, to Julius

Klein, Bureau of Foreign and Domestic Commerce, 29 January 1923, folder "International Radio Problems, 1922" (*sic*), Box 501, HHPL—Commerce.

22. Gaulin to State Department, 31 January 1925, RG 59, 832.74/71, DSNA. Gaulin enclosed a copy of *RADIO*, which is also in the decimal file. Also see Bureau of Foreign and Domestic Commerce, Electrical Equipment Division, Special Circular no. 410, 25 July 1925, RG 151, file 544—radio—Brazil, Box 2727, DCNA, which duplicates much of the material in Gaulin's report. Most of the information in the next few paragraphs is based on the State Department document.

23. Ibid.

24. Leslie J. Page, "The Nature of the Broadcast Receiver and Its Market in the United States from 1922 to 1927" in *American Broadcasting: A Source Book on the History of Radio and Television*, ed. L. Lichty and M. Topping (New York: Hastings House, 1975), pp. 467–73.

25. American Consul Fred Eastin to State Department, 10 July 1925, RG 59, 811.768/1, DSNA.

26. Eastin to State Department, 10 July 1925, RG 59, 811.768/-, DSNA.

27. C. W. Horn, Westinghouse, to Commerce Department, 2 September 1925, forwarded to State Department, RG 59, 811.768/3, DSNA. Horn, who would later be an international expert for NBC, added "the greatest propaganda agency the State Department could make use of is the Westinghouse Short Wave Relay System." The growth of American private shortwave broadcasters such as Westinghouse, their increasing importance as programmers to Latin America, and their metamorphosis through depression and war into the Voice of America are the themes of Fred Fejes, "Imperialism, Media, and the Good Neighbor: New Deal Foreign Policy and United States Shortwave Broadcasting to Latin America," Ph.D. diss., University of Illinois, Urbana, 1982.

28. Bureau of Foreign and Domestic Commerce, Trade Promotion Series no. 109, "Radio Markets of the World, 1930" (Washington: Government Printing Office, 1930); hereafter, "Radio Markets of the World, 1930"; unless otherwise noted, export data that follow are from this report.

29. American Consul to Manaus George Seltzer to State Department, 13 August 1926, RG 59, 832.74/76, DSNA.

30. American Consul to Pernambuco Nathaniel Davis to State Department, 2 October 1926, RG 59, 832.74/77, DSNA.

31. American Consul to Porto Alegre C. R. Naismith to State Department, 20 August 1927, RG 59, 832.76/2, DSNA. Naismith felt that this "should be of interest to American manufacturers of radio apparatus as the erection of this broadcasting station will create later on, a market for radio apparatus and parts—which market does not exist at this time."

32. Morgan to State Department, 5 May 1928, RG 59, 832.74/80, DSNA.

33. *New York Times*, 22 May 1927; *New York Times*, 31 July 1927.

34. American Consul to Sao Paulo C. R. Cameron to State Department, 23 February 1929, RG 59, 832.74/82, DSNA.

35. Bureau of Foreign and Domestic Commerce, Trade Information Bulletin no. 771, "Broadcast Advertising in Latin America" (Washington: Government Printing Office, 1931); hereafter "Broadcast Advertising in Latin America." By 1940, about 50 percent of homes throughout Brazil owned a radio set; about 90 percent of the urban adult male population described themselves as frequent to occasional listeners. See "Radio Survey in Brazil" conducted by Lloyd Free, American Social Services, 1941, in folder 22, Box 111, Papers of John Royal (NBC vice president for international relations), Mass Communications History Center of the State Historical Society of Wisconsin, Madison (hereafter Royal Papers); also see Robert M. Levine, "Elite Intervention in Urban Popular Culture in Modern Brazil," *Luso-Brazilian Review* 21 (Winter 1984): 9–22; Ruben George Oliven, "The Production and Consumption of Culture in Brazil," *Latin American Perspectives* 40 (Winter 1984): 103–15; Maria Isaura Pereira de Queiroz, "The Samba Schools of Rio de Janeiro or the Domestication of an Urban Mass," *Diogenes* 129 (Spring 1985): 1–32; Carlos Eduardo Lins da Silva, "Transnational Communication and Brazilian Culture," in *Communication and Latin American Society: Trends in Critical Research, 1960–1985*, ed. Rita Atwood and Emile G. McAnany (Madison: University of Wisconsin Press, 1986), pp. 89–111.

36. Unless otherwise indicated, information on Mexico is from "Radio Markets of the World, 1930"; "Broadcast Advertising in Latin America"; Bureau of Foreign and Domestic Commerce, Trade Information Bulletin no. 519, "Market for Electrical Equipment in Mexico" (Washington: Government Printing Office, 1928); John Sinclair, "Dependent Development and Broadcasting: The Mexican Formula," *Media Culture and Society* 8 (1986): 81–101; Jorge Mejia Preito, *Historia de la Radio y la Televisión en Mexico* (Mexico: Editores Associados, 1972).

37. George Sweet, Navy Department, to Secretary of State Charles Evans Hughes, 27 March 1923, RG 59, 812.74/189, DSNA.

38. American Consul Walter Boyle to State Department, 11 May 1923, RG 59, 812.74/191, DSNA. The call for easy credit from American equipment suppliers was a common recommendation of diplomats and salesmen in the field during the 1920s and 1930s.

39. American Consul to Veracruz John Wood to State Department, 2 December 1924, RG 59, 812.74/199; American Consul to Guadalajara Dudley Dwyre to State Department, 12 August 1925, RG 59, 812.74/201; American Consul to Chihuahua W. M. Mitchell to State Department, 14 December 1922, RG 59, 812.76/3; American Consul to Mazatlan W. E. Chapman to State Department, 19 October 1923, RG 59, 812.76/4; all DSNA.

40. The radio audience in Mexico now hears of the qualities of an American radio; that an American insecticide will free their kitchens of roaches; that the Contro Mercantil has the best bargains in ladies hats; that a talking-machine hour is sponsored by the Mexico Music Company; that a well known light six is the car of their dreams; and many, many other statements which by repetition can not fail to build up a preference in the minds of consumers. . . . [Radio station]

owners are impressing the large Mexican business organizations with their service, and they are soliciting American advertising . . . they are working hard to establish radio as an institution.

"Broadcast Advertising in Latin America," pp. 28–29.

41. Unless otherwise indicated, information on the Caribbean and Central America is from "Radio Markets of the World, 1930"; "Broadcast Advertising in Latin America"; Irwin Thomas, "The Beginnings of Broadcasting in the British West Indies," Ph.D. diss., University of Missouri, Columbia, 1977; Bureau of Foreign and Domestic Commerce, Trade Information Bulletin no. 563, "Market for Electrical Equipment in Central America" (Washington: Government Printing Office, 1928).

42. Travis Nance (International General Electric) to M. T. McGovern, Westinghouse, 10 November 1922, file 11–14-10, Box 100, Owen D. Young Papers, Van Hornesville, N. Y. (hereafter Young Papers).

43. "List of NBC International Programs 1924–1929," folder 9, Box 38, Central Office Files of National Broadcasting Company (NBC) Records, Mass Communications History Center of the State Historical Society of Wisconsin, Madison (hereafter NBC Central Files).

44. American Consul to Santo Domingo Reed Clark to State Department, 12 March 1930, RG 59, 839.76/2; James Brown, American legation, to State Department, 20 December 1934, RG 59, 839.76/7; both DSNA.

45. John Russell, American legation, to State Department, 3 December 1926, RG 59, 838.74/29, DSNA.

46. Consul-General Philip Holland to State Department, 29 January 1925, RG 59, 814.76/1, DSNA.

47. Secretary of War John Weeks to Hughes, 11 January 1923, RG 59, 819.74/108, DSNA. R. D. Prescott had pointed out in an attachment to this document that

> The members of the American Amatuer (*sic*) Relay League maintain communication throughout all of the United States and also with Canada, Mexico, Hawaii, and Porto Rico. Why not with PANAMA? Only recently has broadcasting been developed and attained to its present high state of efficiency and perfection, and this year nearly every one of the large broadcasting stations located in the Central and Eastern [United] States has been heard in Panama.

The large number of accounts of Latin American radio owners regularly tuning in United States broadcast stations since the early 1920s has been a source of amazement to me during my research; I have cited only a very few of these accounts, which came in from every nation in the Western Hemisphere. As I discuss in later chapters, these accounts have in part led me to conclude more than ever that broadcasting is above all else a global rather than a national phenomenon, and has been so from its very beginnings.

48. Secretary of the Navy Edwin Denby to Hughes, 23 January 1923, RG 59, 819.74/109; American Minister to Panama J. G. South to Hughes, 24 January 1923, RG 59, 819.74/110; Hughes to South, 26 January 1923, RG 59, 819.74/110; all DSNA.

49. South to Hughes, 26 June 1925, RG 59, 819.74/134, DSNA.

50. Unless otherwise indicated, information on Argentina is from "Radio Markets of the World, 1930"; "Broadcast Advertising in Latin America"; Bureau of Foreign and Domestic Commerce, Trade Information Bulletin no. 536, "Market for Electrical Equipment in Argentina" (Washington: Government Printing Office, 1928); Jorge Eduardo Noguer, *Radiodifusion en la Argentina* (Buenos Aires: Editorial Bien Comun, 1985).

51. American Consul-General to Buenos Aires W. Henry Robertson to State Department, 28 June 1923, RG 59, 835.74/58, DSNA. Log sheets from two of these stations are included in this dispatch.

52. W. A. Winterbottom, RCA, memo to Young, 15 October 1923, file 11–14-10, Box 101, Young Papers.

53. American consul to Buenos Aires Raleigh Gibson to State Department, 27 June 1924, RG 59, 835.74/63, DSNA.

54. J. C. White, American legation to Argentina, to State Department, 17 February 1932, RG 59, 835.76/4, DSNA; J. G. Shillock, American legation, to State Department, 20 February 1932, RG 59, 835.76/5, DSNA.

55. Unless otherwise indicated, information on Uruguay is from "Radio Markets of the World, 1930" and "Broadcast Advertising in Latin America."

56. Morris Hughes to State Department, 28 July 1925, RG 59, 833.74/22, DSNA.

57. Transcription discs first came into wide use in the United States around 1930. They usually held fifteen minutes of programming on a side, and the needle moved from the inside out. These discs were important in the development of continuing dramatic radio series such as soap operas, detective shows, and adventure tales. Programs were usually scripted and recorded at the advertising agency that represented the sponsor of the program. The agency would deliver the recorded program to the station or network, which would then assume responsiblity for local, regional, or national distribution via broadcasting. For an excellent, exhaustive, and occasionally obsessive discussion of radio broadcasting and recording technologies during this period, see Michael Biel, "The Making and Use of Broadcast Recordings Prior to 1936," Ph.D. diss., Northwestern University, Evanston, 1977.

58. Unless otherwise indicated, information on Bolivia and Paraguay is from "Radio Markets of the World, 1930"; "Broadcast Advertising in Latin America"; Raul Rivadeneira Prada, *La Television en Bolivia* (La Paz: Editorial Quipus, 1986).

59. American Consul to La Paz Jesse Cottrel to State Department, 9 December 1925, RG 59, 824.74/10, DSNA. The relatively small number of radio transmitters in operation in the 1920s meant that the reception of stations from exceedingly great distances (particuarly during ideal atmospheric conditions) was not as unusual as we would now believe; on the contrary, such reception was a regular facet of the overall listening experience.

60. American Consul to Asunción R. M. Scotten to State Department, 24 April 1926, RG 59, 834.76/2, DSNA. Scotten suggested that Ameri-

can radio manufacturers provide easy credit for the purchase of a better transmitter, which would subsequently increase sales of American sets.

61. Unless otherwise indicated, information on Chile is from "Radio Markets of the World, 1930"; "Broadcast Advertising in Latin America"; and Bureau of Foreign and Domestic Commerce, Trade Information Bulletin no. 515, "Market for Electrical Equipment in Chile" (Washington: Government Printing Office, 1928).

62. Unless otherwise indicated, information in this section on Peru and Ecuador is from "Radio Markets of the World, 1930"; "Broadcast Advertising in Latin America"; and Bureau of Foreign and Domestic Commerce, Trade Information Bulletin no. 508, "Market for Electrical Equipment in Peru" (Washington: Government Printing Office, 1927).

63. Hughes to American legation, Lima, 30 March 1921, RG 59, 823.74/24, DSNA.

64. American Ambassador to Peru Miles Pointdexter to Hughes, 11 August 1923, RG 59, 823.74/48, DSNA.

65. Unless otherwise indicated, information on Colombia, Venezuela, and the Guianas is from "Radio Markets of the World, 1930"; "Broadcast Advertising in Latin America"; Bureau of Foreign and Domestic Commerce, Trade Information Bulletin no. 511, "Market for Electrical Equipment in Columbia and Venezuela" (Washington: Government Printing Office, 1927); Reynaldo Pareja, *Historia de la Radio en Colombia 1929– 1980* (Bogota: Servicio Columbiano de Communication Social, 1984); and Alfredo Cortina, *Contribucion a la Historia de la Radio en Venezuela* (Caracas: Instituto Nacional de Hipodromos, 1982).

66. American Vice-Consul to Caracas Harry J. Anzinger to State Department, 4 June 1924, RG 59, 831.74/109, DSNA.

67. Unless otherwise indicated, information on Africa is from Geoffrey Kucera, "Broadcasting in Africa: A Study of Belgian, British and French Colonial Policies," Ph.D. diss., Michigan State University, East Lansing, 1968; Bureau of Foreign and Domestic Commerce, Trade Promotion Series no. 101, "Market for Electrical Equipment in the Union of South Africa" (Washington: Government Printing Office, 1930), pp. 46–51; and "Radio Markets of the World, 1930."

68. Unless otherwise indicated, information on Asia is from Bureau of Foreign and Domestic Commerce, Trade Information Bulletin no. 505, "Market for Electrical Equipment in Japan" (Washington: Government Printing Office, 1927), p. 18; Bureau of Foreign and Domestic Commerce, Trade Information Bulletin no. 513, "Market for Electrical Equipment in India" (Washington: Government Printing Office, 1927), pp. 21–26; Bureau of Foreign and Domestic Commerce, Trade Information Bulletin no. 487, "Market for Electrical Equipment in Australia" (Washington: Government Printing Office, 1927), pp. 33–34; Bureau of Foreign and Domestic Commerce, Trade Information Bulletin no. 727, "Market for Electrical Equipment in the Netherlands East Indies" (Washington: Government Printing Office, 1930), p. 33; John D. Stephens, "Islands, Ether and Echoes,"

Pacific Islands Communications Journal 12 (1983): 79–87; and "Radio Markets of the World, 1930."

69. Stephens, "Islands, Ether and Echoes," p. 83. Additional information on American radio exports to Africa and Asia during the 1920s can be found in James Schwoch, "The United States and the Global Growth of Radio, 1900–1930: In Brazil and in the Third World," Ph.D. diss., Northwestern University, Evanston, 1985, pp. 192–205.

70. Among the many influential works on the culture of consumption are Richard W. Fox and T. J. Jackson Lears, eds., *The Culture of Consumption: Critical Essays in American History 1880–1980* (New York: Pantheon, 1983); Susan Porter Benson, *Counter Cultures: Saleswomen, Managers, and Customers in American Department Stores 1890–1940* (Urbana: University of Illinois Press, 1986); David E. Nye, *Image Worlds: Corporate Identities at General Electric* (Cambridge: MIT Press, 1985); Howard Segal, *Technological Utopianism in American Culture* (Chicago: University of Chicago Press, 1985); Roland Marchand, *Advertising the American Dream: Making Way for Modernity, 1920–1940* (Berkeley: University of California Press, 1985); Cecelia Tichi, *Shifting Gears: Technology, Literature and Culture in Modernist America* (Chapel Hill: University of North Carolina Press, 1987); T. J. Jackson Lears, "Radical History in Retrospect," *Reviews in American History* 14 (March 1986): 17–24; and Lears, "The Concept of Cultural Hegemony: Problems and Possibilities," *American Historical Review* 90 (June 1985): 567–93.

5

Radio Broadcasting and Global Media Culture

If radio broadcasting was a global phenomenon from the start (as I suggest in the text and several notes of the preceding chapter), then an analysis of the American radio industry and its Latin American activities from 1900 to 1939 must eventually recast its scenes on a global stage and with a global cast of characters. In this chapter, a questioning of the centrality of the nation-state as protaganist begins with a reconsideration of the relationship between capitalism and the nation-state and the historical implications that such a reconsideration raises. The process of reconsideration begins with a deliberation on the protection that the nation-state offers to capitalism:

> did the state or did it not promote capitalism, further its progress? Even if one has reservations about the degree of maturity of the modern state, and if, with contemporary parallels in mind, one finds it very inadequate, it must be admitted that between the 15th and 18th centuries the state concerned everything and everybody: it was one of the new forces in Europe. But can it *explain* everything, did it govern everything? The answer is quite emphatically no. Indeed one can even argue for a reversal of the terms. The state undoubtedly encouraged capitalism and came to its rescue. But the formula can be reversed: the state also discouraged capitalism which was capable in turn of harming the interests of the state. Both statements could be true, one after another or simultaneously because real life is always complicated, in both predictable and unpredictable ways. Whether favorable or unfavorable, the modern state was one of the realities among which capitalism had to navigate, by turns helped or hindered, but often progressing through neutral territory. How could things have been otherwise?[1]

Somehow, along the way from changing past lives into lived past, historians often seem to forget (or at least fail to incorporate) Fernand Braudel's dictum that real life is always complicated, in both predictable and unpredictable ways. But how could things be otherwise? History is not merely an attempt to reconstruct real life faithfully from the past, but also a present-day accounting for the pace and direction of change over time. As such, it is simultaneously a descriptive and ideological process. Ultimately, history is concerned with the empowerment of particular ideologies in the present by an anchorage of here-and-now with a great past and a continuing story. Facts, evidence, and method become the chains that hold the present in place.[2] Although this recognition of the simultaneity of the historical process is certainly not a new revelation,[3] historical theory too often remains separate from historical practice. In other words, historical writing usually tends to fall into an either/or situation: it is either theoretical (centering on the ideological processes and the methodologies that underlie ideologies) or practical (offering descriptive data through a narrative structure itself inherently ideological without a full recognition or acknowledgment of the methodology/ies and ideology/ies such a narrative structure provides). Studies that develop a both/and approach — in other words, historical research that contains both theory and practice — are relatively uncommon, particularly in the history of American foreign relations. American diplomatic history has centered its great past upon unquestioned assumptions of nationalism, and although scholars who work in areas such as U.S. mass culture and Latin America may theorize that they are less nation-bound than other scholars, in practice they often tend to be more so. Whether writing as critics or as apologists of the past, this ideological assumption infuses their history as much as (if not more than) any other.[4] In many ways the preceding chapter of this book unquestioningly assumes a larger past of U.S. economic nationalism, despite its focus on cultural activities.

Such an assumption does not diminish the importance of chapter 4, nor does it diminish the importance and relevance of similar scholarship on American foreign relations. What the assumption of economic nationalism does, however, is place unintentional limitations on scholarly thought, particularly in areas of inquiry less concerned with crisis and transition as entities in and of themselves. One problem with the assumption of economic nationalism is that it tends to place the modern state in an always-center-stage position. The power of the state, in this case, the power of the United States—ultimately represented or filtered through its public sector[5]—wielded over the nations of Latin America, tends to be a constant premise and conclusion. Chapter 4 exemplifies this attitude by casting what I have termed the "carpenters" of the American radio industry's international expansion in leading roles. In this way, the present is tied to the past through the lack of narrative closure (the ongoing struggle among nation-states in which the United States always retains its position of power), which becomes a form of closure in and of itself. For example, continuing dissemination of American technical know-how coupled with economic expansion and the perceived desirability of consumer culture—all under the aegis of radio broadcasting—served chapter 4 as a theme of narrative nonclosure that tied the past to the present under the guise of competing nation-states, with one nation-state emerging as dominant. The areas and terrains of struggle, rather than the relations of power, are what provide the locations of historical change; although such change can be seen in areas of culture, class, and society, the various nation-states always remain at the center, circumscribing all other categories and contexts. It is through the continuing present that historians prove that the great story and the larger past exist; therefore, such a narrative nonclosure is an integral part of writing history.

The history of American foreign relations has been more often than not a single-factor larger past tied to the continuing story of the modern nation-state as protagonist, either as hero or antihero. Where the United States is a hero, the linkage of economic theory has usually been tied to the concept of modernization. In this model, the United States becomes the standard-bearer that clears the way for other nation-states to follow on the path to progress. An antihero role for the United States is often tied to the concept of dependency theory; the United States sets the agenda for other nation-states and thereby retains a position of power through creation of controlling interests. Such a history has been rich and valuable and has revealed much; for example, chapter 4 helps reveal the growing interest of American policymakers in using radio as a cultural component in the overall expansion of American economic nationalism (but even here "American economic nationalism" always remains at center-stage). The events of the 1920s can be tied to a larger past, that is, the internal economic crises of the 1870s and 1880s and the new industrial and cultural era that emerged from that period. The history can also account for the roots of the present-day New International Information Order; it can account for the maturation of a consumer culture in the United States, as well as the adolescence of a consumer culture in Latin America. But models built centrally on the concept of the nation-state cannot fully account for capitalism on its own terms. Although capitalism certainly functions in continuing combination with the state, how does it simultaneously function away from the state, in what Braudel called the "neutral territory" where the state does not function and is not always welcome?

Of course, a major body of scholarship—dependency theory— has been developed in the past thirty years that has U.S.-Latin American relations at the core of its concerns and is interested in questions concerning capitalism.[6] Dependency theory represents a broad, systematic accounting for international capitalism in relation to various nation-states through the course of Latin American history beginning with the European penetration of the Western Hemisphere, especially since Latin American political independence movements. With its emphasis on the relations of economies from one nation to another, the problems of producing primary goods, product life-cycles and the rising importance of cheap labor, and the international class system that linked local, national, and multinational capital, dependency theory helped move the history of U.S.-Latin American relations out of a relatively narrow focus on political relations among governments and into a larger and more intellectually stimulating concern with international relations along political, economic, cultural, and social lines. In addition, dependency theory cemented the history of the developed world to the underdeveloped world. Europe and the United States historically were rich because they had made Latin America and the third-world poor; backwardness in third-world political economies was a historical structure rather than a primitive origin.

These contributions to knowledge had a shared trait with the "enemy" scholarship: the unrecognized assumption of the primacy (the always-center-stage) of the nation-state as identified through the national economy. Even though dependency theorists have recognized and argued for the importance of the noneconomic spheres of activity, dependency studies have focused overwhelmingly on issues of economic history rather than on issues of intellectual history or cultural history. Society and culture become end products of economic activities and not independent or interedependent factors capable of center-stage status on their own terms. Dependency studies invariably surmise that the economic influences the cultural, but rarely do they see things the other way around. A predeliction for evidence and data organized in categories wholly enclosed within the concept of the nation-state—for example, the gross national product—exacerbates this tendency. Dependency studies conclude that "external influence is not solely confined to economic activities; it extends to cultural, legal, and political spheres as well."[7] True enough, but the underlying and unquestioned assumption is laid bare precisely in the word *extends*; what better term to show the always-center-stage position of economic nationalism in dependency theory? The economic, as identified and quantified through the nation, becomes the always-deterministic of the narrative structure of dependency studies.

Despite a radical and revealing historical rewrite of the areas and terrains of struggle, dependency studies paradoxically share a conceptually limiting myopia with their intellectual and political opposites. This does not mean dependency theory is valueless; far from it. Nor do I imply that any study that only focuses on economics is problematic, worthless, or incomplete. I do believe, however, that dependency studies taken as a whole also have difficulty in showing change over time in power relations where the changes are outside of the realm of the nation-state, as well as difficulty in describing and analyzing the activities of capitalism on its own terms, capitalism in neutral territory, capitalism as the agent of narrative nonclosure. In order to account fully for capitalism on its own terms, one has to let go of the nation-state periodically, to roam the fringes of the stage, point the spotlight elsewhere at times, and then remember what one has seen. Both mainstream accounts and dependency studies, by virtue of their common ideology of economic nationalism, have limitations as a theoretical construct for historical narrativity concerning capitalism. Ultimately, no single-factor explanation of capitalism can be offered as complete; however, the analysis of capitalism offered through a world-systems approach can be adapted to offer another larger past for the history of the American radio industry and Latin American broadcasting. In the discussion that follows, the writings of Fernand Braudel provide the focus for the explication of a world-systems approach to radio broadcasting and global media culture.

The following discussion and elaboration of a world-systems approach offers not an alternative, but rather a dual past; in other words, it does not stand in opposition to economic nationalism so much as in relation to, and subtending, that other past. I do not offer a simplification of Braudel's work to be used by uninformed researchers. Anyone interested in Braudel's narrativity should begin by making the commitment to read his work and the work of other world-systems scholars such as Immanuel Wallerstein rather than only borrowing from my discussion. I also stress the word *adapt* rather than *adopt*; readers familiar with Braudel will occasionally find evidence of my adaptation (for example, my argument that world time has "speeded up," which would contradict a strict, formal adoption of Braudel's narrative structure). Despite occasional shifts of emphasis, I believe my adaptation is faithful to the spirit of the original text.

What follows is not intended as a full-blown model for global analysis of media culture that researchers might plug into so much as a sketching of sensible avenues of inquiry based on concerns and questions of world-systems scholars. Although using early modern European historians such as Braudel and Wallerstein to help explain twentieth-century U.S.-Latin American relations might seem a prosaic undertaking, the necessity of these historians to account for the emergence and rise of the modern nation-state has resulted in a flexible narrative that does not always place the nation-state in a central position. In addition, the always-international nature of broadcasting—its total disregard for political boundaries in its dissemination,[8] a trait that all media demonstrate somewhat and broadcasting, by virtue of its system of distribution, demonstrates most extremely—makes such a flexible structure a valuable commodity in writing history.[9] The adaptation that follows begins with a discussion of Braudel's constructions of time and space.[10]

In *Civilization and Capitalism* Braudel writes at three levels of time: the *longue durée* (often translated as "the structure," although the "long term" or "long duration" might be more accurate), the conjuncture, and the event. The structure is the longest of long terms: centuries of routine shaped and influenced by diet, disease, climate, land, and sea.[11] The long term is the slowest to show change; it is also that which is changed irrevocably. Braudel ends *Civilization and Capitalism* in the early 1800s (although he does offer a conclusion based on present-day experiences)[12] partly due to his recognition that the long term of everyday life had in fact finally begun to be changed irrevocably in the coming of the industrial era.[13]

The long and short terms coexist most clearly at a middle level of time, the conjuncture. The conjuncture is a shorter period that somehow brings about a level of change discernible in the long term, although not necessarily irrevocably in the long term. Braudel warns it is extremely complex and theoretically incomplete, and then offers economic cycles named for the economic researchers who theorized them—Kitchin, Juglar, Labrousse, Kuznets, and Kondratieff—as the most "coherent" of conjunctures.[14] Although the actual temporal duration of a conjuncture can vary and even be ambiguous, Braudel conceives of the conjuncture as a medium-length temporal unit of ten, twenty, or even fifty years.[15]

Finally, Braudel identifies what he sees as the shortest, and the least significant, temporal unit: the event.[16] The event, the shortest period of time, could be a decision, a decree, a meeting, a coronation, a sailing, a harvest, a war, or even a truce. Braudel tends to downplay the event, and has received justifiable criticism for doing so.[17] Above and beyond this criticism, however, Braudel should be applauded for bringing so much to bear—in this case, three distinct temporal levels—on the pace and direction of change.

Certainly, a contemporary adaptation of Braudel must acknowledge that world time has speeded up; in other words, changes at the levels of structures, conjunctures, and events occur at a more rapid rate than in the world before the industrial revolution—or in any case, the preponderance of evidence and documentation available to modern historians gives the illusion of such speed. Today's rapid dissemination of electronic communications coupled with the incredible number of sources that can quickly receive disseminations probably increase the significance of events in influencing conjunctures and structures of historical time. This does not mean that thinking of time at three levels is now frivolous or arcane, however. In addition, the electromagnetic spectrum (and also the global dissemination of electronic communications) holds many similarities with the physical structures Braudel identifies,[18] in that the spectrum is a single, shared global resource demanding certain levels of international cooperation and also providing a location for political, social, cultural, and economic activities. World time can still be narrativized as functioning at three temporal levels. For example, using the experiences of my own world—an adult resident of the United States, who is aware of current affairs—as it was in October 1987, I can point to the most hectic week in Wall Street history as the event; the international monetary policies of the 1970s and 1980s as the conjuncture; and the long-term ideology of (and long-term attempts to slowly withdraw from) precious metals as the determinant factor in comparative evaluation of local, regional, and national currencies as the structure that dominated television, radio, and print news over the last two weeks of that month. While a strict adoption of Braudel runs the risk of artifice and imposition, a careful adaptation of his narrative conceptualization of time can be helpful and valuable in accounting for the history of the nineteenth and twentieth centuries.

Along with three levels of historical time, Fernand Braudel also identifies three levels of material space: everyday life, the market economy, and capitalism.

> J. K. Galbraith talks about the "two parts of the economy," the world of the "thousands of small and traditional proprietors" (the market system) and that of the "few hundred . . . highly organized corporations." Lenin wrote in very similar terms about the coexistence of what he called "imperialism" (or the new monopoly capitalism of the early twentieth century) and ordinary capitalism, based on competition, which had, he thought, its uses. . . . I agree with both Galbraith and Lenin on this, with the difference that the distinction of sectors between what I have called the "economy" (or the market economy) and "capitalism" does not seem to me to be anything new, but rather a constant in Europe since the Middle Ages. There is another difference too: I would argue that a third sector should be added to the pre-industrial model—that lowest stratum of the non-economy, the soil into which capitalism thrusts its roots

but which it can never really penetrate. This lowest layer remains an enormous one. Above it, comes the favored terrain of the market economy, with its many horizontal communications between the different markets: here a degree of automatic coordination usually links supply, demand, and prices. Then alongside, or rather above this layer, comes the zone of the anti-market, where the great predators roam and the law of the jungle operates. This—today as in the past, before and after the industrial revolution—is the real home of capitalism.[19]

Everyday life is as it implies; the routine of past and present shaped by long, mostly forgotten learning of habits, and a level of life at which the impact of capitalism, although certainly noticeable, is nevertheless the least. The market economy does not describe what is often called "the market" in the 1980s, but instead corresponds more closely to that which is now sometimes labeled "entreprenuership": that level of material life and economic transaction often, although by no means always, based on finance, found in virtually all societies, past and present, East and West, North and South, in the villages, shops, towns, fairs, bazaars, and souks.[20] In many of these transactions an implicit acknowledgment of money in the abstract underlies the exchange or barter of goods for goods, goods for services, services for goods, or services for services. This level of material life is influenced by a broader grid of capitalism and is usually governed by the coordination of supply, demand, and prices. However, in many ways the market economy can fall outside the full range of capitalist practices. Capitalists can find the market economies of certain areas tedious and frustrating terrains for exploitation; and the market economy can, on infrequent occasions, even present obstacles to the advancement of capitalism, at least during events and conjunctures if not in the long duration.

Finally, the real home of capitalism: international commerce.[21] Activity at an always-international scale is a historical trademark of the capitalist process, whether it be early modern European capitalists or twentieth-century American radio capitalists. To become capitalist is to ultimately begin to transcend national identity while still beng able to use national identity as a supporting system for global activites. This process of transcendence coupled with utilization signifies capitalism's ability to control the ideology of national identity for its own best interests—

perhaps not for each and every event, but over the long duration. The ability to use national identity is but one example of the flexibility and adaptability that is also a historical trademark of capitalism, a trademark that provides for its survival in crisis and its expansion in propserity. This flexibility is of the utmost importance, for it ensures the survivability and prosperity of capitalism beyond the boundaries and powers of the nation-state.[22]

A contemporary adaptation of Braudel's three levels of material space must recognize that contemporary everyday life, the lowest level of the noneconomy, is now much more permeated with capitalism than it was from the fifteenth through eighteenth centuries. An adaptation must also recognize that movement between the market economy and capitalism is, if anything, probably even more spontaneous and adaptive than Braudel found in his historical analysis; again, this is in part attributable to an "age of information" and the special advantages that rapid communication offers to those individuals and institutions traveling the international avenues of capitalist enterprise. But these adaptations do not diminish the value and utility of Braudel's dual trios of structure, conjuncture, and event, and everyday life, market economy, and capitalism. The inclusion of this narrative with mainstream and dependency approaches to writing American diplomatic history can move around the ideology of economic nationalism while at the same time recognizing and respecting the importance of that ideology. The following history of capitalism on its own terms in the development of the American radio industry in Latin America prior to 1940 constitutes an early contribution toward demonstrating a world-systems approach in media culture.

When one moves beyond the relationship between capital and the state in the history of the American radio industry and U.S.-Latin American relations from 1900–1939, the interactions between the market economies of Latin American radio and the international capitalism of the American radio industry become visible. A reexamination of the growth of Latin American broadcasting with a world-systems approach casts developments in a new light, and one sees that radio broadcasting developed in large urban areas with links to local market economies. Within these local market economies, broadcasters functioned like shopkeepers, local tradesmen, and merchants. Radio broadcasting in Latin America thrived under these arrangements. The following market economies often developed around large urban areas in Latin America, such as Buenos Aires, Mexico City, Rio de Janiero and Sao Paulo, Lima, Caracas, or Santiago. In addition, they sprang up in less populated areas that nevertheless had a geographic specificity that encouraged such activity. These areas included certain Caribbean islands and the United States-Mexican border. Whether urban or rural, all of these locales of radio activity were characterized by a number of local indigenous broadcasters who had initially carved out their own terms of broadcasting, and were subsequently influenced (in a broad sense of that term) by the multiple and flexible activities of the American radio industry.

One urban market economy of radio broadcasting emerged in Buenos Aires, largely exemplified by the endeavors of the Pekam Company (although they were only one of several indigenous broadcasters). Incorporated in Argentina, Pekam was a major manufacturer and broadcaster through the 1920s; the company's sets and transmitters were spread throughout Argentina, Brazil, Bolivia, Paraguay, Uruguay, and Chile, although it did not dominate any of those markets.[23] Pekam (and by extension other Argentines interested in radio) had been able to integrate the development of radio manufacturing and broadcasting into the local market economy of Buenos Aires, and to a lesser extent all of Argentina and the southern cone of South America. General Electric representatives in Buenos Aires and Montevideo complained in 1922 to their superiors in Schenectady that local shops were not interested in purchasing large stocks of General Electric radio equipment, or even carrying the equipment on consignment. Local merchants had already stocked up on all varieties of radio equipment available, whether it be from North America, Europe, or produced locally: "Not only the larger houses but every small house down to the most miserable *boliche* are overstocked in radio material of all kinds."[24] RCA representatives in Buenos Aires insisted in desperation that "almost overnight, there sprung up a great sales competition through importation and local manufacture which we were unable to fight. . . ."[25]

These complaints and conditions partly spurred the establishment of Radio Sud America, an Argentine company with backing from RCA and the rest of the members of the four-nation wireless consortium (the AEFG consortium between RCA, Marconi, Tele-funken, and French wireless corporations). Radio Sud America was set up to sell the equipment of the consortium in the Argentine market, a market whose consumers were overwhelmingly concerned with broadcast reception.[26] The suggestion that the consortium introduce a broadcast component was advanced by George Davis of General Electric, who also suggested that if RCA, General Electric, American Telephone and Telegraph, Westinghouse, and International Telephone and Telegraph could all work together on the entire South American broadcast market, they might form an export cartel and thereby take advantage of the Webb-Pomerene Act. The act provided for the legal creation of cartels and trusts provided they confined their activities to global rather than domestic commerce. Such an action would produce dependable percentages of sales for each participant and also "reduce the evil results due to unrestricted sales of broadcasting transmitters and parts."[27]

The evil results Davis mentioned were in fact the impact of the American exhibitions at the Brazil centennial in 1922.[28] The AEFG group had considered setting up individual broadcast displays at the centennial but decided instead that it was better for all to first develop a unified plan to enable the consortium to introduce radio broadcasting to all of South America at the same time. Gerard Swope of General Electric concluded that "it would seem very inadvisable for the various members of the AEFG group to be competing with each other...no particular benefit can be derived, and it will only create a very disturbing situation. . . ."[29] AEFG officials, including RCA executives, agreed with Swope's advice, but Westinghouse went ahead and shipped radio equipment to the centennial (despite the fact they were now members of RCA and therefore at least tied legally to the consortium), and Western Electric later followed Westinghouse's lead, to the consternation of policymakers at RCA from General Electric. General Electric scrambled to enter its own equipment after Westinghouse had acted on its own, but General Electric executives felt deceived and also felt that their own effort fell short.[30]

Radio Sud America was in part designed to prevent such problems from surfacing in the future. However, because of the initial success of local manufacturers such as Pekam, as well as the wide selection of sets and manufacturers in the Buenos Aires market, in 1923 Radio Sud America had to temporarily sell equipment at the same price as sets produced locally. Although this meant selling at a loss, it also had the long-range effect of drying up demand for locally produced radio equipment; most Argentines perceived American-manufactured equipment as superior, and the opportunity to purchase such equipment for the same price as that manufactured locally was too good to pass up.[31] The consortium also tried on several occasions to strictly enforce its patent rights on vacuum tubes. Such enforcement could possibly put an outright end to local manufacture (or so AEFG executives believed), but strict enforcement proved impossible in Buenos Aires and elsewhere. RCA executives were generally against issuing licenses to Argentine corporations for manufacture with RCA patents; they feared it implied that Argentine equipment was equal to American, and the ideology that associated the United States with technological superiority had already proven an effective selling technique for American radio equipment in South American markets.[32]

While the American radio industry—and the AEFG consortium—achieved some sporadic success in the internationalization of radio developments, they also received reports from the Buenos Aires that detailed the problems and frustration of Radio Sud America. This company had first been organized to sell RCA equipment as well as the equipment of other consortium members, but plans went awry on a number of fronts, all largely because of the native Argentine's control of the local radio market economy. In part, this control came about from "unusual" business practices by the Argentines. Radio Sud America officials complained that they encountered a number of distribution problems, had trouble finding reputable dealers outside of Buenos Aires, and could not expand their sales network in Argentina for "we would have been forced to take in houses of the dealer class; dealers who are not always responsible and who could not have been depended on to maintain prices."[33] The parent companies of the consortium had partly compounded the problems by exporting a number of parts such as storage batteries, which could be purchased from local manufacturers or established exporters for less than the Radio Sud America price. In fact, the attempts to sell equipment at the initial prices the consortium suggested led to a situation in which "When Radio Sud America launched her sales campaign in November 1922 the then few competitors were elated over our high prices. Some of them immediately arranged to increase their capital and in an incredibly short space of time many new companies came into existence. They believed that with our high prices they had nothing to fear from us. . . ."[34]

The beginnings of broadcasting in Buenos Aires by Radio Sud America only exacerbated the situation:

> after it became known that good broadcasting was being done by our station . . . we began to hear of the radio manufacturers. The advertisements of new manufacturers appeared almost daily and the boom had started. Anybody, who could obtain the information and necessary financial backing, went into the business. Many of our articles were copied and sold at a price much lower than ours. They began to boom "National Industry," as a part of their advertising campaign. The small dealer displayed his wares topped by a "Made In This Country" sign and asked that the public purchase to protect home industry. . . . No attention was paid to the patent situation, in fact patents controlled by foreign interests were treated as a joke . . . at the time of writing this report there are more than 30 manufacturers interested in radio in Argentina . . . the manufacturer is little more than an assembler. . . . He does not have to pay the enormous sums for development—this is done for him . . . He could undersell us, and the fact that we practically financed the broadcasting of the country, was really a benefit to him.[35]

Officals at Radio Sud America, empowered by their superiors with representing RCA and the consortium's broadcast efforts not only in Buenos Aires and Argentina but also Uruguay and Chile, must have felt at wit's end. They had tried operating a broadcasting station, they had imported Spanish-language radio literature, they had hosted expositions and sent out salesmen to drum up business with staged displays in local shops, but they could not corner the market. Had E. C. Benedict of Amazon Wireless been with them, he most likely would have felt a slight sense of déjà vu. Probably the topper came late in 1922 when Radio Sud America found that its broadcast signal was not alone on its wavelength; an Argentine broadcaster deliberately sent a signal over the Radio Sud America frequency, rendering broadcasts nearly indecipherable, and then demanded a ransom from Radio Sud America to stop his interference.[36] This is most likely the first instance of signal jamming anywhere in the world. Contemporary readers familiar with the current problems of Latin American industries with regard to foreign competition might marvel at this response to international capitalism, in which patents were often ignored, and every move by the capitalists seemingly countered by the indigenous (and ingenious) local radio activities. Yet is the situation really so far removed from, say, the current policy of Brazil on the development of the microcomputer industry? Although there are indeed differences, in both cases local industry built around the manufacture of a crucial component in the overall establishment of a larger social, political, economic, and cultural process—broadcasting and consumer culture in Argentina in the 1920s, the information age in Brazil in the 1980s.[37] And in both cases the responses by capitalism demonstrate those qualities Fernand Braudel so carefully linked to historical capitalism—spontaneity, flexibility, adaptability, and the ability to react to change at a moment's notice—as the American radio industry would move more and more toward control of programming, and as the globalization of the computer industry relies more and more on the control of software. It is no wonder that the areas and terrains of struggle have shifted from control of patents to control of copyright.

But for Radio Sud America, fighting for its patent rights still seemed to be a viable option. Through 1922 and 1923, Radio Sud America argued loud and long in Buenos Aires on behalf of its superiors in New York, London, Paris, and Berlin that local industries used unlicensed patents; their protests had little if any effect. Finally, Radio Sud America adopted the drastic measure of a liquidation sale in May 1924. A number of factors caused the decision. First, the consortium had found it difficult, if not impossible, to sell all of their radio equipment through one South American outlet, particularly with the rapid development and modernization of broadcast sets and parts. Consortium members eventually came to believe that each would probably do better in mutual competition, but agreed that the large number of local manufacturers, assemblers, and jobbers would be a real future problem for all of the consortium members. Therefore, Radio Sud America sold its equipment at a slight loss starting in October 1923 until the liquidation sale of the following May. "The result was a great commotion in the market. Some of the [local] distributors protested, others did not seem to care, as a body they lost control of the situation."[38] Several Argentines were run out of the radio manufacturing business, and those still remaining effectively traded their control over this aspect of their own market economy for the stability that international capital could offer in the form of RCA, Marconi, Telefunken, and French companies. The dissolving of Radio Sud America and the termination of consortium agreements concerning South American broadcasting allowed RCA to coordinate its new radio sets and equipment more effectively with South American equipment markets.[39] While international capital in the radio industry, as led by RCA, did not immediately succeed in capturing the market economy of Buenos Aires, RCA (and by extension American radio capitalists) found their own flexibility and ability to react to unusual conditions held sway in the long term.

The native broadcasters of the Buenos Aires market economy also anticipated many developments that history — or conventional pedagogy of media studies — has attributed to American broadcasting, including special broadcasts of cultural importance and also the inception of broadcast advertising. Local Argentines had begun a regular broadcast service as early as 1918, transmitting plays and events from a large theater in Buenos Aires. This activity predates KDKA Pittsburgh, often acknowledged as the first regular broadcasting station, by about two years.[40] Broadcast programs by 1922 included news reports sponsored by large newspapers and a number of debates and discussions of the Argentine congress. The Pekam broadcasters regularly carried opera from Buenos Aires as early as 1920, and in the spring of 1922 they suggested that "The installation of microphones in theatres and other public halls is not only a means of spreading knowledge of art but could also be used for commerical propaganda . . . whenever there is a public show, any commercial company which desires to announce or to extend a knowledge of its products can transmit a certain number of words. . . . In this way, those who desire to use the apparatus for this purpose will make a small payment for each work transmitted."[41]

Thus, international capital in the radio industry, centered in the United States ("each time a decentering occurs, a recentering takes place")[42] had to negotiate the development of broadcast advertising at the level of the market economy; these conditions in

Buenos Aires predate the genesis of broadcast advertising in the United States—specifically the "WEAF Queensboro Commercial"—by a few months. As is now known, international capital in the radio industry was eventually, in the long run, able to provide a semblance of order and coordination along its own lines of rationality; yet temporal analysis at the level of the event shows that such a coordination was not automatic. Neither was it dependent only upon the power of the state in the form of the American government nor the power of economic nationalism in the form of dominant American ideology and consumer culture. Indeed, the exchange transaction at the heart of American broadcasting existed in the local market economies of Latin America before its existence at the center of radio's capitalization. The rise of capitalist order and rationality in radio and consumer culture at the global level is a result of that flexibility and adaptability dating from the 1920s to thirteenth-century Italy; a rationality built not so much around the logic of spontaneous exchange (that was the logic of the Buenos Aires radio market economy, like all market economies), but rather the logic of international capitalism: the logic of speculation, monopoly, anti-market, and power.[43]

Although international capitalists at the center of the radio industry did not always provide the initial vision for radio's economic well-being, they did always see their work as a global rather than a merely domestic activity. Radio capital especially sought out links with the local market economies of Latin American broadcasting. By the 1930s, it had become clear to the American radio industry that these links could be forged through programming as well as technology. Indeed, the creation of the American broadcast networks in the latter part of the 1920s represents the growing awareness of this avenue of control.[44] Quinton Adams of the National Broadcasting Company remarked in 1934 that "it is not too difficult to forsee the possibility of an NBC of the Argentine, an NBC in Brazil, etc., with control here . . . activity abroad should be considered along with the domestic."[45] Adams was not a maverick at NBC; three years later, an internal study group concluded that NBC should approach Havana as it would

> any city in the U.S. from the standpoint of a network outlet. It is
> a city of approximately 700,000 inhabitants using American

products almost exclusively. . . . Havana as an NBC outlet has always seemed logical . . . with more prosperous conditions now existing in Cuba, there is a possibiity that our Sales Department can work up an interest in Havana by some of their clients . . . we should endeavor to sell this city as an outlet. Similar arrangements are being made with Mexico City.[46]

Expansion into local market economies was important for American radio capitalists, despite the fact they often found the everyday conditions of Latin American radio appalling. For example, the Cuban radio situation seems a classic and chaotic example of Braudel's middle space, the market economy. Although there were about sixty licensed broadcast stations in Cuba by the late 1930s, NBC also found that

it is generally conceded that scattered throughout the island an unknown number of "bootleg" stations are operating without an official license. . . . Due to the lack of suitable talent, programs are for the most part composed of recordings. A few of the Havana stations present live talent shows but even the best fall far short of American standards. The general run of stations, however, present an indeterminable series of recordings of dance orchestras with as much time devoted to commercial announcements as to music. . . . The intense competition that exists for the sale of time keeps the rates on most of the stations down to a few dollars an hour. Rate cards, when they exist, are not adhered to and sales of time are made on a "deal" basis.[47]

During a 1939 fact-finding trip, C. W. Horn (now at NBC) wrote NBC President Lenox Lohr to tell him firsthand about everyday Cuban radio.

Most of the stations are run on the barter system. One engineer I know takes care of the technical work on 8 stations and receives pay from only 2 stations. The others pay him in time on the air which he peddles to merchants for clothing, food, and other necessities including a new Plymouth auto. The G.E., Westinghouse, and RCA distributors give credit for tubes and parts for which they receive pay in time on the air mostly in the form of announcements. One station here has 1,400 announcements daily. The announcements are recorded and rattled off a score at a time from records. Only a couple of stations break even or make a little. . . . It is a paradise in respect to musicians, if you can call them that, for they pay them about a dollar a day. Much of the talent is free or gets a small handout. There are not ethics and every one cuts the other fellow's throat. It is the exact opposite of our method of operating. Technically it is just as bad . . . try to talk engineering standards with them and they won't even listen much less understand . . . but what is a kilocycle or two of deviation among friends.[48]

From a world-systems perspective, the problem for Quinton Adams, C. W. Horn, Lenox Lohr, NBC, and the international capitalists of the American radio industry was not so much how to introduce an "American model" that included private ownership, advertising, and entertainment; it was how to deal with the strengths and weaknesses of Latin American market economies and to integrate them rationally into a larger, global system of capitalism.

The development and international expansion of American broadcast program fare proved important in the globalization of Latin American radio market economies. Along with the ideology of American technological superiority, the belief in the cultural value and higher quality of American broadcast programming and American popular entertainment became widespread in Latin America, in part through the global spread of a culture of consumption. Some special programs were developed by American networks specifically for Latin American stations and networks. For example, RCA's "Magic Key" was an ambitious weekly program of the 1930s that featured live remote broadcasts from all over Latin America, and was circulated throughout North and South America by NBC. "Magic Key" aired on certain Latin American stations and also on the Blue Network, the second-level domestic NBC network. NBC investigated the possibilities of building a permanent land-line link with major broadcast stations in Mexico City, in part to facilitiate carrying "Magic Key."[49]

Latin American radio audiences were also enthusiastic about reports and programs on Hollywood, and the American networks responded to that interest with a number of special broadcasts, reports, and programs. General Electric began using Hollywood film stars on a regular basis in its Latin American advertisements as early as 1932, and they asked NBC to develop a program, featuring Hollywood stars, specifically for sponsorship and distribution to Latin American broadcast stations.[50] NBC audience researchers found the Latin American listeners "are definitely movie conscious and follow avidly the doings of Hollywood celebrities. . . ."[51] and by the end of the decade both NBC and CBS regularly featured film stars in their Latin American programs (now transmitted by shortwave) and also helped prepare transcription discs of Hollywood-produced radio programs for Latin American broadcasters.[52]

Along with the development of programming and audiences by the American radio industry, the identification of cooperative Latin American broadcasters became important for the American-led globalization of Latin American broadcasting. Such identifications were determinant events in the discreet establishment of a capitalist hierarchy that was centered in the American radio industry but served—to a certain extent—some Latin American broadcasters. The Latin American broadcasters could even become capitalists themselves—not located at the center of the heirarchy, but has that ever really mattered? It is the access to the conduits of capitalism, the lines of communication and credit, that has always counted. True, it counts for more to be at the center, whether it be Venice, Genoa, Amsterdam, London, or New York, but to be a part of the heirarchical system is the key. And the market economy, in the past and still in the present, can provide the context for the appearance of capitalism.[53]

Throughout Latin America, certain broadcasters stepped forward, out of their market economies (although by no means detaching themselves from those arenas of activity) and into the international arena offered by NBC and by extension the radio capitalists centered in the United States. The American radio industry welcomed some "radio elites" of Latin America, but disdained others. In Mexico, NBC worked closely with Emilio Azcarraga, who ran some of the most powerful stations in Mexico and co-financed a plan for regular program exchanges with NBC; he also introduced television to Mexico after World War II. In addition to his broadcasting activities, Azcarraga owned a music publishing company, controlled most of the copyrights on Mexican music, and operated a large talent agency. He also represented RCA and RCA Victor in Mexico City. NBC valued its relationship with Azcarraga as much as they valued a relationship with any American affiliate.[54] Azcarraga also exemplifies how capitalism is above all else marked by its spontaneity, its adaptation, its ability to react to change at a moment's notice and keep options open, for that is precisely what he did as American consumer culture entered Mexico through records, sheet music, and radio.

Other Mexican broadcasters posed problems, however. A number of broadcasters—some Mexicans, others Americans—set up powerful stations on Mexico's side of the American-Mexican border during the 1930s and served all who cared to listen regardless of nationality. The "border blasters"[55] had impressive transmitter power, ranging from a hundred thousand to a million watts, and signal strength to reach most of the United States and Canada under normal evening atmospheric conditions. Audience measurement comparisons with "normal" American networks and stations is virtually impossible because the border blasters never subscribed to conventional audience measurement services such as Hooper or Nielsen. They instead measured audiences by response to the direct mail products pitched by radio personalities. These renegade broadcasters answered to no authority except their own—and of course the "authority" of spontaneous exchange that characterizes local market economies. Lewis Boyle, the State Department consul in Sonora, described one of these broadcast renegades: "The owner . . . is a well-known minor Mexican politician. . . . He is a bar owner and an owner and operator of most of the houses of prostitution in Agua Prieta. He is at present constructing a motion picture theatre. . . . I believe him to be a thorough-going scalawag and rascal. . . . I know from time to time commercial announcements are made over his station . . . the programs usually consist of commercial announcements interspersed with phonograph records."[56]

Other such broadcasters included the infamous John Brinkley, who had been run out of Kansas despite the enormous popularity of his "patent medicine" radio broadcasts. Brinkley simply set up shop across the border in Mexico and continued to reach vast numbers of American and Mexican listeners.[57] Mexican border station XED for a time sold Mexican lottery tickets by mail to Americans, who would then listen in to XED to hear results.[58] Although in general, the American radio industry preferred to carry out its Latin American activities unencumbered by the machinations of local and national governments, American networks turned to the American government (including the FCC and the State Department) and also the Mexican government for help in controlling and preventing the behavior of the border broadcasters. The Mexican government cooperated by approving a number of regulations that in part controlled the border broadcasters through frequency regulation and guidelines for program content.[59] But despite the border renegades, there were many cooperative broadcasters like Azcarraga in Mexico: XEL Saltillo, XEU Veracruz (whose owner was the local Victor distributor) and XETF (whose owners distributed Philco radios in Veracruz), and XES Tampico (again owned by the Victor distributor).[60]

Latin American radio elites—sometimes accommodating, sometimes renegade—interested in working with the American radio industry could also be found in Central America, in the Caribbean, and on the South American continent. In Guatemala, Javier Figueroa threatened in 1929 to build a station of five thousand watts "to drown out every other station in Guatemala, Honduras, Salvador, and parts of Mexico. They will need no studio, as they can pick up programs from almost any part of the world." Figueroa offered to drop the plans if American manufacturers bought him out, and he believed the fact that his brother was the local chief of police gave him added muscle. However, the American legation simply had the Guatemalan government strictly enforce the frequency guidelines of the 1927 Washington Conference, and the American radio industry shipped Figueroa no equipment.[61] In Haiti, Henry Charbonnel was very cooperative and tried to set up a station that would carry NBC and CBS programs. Although American networks were sympathetic, Charbonnel eventually did not have the venture capital for his end of the bargain.[62] But things went smoothly in Venezuela: the local Victor distributor, Arthur Santana, had begun broadcasting in 1925 and often carried American programs in the 1920s and 1930s.[63]

The American radio industry found the South American broadcasters generally better able to deal with their hierarchy than those of Central America and the Caribbean (with the exception of Mexican broadcasters such as Azcarraga). In Argentina, NBC cooperated with Benjamin Gache of Radio Splendid, Alfredo Perez of Radio Stentor, and Jaime Yankelevich, who owned several stations. When the Argentine government established a commission in 1938 to study radio, Gache was appointed, and at NBC Horn confided to Lohr that

I note a name of a friend of ours on the commission. . . . I am watching this very carefully . . . if broadcasting from Buenos Aires is greatly limited or restricted, there may also be an opportunity for a high power station in Montevideo across the bay, which could easily serve Buenos Aires with 500 kilowatts. The lesson that we learn from such events as are taking place in Buenos Aires, is the necessity of knowing thoroughly the political and other relationships of the stations before we make any permanent tie-up with foreign stations. There has always been trouble in the Argentine in this respect. . . . We have managed to keep in touch with the several large stations. I am doing the same thing in Cuba. . . .[64]

Broadcasters in Brazil were also interested in establishing contacts with NBC. Albert Byington, who controlled a network of about twenty stations in Brazil in the 1930s, wanted to exchange programs with NBC on a regular basis but, like Henry Charbonnel in Haiti, Byington could not afford his end of the costs. He attempted unsuccessfully to secure funds from the U.S. Department of Agriculture to support the effort.[65] Another Brazilian broadcaster, Carlos Baccarat, approached NBC several times in the hope of securing closer relations, including the following appeal in 1941.

We have all the bigger sponsors which use Radio in this country, amongst them many American concerns such as Fort [*sic*] Motor Company, General Motors, Lever Brothers, Colgate-Palmolive, Westinghouse, Carter Pills, General Electric, and many others, all having renewed their contracts for the last 4 years and many European sponsors as Bayer Asprin, Coty Perfumes, Dunlop, Anglo-Mexican, the proof of our station being the Number One in this area. . . . Our President an old timer in the Radio Game has been in the States back in 1928 for one year studying the American Broadcasting on its old days and is acquainted with the americans [*sic*] way of work, knowing your country all the way throughout.[66]

Although Baccarat's mastery of English may have been lacking, he had no trouble expressing himself as a capitalist in the heirarchy radio had built around the new consumer culture of the United States and the rest of the modern world. Although further research on other media forms is necessary, it appears that radio developed, in the short term, at the level of the market economy in Latin

America, later to be superseded in the long term by international capital—especially after World War II.

Although the heirarchy of international capitalism continues to progress through the vast neutral and uncharted territory ignored or unexamined by the state, the media-based market economy is by no means a thing of the past in Latin America. For example, during the 1980s a large number of video rental stores, often ignoring international regulations such as copyright (just as their radio ancestors ignored many regulations prohibiting set ownership and many technical regulations and guidelines for transmission) sprang up in the market economies of major urban areas. The American film industry has sued Brazilian video clubs in an effort to stop this activity, but like the patent enforcement of Radio Sud America, the suits have been less than successful. Some relief came through licensing with a Globo TV subsidiary. Raids on bootleg video stores in Argentina did little to dent the influx of new bootleg tapes. Pirates in Puerto Rico did a booming business by dubbing Spanish dialogue onto bootlegged American network broadcasts and subsequently distributing them in Colombia. Colombian President Belisario Betancur opted against litigation to protect American copyrights strictly, for he feared the unemployment problems such litigation might bring; by the mid-1980s, more than forty thousand families in Colombia earned a living in the video market economy. The market economy grows; the globalization efforts continue. And international capital, always spontaneous, always adaptive, responds in part through the new plans offered by the Pan American Satellite Corporation (PANAMSAT), a privately held satellite common carrier to provide service from the United States to Latin America and expecting, by 1990, to carry Hollywood entertainment production to Latin American hotels, resorts, restaurants, and future cable outlets.[67]

The American government, as well as the large American business associations concerned with copyright and international trade, have launched a concerted effort to stem the tide of infringements on intellectual property rights held by American corporations, including broadcast rights. In 1985, a new trade association, the International Intellectual Property Alliance (a consortium association formed by the Computer Software and Services Industry Association, the American Film Marketing Association, the

Association of American Publishers, the Computer and Business Equipment Manufacturers Association, the International Anti-counterfeiting Coalition, the Motion Picture Association of America, the National Music Publisher's Association, and the Recording Industry Association of America) complained that intellectual copyright losses in the ten worst-offender nations (a most-wanted list including Brazil and Mexico) cost American industry more than $1 billion annually. The International Intellectual Property Alliance continues to monitor copyright infringements, and considers video and film piracy to be among its greatest areas of concern.[68]

American government policymakers are approaching the problem by encouraging other nations to begin to properly protect the intellectual property rights of their own "legitimate" citizens and corporations. The United States General Accounting Office noted in April 1987 that the developing countries of the world need

> to adopt adequate protection before their rapidly advancing economies spawn pirate industries of a magnitude equivalent to those in, for example, South Korea or Taiwan . . . as one set of economies advances to a point where the economic importance of legitimate businesses based on intellectual property causes the government to strengthen protection, they will be replaced by another group of countries prepared to take advantage of the easy profits to be made through piracy . . . improved intellectual property protection can encourage economic development . . . permitting piracy to continue discourages the development of creative industries . . . adequate protection practices also help to create the investment climate necessary to attract and/or maintain foreign direct investment and the attendant technology transfers that developing countries need.[69]

In the 1920s and the 1930s, the international capitalism built around media culture and centered in the American radio industry worked toward the long-term rationalization of local Latin American market economies based on radio broadcasting through protection of patents, formation of industry groups such as the AEFG consortium, the promotion of American consumer culture, the enlistment of local Latin American radio elites and their incorporation into the international avenues of media enterprises, and of course the support of an accommodating public sector. In the 1980s, the terrain of struggle shifted from radio broadcasting and patent rights to video and software piracy and protection of intellectual property and copyrights. Yet the structure of opposition—international capital stymied by the vagaries and self-determination of local Latin American market economies—remains in place. True, the AEFG Radio Consortium of the early 1920s no longer exists, but the International Intellectual Property Alliance does. There may no longer be a horde of Argentine radio broadcasters and radio manufacturers who ignore international patents and jam up broadcast frequencies, but there are the broad-based activities of video pirates and tape bootleggers from Puerto Rico to Chile and everywhere between. The larger past and continuing present of nation-state struggles chronicled by mainstream and dependency studies truly is subtended by a larger past and continuing present of event, conjuncture, long duration, and everyday life, local market economy, and international capitalism: the great story of capitalism and media culture continues in a world-systems narrative also.

The Value of a Dual History

At the centre of the world-economy, one always finds an exceptional state, strong, priveleged, dynamic—simultaneously feared and admired. In the fifteenth century it was Venice; in the seventeenth, Holland; in the eighteenth and still the nineteenth, it was Britian; today it is the United States. How could these "central" governments fail to be strong? . . . There were strong governments then, in Venice, even in Amsterdam, and in London, capable of asserting themselves at home, of keeping the "common people" of the towns in order, of raising taxes when the situation required, and of guaranteeing commercial credit and freedom; capable too of asserting themselves abroad; it is to these governments, who never hesitated to employ violence, that we can readily apply, at a *very early* date and without fear of anachronism, the words *colonialism* and *imperialism*. This did not prevent—far from it—such "central" governments from being more or less dependent on a precocious form of capitalism already sharp in tooth and claw. Power was shared between the two. Without ever being swallowed up, the state was thus drawn into the intrinsic movement of the world-economy. By serving others and serving money, it was serving its own ends as well.[70]

The history of the American radio industry and Latin American broadcasting has, as a major character, a strong, aggressive, dynamic, feared-and-admired state; it also has market economies and international capital subtending that state and occupying a larger, less understood, more discreet and uncharted territory. Yet researchers should by no means abandon their interest in the state—particularly the aggressive state—for the state can obtain and exercise a relative degree of autonomy at the level of the event and the conjuncture, if not in fact in the long duration. In addition, market economies can operate against capitalist heirarchies. In the short term, the opposition is specific to a certain aspect of the world economy, but in the long term particular areas seem to reemerge constantly as terrains of struggle, including questions of patents, copyright, and culture. Whether in fact a structure of opposition regarding cultural activities exists between the market economy and international capital in the long duration is a question often obscured by the flexibility and adaptability of capitalism; nevertheless, an examination of the American radio industry and Latin American broadcasting (especially when tied to current events, such as video copyrights and illegal distribution) suggests the long-term existence of such a structure. More often than not, that structure is more clearly visible when researchers can step away from the always-center-stage status of capital and the state, but again that does not mitigate against studies of governments and private enterprise in tandem.

What is needed is a history of capitalism that is both a part of, and also separate from, the history of the state. Although historical crises are centered on the state, and indeed every centering implies a de-centering, it has been the state rather than capitalism that has centered and decentered in relationship to its peers—other governments. Capitalism, the always-international, past and present, is what discreetly surrounds the modern nation-state and remains autonomous, spontaneous, and an elusive subject beyond the empowerment of narrative closure. Hopefully, further research with multiple historical narratives can develop a more revealing and effective strategy for a lasting deconstruction of capitalism. Although the narrative closure of capitalism remains elusive, to refuse the questioning of its enduring power seems unthinkable. The asking of a multitude of questions might someday change our great past and bring about a lasting discourse that resolves in the long duration the social inequities that are invariably part of the conclusion of the capitalist narrative. After all, Fernand Braudel (like all good historians) wrote his narrative not only so we might know, but also so we might ask even more.

Notes

1. Fernand Braudel, *Civilization and Capitalism 15th-18th Century*, vol. 2: *The Wheels of Commerce*, trans. Sian Reynolds (New York: Harper and Row, 1984), pp. 553–54; emphasis in original. This chapter makes extensive use of the following works of Fernand Braudel: *Civilization and Capitalism, 15th-18th Century*, vol. 1: *The Structures of Everyday Life: The Limits of the Possible*; vol. 2: *The Wheels of Commerce*; vol. 3: *The Perspective of the World*, trans. Sian Reynolds (New York: Harper and Row, 1984); and *Afterthoughts on Material Civilization and Capitalism*, trans. Patricia M. Ranum (Baltimore: Johns Hopkins University Press, 1976). These four volumes are hereafter cited as *Structures*, *Wheels*, *Perspective*, and *Afterthoughts*.

2. Robert Berkhofer, "Comparing Pasts and Models: Toward a Comparative Metahistory." Paper presented at the Conference on Comparative Approaches to Social History, Northwestern University, Evanston, April 1986.

3. Although tracing the history of historical writing is a mammoth undertaking in itself, the widespread recognition of the complex and shifting ideological nature of history is at least as old as the work of Marc Bloch; for example, see his *The Historian's Craft*, trans. Peter Putnam (New York: Vintage, 1953); and Jacques Le Goff and Pierre Nora, eds., *Reconstructing the Past: Essays in Historical Methodology* (Cambridge: Cambridge University Press, 1985).

4. Thomas McCormick, "Drift or Mastery? A Corporatist Synthesis for American Diplomatic History," *Reviews in American History* 10 (December 1982): 318–30. On the origins of the concept of nation-state, see Benedict Anderson, *Imagined Communities: Reflections on the Origin and Spread of Nationalism* (London: Verso, 1983).

5. Whether it be directly through studies of government assisting industry or indirectly through the extensive use of government documents as evidence to discuss private enterprise.

6. The literature of dependency theory is immense, and what follows is not an exhaustive list. I have personally been influenced by many works, including Peter Evans, *Dependent Development: The Alliance of Multinational, State, and Local Capital in Brazil* (Princeton: Princeton University Press, 1979); Celso Furtado, *Formacao Economica do Brasil* (Berkeley: University of California Press, 1965); Andre Gunder Frank, "The Development of Underdevelopment," in *Imperialism and Underdevelopment: A Reader*, ed. R. I. Rhodes (New York: Monthly Review

Press, 1970); Paul Baran, "On the Political Economy of Backwardness," in *The Political Economy of Development and Underdevelopment*, ed. Charles Wilbur (New York: Random House, 1979); Keith Griffin, *Underdevelopment in Spanish America* (Cambridge: MIT Press, 1969); among other important scholars of this field are Fernando Cardoso, Teotonio Dos Santos, James Petras, Florestan Fernandes, Samir Amin, and Guillermo O'Donnell. Scholarship dealing with dependency theory and mass communications includes Oliver Boyd-Barrett, "Media Imperialism: Towards an International Framework for the Analysis of Media Systems," in *Mass Communication and Society* ed. J. Curran et al. (Beverley Hills: Sage, 1979); Chin-Chuan Lee, *Media Imperialism Reconsidered: The Homogenizing of Television Culture* (Beverley Hills: Sage, 1980); Fred Fejes, "Media Imperialism: An Assessment," *Media Culture and Society* 3 (1981): 281–88; Herbert Schiller, "Decolonization of Information," *Latin American Perspectives* 5 (1978): 35–48; Anthony Smith, *The Geopolitics of Information: How Western Culture Dominates the World* (London: Oxford University Press, 1980); Dallas Smythe, *Dependency Road: Communications, Capitalism, Consciousness and Canada* (Norwood: Ablex, 1981); and Mark Tolstedt, "Micronesian Broadcasting and U.S. Strategic Interests: The Evolution of a Dependency," Ph.D. diss., Northwestern University, Evanston, 1986, which contains an excellent literature review of dependency theory and mass communications research. I am not the first media researcher to question the efficacy of the dependency model; for example, see Armand Matellart, *Transnationals and the Third World: The Struggle for Culture* (South Hadley: Bergin and Garvey, 1983), chap. 1.

    7. Tolstedt, "Micronesian Broadcasting," p. 35.

    8. I have discussed several examples of this in the preceding chapter.

    9. In addition to *Structures*, *Wheels*, *Perspective*, and *Afterthoughts*, what follows also draws upon Le Goff and Nora, *Reconstructing the Past*; Lynn Hunt, "French History in the Last 20 Years: The Rise and Fall of the *Annales* Paradigm," *Journal of Contemporary History* 21 (1985): 209–24; Olwen Hufton, "Fernand Braudel," *Past and Present* 112 (1987): 208–13; Olivier Zunz, "Problem-Oriented History: A French-American Dialogue," *Reviews in American History* 14 (1986): 175–80; Robert S. DuPlessis, "The Partial Transition to World-Systems Analysis in Early Modern European History," *Radical History Review* 39 (1987): 11–27; Immanuel Wallerstein, *The Modern World-System: Capitalist Agriculture and the Origins of the European World-Economy in the Sixteenth Century* (New York: Academic Press, 1974); Wallerstein, *The Modern World-System II: Merchantilism and the Consolidation of the European World-Economy, 1600–1750* (New York: Academic Press, 1980); Wallerstein, *Historical Capitalism* (London: Verso, 1983); Frank, "The Development of Underdevelopment"; Michael Nerlich, *Ideology of Adventure: Studies in Modern Consciousness, 1100–1750*, vols. 1 and 2, trans. Ruth Crowley (Minneapolis: University of Minnesota Press, 1987); and Otto Mayr, *Authority, Liberty and Automatic Machinery in Early Modern Europe* (Baltimore: Johns Hopkins University Press, 1986).

10. The elaboration of Braudel's uses of time and space herein owes much to discussions that occurred at a conference presentation at the Society for Cinema Studies in Montreal in May 1987 and a lecture at the Department of Communication Arts at the University of Wisconsin in October 1987; my thanks for two intelligent and enthusiastic audiences.

11. I began with daily life, with those aspects of life that control us without our even being aware of them: habit or, better yet, routine — those thousands of acts that flower and reach fruition without anyone's having made a decision, acts of which we are not even fully aware. I think mankind is more than waist-deep in routine. Countless inherited acts, accumulated pell-mell and repeated time after time to this very day, become habits that help us live, imprison us, and make decisions for us throughout our lives . . . it is the life that man throughout the course of his previous history has made a part of his very being, has in some way absorbed into his entrails, turning the experiments and exhilirating experiences of the past into everyday, banal necessities. So no one pays close attention to them any more.

Braudel, *Afterthoughts*, pp. 7–8.

12. Braudel, *Perspective*, chaps. 6 and 7.

13. "The long term and the short term coexist; they cannot be separated . . . we all live in both the long term and the short term: the language I speak, the trade I practice, my beliefs, the human landscape surrounding me are all inherited; they existed before me and will go on existing after me," ibid., p. 85.

14. Ibid., pp. 71–72. For an application of the Kondratieff cycle to information technology studies, see Chris Freeman, "Long Waves of Economic Development," in *The Information Technology Revolution*, ed. Tom Forester (Cambridge: MIT Press, 1984), pp. 602–16.

15. Hunt, "French History," p. 211.

16. Olwen Hufton has tried to describe Braudel's relationship to the event:

The third level of time is the most difficult of all to describe . . . reference to phenomena such as abnormal harvests or short industrial slumps of temporary dislocation which might, although I have never seen it explicitly spelt out, be the product of political factors: war, occupation, etc. It is easily envisaged by reference to a particular agricultural year produced by extraordinary conditions affecting society until another harvest brought alleviation and restored normalcy, or by reference to a temporary slump within a burgeoning industry, due perhaps to overproduction, changes in market fashion, disruption of trade through war.

Hufton, "Fernand Braudel," p. 211.

17. Lynn Hunt says that for Braudel, "events are dust," "French History," p. 212.

18. In addition to previously cited works by Braudel, also see *The Mediterranean and the Mediterranean World in the Age of Philip II*, vols.

1 and 2, trans. Sian Reynolds (New York: Harper and Row, 1973), for his analysis of the physical structures of the Mediterranean area.

19. Braudel, *Wheels*, pp. 229–30.

20. Braudel gives a glimpse of the market economy of Rome during the seventeenth century in an illustration showing more than a hundred street peddlers (all with their own specialities) in *Wheels*, p. 380.

21. Capitalist interests, in the past as in the present, naturally extend beyond the narrow boundaries of the nation; and this prejudices, or at any rate complicates, the dialogue and relationship between state and capital. In Lisbon, which I choose out of a number of powerful cities to illustrate the point, the capitalism of the real businessmen, the powerful merchants, was quite invisible to the townspeople. This was because the real transactions went on overseas: in Macao, the secret gateway to China; in Goa in India; in far-off Russia (when one wanted to sell an exceptionally large diamond for instance) or in Brazil, the great realm of slaves and plantations, of gold-diggers and *garimpieros* [diamond hunters]. Capitalism always wore seven-league boots.

Braudel, *Wheels*, pp. 553–54.

22. Let me emphasize the quality that seems to me to be an essential feature of capitalism: its unlimited flexibility, its capacity for change and *adaptation*. If there is, as I believe, a certain unity in capitalism, from thirteenth-century Italy to the present-day West, it is here above all that such unity must be located and observed. . . . On a world scale, we should avoid the over-simple image often presented of capitalism passing through various stages of growth, from trade to finance to industry—with the "mature" industrial phase seen as the only "true" capitalism. In the so-called merchant or commercial capitalism phase, as in the so-called industrial phase (and both terms cover a multitude of forms) the essential characteristic of capitalism was its capacity to slip at a moment's notice from one form or sector to another. . . .

Braudel, *Wheels*, p. 433; emphasis in original.

23. "Radio Markets of the World, 1930."

24. Minutes of a meeting of the Buenos Aires branch of General Electric of South America, 28 September 1922, file 11–14-10, Box 101, Owen D. Young Papers, Van Hornesville, N. Y. (hereafter Young Papers).

25. "Report Covering the History of Radio Sud America" (an RCA subsidiary), 17 June 1924, file 11–14-10, Box 101, Young Papers (hereafter "History of Radio Sud America"). This document—which runs more than a hundred pages—was prepared for Young when he negotiated the liquidation of the broadcast component of the AEFG consortium, events discussed in greater detail on pp. 137–39.

26. American Consul General W. Henry Robertson to State Department, 16 April 1923, Record Group (RG) 59, 835.74/55; J. W. Riddle, American legation, to State Department, 9 May 1923, RG 59, 835.74/56; Robertson to State Department, 28 June 1923, RG 59, 835.74/58; Raleigh Gibson to State Department, 27 June 1924, RG 59, 835.74/63; all Department of State, National Archives, Washington (DSNA); "History of Radio Sud America."

27. George Davis, General Electric, to Young, 17 June 1922, file 11–14-10, Box 100, Young Papers.

28. See the chapter 4 for a discussion of the introduction of broadcasting by American corporations at this event.

29. Gerard Swope, General Electric, to W. B. Van Dyke, International General Electric, 12 April 1922, file 11-14-10, Box 99, Young Papers.

30. A. Oudin, RCA, to Davis, 21 April 1922; Van Dyke to Young, 12 May 1922; both file 11–14-10, Box 99, Young Papers. This all took place while Young was away in Europe meeting with other members of the AEFG consortium. For a summary memo, see Van Dyke to A. S. Durrant, International General Electric, 12 July 1922, file 11–14-10, Box 100, Young Papers.

31. N. E. Nielsen, Radio Sud America, report to International General Electric Company, 16 June 1923, file 11–14-10, Box 101, Young Papers.

32. Memo, H. C. Mitchell (General Electric representative in Argentina), 28 June 1922; memo by Mitchell, 13 July 1922; W. A. Reece, General Electric representative in Argentina, to R. G. Henderson, International General Electric Company, 17 July 1922; all file 11–14-10, Box 100, Young Papers. Reece included a snapshot of the exterior of the Pekam broadcast studio.

33. "History of Radio Sud America," p. 17.

34. Ibid., p. 8.

35. Ibid., pp. 26–28.

36. Ibid., appendix on broadcasting.

37. John Westman, "Modern Dependency: A 'Crucial Case' Study of Brazilian Government Policy in the Minicomputer Industry," *Studies in Comparative International Development* 20 (Summer 1985): 25–47; Antonio Jose J. Bothelho, "Brazil's Independent Computer Strategy," *Technology Review* (May-June 1987): 36.

38. "History of Radio Sud America," p. 18.

39. "General Harbord Announces New South American Radio Plans," RCA press release, 24 July 1924, file 11–14-10, Box 101, Young Papers; "Harbord Reviews His South American Trip," *World Wide Wireless*, May 1925, p. 6.

40. "History of Radio Sud America," appendix on broadcasting.

41. Mitchell's report of 28 June 1922, file 11–14-10, Box 100, Young Papers. In addition, a tax on advertising gave the municipal government 5 percent of the gross.

42. Braudel, *Afterthoughts*, p. 85. I believe the development of broadcasting at the global level, as encouraged by the American radio industry in tandem with American policies for international communications conferences in the 1920s, laid to rest once and for all the question of where the international capitalization of radio had centered. In addition, it is hardly coincidental that the centering of the new means of global communication in the United States was concurrent with the recentering of international finance from London to New York City.

43. Braudel, *Wheels*, pp. 575–76; 229–30; 433.

44. For background on the formation of NBC, see Josephine Young Case and Everett Needham Case, *Owen D. Young and American Enterprise* (Boston: Godine, 1982), pp. 350–56; Kenneth Bilby, *The General: David Sarnoff and the Rise of the Communications Industry* (New York: Harper and Row, 1986), pp. 84–110.

45. Memo of 27 April 1934, folder 6, Box 27, NBC Central Files.

46. Report by NBC study group on radio progress in Cuba, 25 March 1937; and supplementary memo to that report written by C. W. Horn, 21 May 1937; both folder 1, Box 53, Central Office Files of the National Broadcasting Company (NBC) Records, Mass Communications History Center of the State Historical Society of Wisconsin, Madison (hereafter NBC Central Files).

47. "Report on Cuba," NBC Statistical Department, May 1937, folder 1, Box 53, NBC Central Files.

48. Horn to NBC President Lenox Lohr, no day, March 1939, folder 50, Box 67, NBC Central Files.

49. Fay Gillis Wells, oral history, p. 29, Broadcast Pioneers Library, Washington, D.C.; Lohr to RCA President David W. Sarnoff, 24 October 1938, folder 62, Box 48, NBC Central Files. Of course, AT&T, at the time involved only in domestic telephony, could not carry a network signal via its long lines any further than Laredo, Texas.

50. Harry C. Maynard, International General Electric, to NBC Vice President John Royal, 4 May 1932, folder 9, Box 114, Papers of John Royal, Mass Communications History Center of the State Historical Society of Wisconsin, Madison (hereafter Royal Papers).

51. Memo by NBC study group on Cuba, 25 March 1937, folder 1, Box 53, NBC Central Files.

52. Enrique Reid, Pan American Union, to Ben Cherrington, Department of State, 22 June 1939, RG 59, 810.42711radio broadcasts/1, DSNA. On the interaction between Hollywood and American radio networks, see Michele Hilmes, *Hollywood and Broadcasting: From Radio to Cable* (Urbana: University of Illinois Press, 1990); Richard Jewell, "Hollywood and Radio: Competition and Partnership in the 1930s," *Historical Journal of Film, Radio and Television* 4 (1984): 125–41; and Charles Eckert, "The Carole Lombard in Macy's Window," *Quarterly Review of Film Studies* 3 (1978): 3–21.

53. Braudel, *Wheels*, p. 519.

54. Biography of Emilio Azcarraga (written in 1957) held at the Mass Cmmunications History Center of the State Historical Society of Wisconsin, Madison; Lohr to Sarnoff, 24 October 1938, folder 48, Box 62, NBC Central Files. My appreciation to archivist Carolyn Mattern for showing me the Azcarraga biography.

55. Gene Fowler and Bill Crawford, *Border Radio* (Austin: Texas Monthly Press, 1987) is a superb accounting of these stations and their program activities. One of the best-known border radio personalities was Wolfman Jack, who experienced border radio at the end of its heyday in the 1960s. W. Lee "Pappy" O'Daniel, governor of Texas in the 1940s,

combined border radio broadcasts with advertisements on the sides of bags of flour to run a successful political media campaign. John Brinkley and Norman Baker, two American medical "entrepreneurs," were among the pioneers of border radio as they publicized their colon, prostate, and cancer clinics and cures via the airwaves; in addition, evangelists, preachers, fortune tellers, psychics, and temperance advocates abounded on these stations. On Brinkley, also see Ansel Harlan Resler, "The Impact of John R. Brinkley on Broadcasting in the United States," Ph.D. diss., Northwestern University, Evanston, 1958; and Gerald Carson, *The Roguish World of Dr. Brinkley* (New York: Holt, Rinehart, and Winston, 1960). On Norman Baker, see Thomas Hoffer, "Norman Baker and American Broadcasting," M.A. thesis, University of Wisconsin, Madison, 1969.

56. American Consul Lewis Boyle to U.S. Ambassador to Mexico Josephus Daniels, 28 September 1939, RG 59, 812.74/310, DSNA.

57. Brinkley had the dubious distinction of an entire State Department decimal file devoted to his Mexican radio activities (RG 59, file 812.76Brinkley, DSNA).

58. U.S. Senator (Texas) Morris Shepard to Hull, 18 March 1932, RG 59, 812.76/133; U.S. Postal Inspector K. P. Aldrich to Hull, 27 February 1937, RG 59, 812.76/277; both DSNA.

59. Horn to NBC President Merlin Aylesworth, 12 June 1931, RG 59, 812.76/71; American Consul General James Stewart to Hull, 3 December 1937, RG 59, 812.761/15; both DSNA. The Mexican government in 1937 zealously discouraged "the transmission of comical numbers which aim to secure the amusement of the audience by recourse to low comedy, puns, exclamations and noises, uncouth jokes . . . sirens, bells, claxons, horns or similar instruments shall not be used to attract the attention of the radio listeners or to announce the broadcasts as this adversely affects the quality of the programs. . . . Announcers must not insistently repeat the name or brand of the article that is wished to advertise. . . ." Clearly, most of the power structure of state and local capital in Mexico and Latin America was quite eager to cooperate with the global heirarchy constructed for all by the American radio industry.

60. American Consul to Saltillo Samuel Sobokin to State Department, 11 March 1931, RG 59, 812.76/55; American Consul to Veracruz Leonard Dawson to State Department, 11 March 1931, RG 59, 812.76/58; American Consul to Tampico C. E. Macy to State Department, 2 April 1931, RG 59, 812.76/62; all DSNA.

61. American Consul General Philip Holland to State Department, 30 January 1929, RG 59, 814.76Figueroa/2, DSNA.

62. Harold Finley, American legation, to Hull, 6 May 1938, RG 59, 838.76/3; State Department memo, 17 December 1938, RG 59, 838.76/8; memo, Francis Colt DeWolf, State Department, 12 January 1939, RG 59, 838.76/8; all DSNA.

63. American Consul Harry Anzinger to State Department, 4 December 1924, RG 59, 831.74/114, DSNA.

64. Horn to Lohr, 4 August 1938, folder 58, Box 58, NBC Central Files.

65. Frank Russell, NBC, to Niles Trammell, NBC, 7 June 1939; and Ovid Riso, RCA Victor, to NBC Vice President Frank Mason, 7 July 1939, folder 53, Box 66, NBC Central Files.

66. Carlos Baccarat (owner of radio broadcasting station in Santos, Brazil) to Royal, 4 December 1941, folder 23, Box 111, Royal Papers.

67. The trade journal *Broadcasting* has covered the PANAMSAT developments; for examples, see "Intelsat OK's PANAMSAT Plan," 15 December 1986, p. 50; "U.S., Intelsat Wrestle with PANAMSAT Application," 13 October 1986, pp. 62–63; and "Intelsat Approves System Coordination," 2 March 1987, p. 76; "PANAMSAT Bemoans Competitive Position vis-a-vis INTELSAT," *Broadcasting*, 23 November 1987, p. 82; "PANAMSAT Cleared for Launch in '88," *Satellite Communications* December 1987, p. 15; on the Latin American video market economy, see "Yanks Ready Legal Grip on Argentine Home Video," *Variety*, 9 May 1984; "Piracy Still Cutting Home Video Profits: Illegal Tapes Rush Latin American Markets," *Variety*, 23 November 1985; "Piracy Law Hits Brazil," *Variety*, 17 October 1983; "The Monster with Two Heads?" *Forbes*, 8 April 1985; "Illegal Homevid in Latin Orbit," *Variety*, 7 March 1985. I am indebted to Maria Uribe, a graduate student from Colombia at Northwestern University during 1985–86, for teaching me about the Latin American video rental market.

68. U.S. Congress, Office of Technology Assessment, *Intellectual Property Rights in an Age of Electronics and Information*, OTA-CIT-302 (Washington: Government Printing Office, 1986), chap. 8.

69. U.S. General Accounting Office, *International Trade: Strengthening Worldwide Protection of Intellectual Property Rights*, GAO/NSIAD-87–65 (Washington: Government Printing Office, 1987), pp. 42–44. Also see U.S. Senate, Committee on Foreign Relations, *International Telecommunications and Information Policy: Selected Issues for the 1980s*, 96th Cong., 1st sess. (Washington: Government Printing Office, 1983).

70. Braudel, *Perspective*, p. 51; emphasis in original.

Epilogue

When many individuals consider the American radio industry and U.S.-Latin American relations from 1900 to 1939, the growing propaganda wars on shortwave frequencies during the late 1930s immediately come to mind as the genesis of the American radio industry's activities in Latin America. The events surrounding the various shortwave broadcasts emanating from the United States, Germany, Italy, Great Britain, France, Japan, and the Soviet Union were subjected to serious research as the broadcasts occurred[1] and these events (along with present-day shortwave radio politics and propaganda) continue to be important topics for analysis.[2] These shortwave propaganda broadcasts of the 1930s had both a worldwide and also a specific Latin American audience. From an American perspective, they mark the inception of U.S. government involvement in international shortwave radio broadcasting; the close cooperation between private American shortwave broadcasters and the government during World War II led directly to the postwar establishment of the Voice of America.

Although the development of private American shortwave broadcasting to Latin America is certainly a significant event in the history of U.S.-Latin American communication relations, Latin American reception of American broadcasts did not suddenly emerge in the late 1930s, but rather has been a part of "American" broadcasting since the early 1920s. Latin American radio enthusiasts did not become listeners of American stations only with the advent of 1930s' shortwave; quite the opposite is true. The Latin American audience has listened to American broadcast programming as well as their own stations since the very beginning of radio broadcasting, and these audiences have always been recognized by American public and private policymakers involved in the radio industry. They remain an important audience for American television programming, American films, American music, and a major outlet for the global spread of consumer culture. Broadcasting was a global activity from its very beginnings.

Latin American listeners usually do not occupy the forefront of attention of the American media industry, but they are never forgotten or ignored. In the early 1920s, Latin American broadcast enthusiasts picked up the distant signals of stations from the United States and also picked up the American experimental shortwave broadcasts of the mid-1920s. By the late 1930s, Latin Americans could listen to several American shortwave program-mers as well as several European programmers; throughout the 1920s and 1930s, they also had their own broadcast stations. The fact that their own broadcast fare was in many ways similar to that from the United States was in part attributable to the interaction of capital and the state in the spread of American radio (chapters 3 and 4), and in part attributable to the structure of relations between market economies and international capital as that struc-ture manifested itself concerning radio broadcasting (chapter 5).

But what about the relationship between capitalism and the American radio industry during the period preceding broadcast-ing? Why did Owen Young succeed where E. C. Benedict had failed? Perhaps capitalism, despite its spontaneity, flexibility, adaptabilty, and power to choose, nevertheless remains somewhat dependent on certain structures that it did not originally create.[3] Despite the efforts of E. C. Benedict and many others, and despite the prior existence of social and political heirarchies and markets of production and consumption, capitalism was a latecomer to the American radio industry, finally arriving permanently with the swirl of events that led to the formation of RCA in 1919. RCA, formed to provide American leadership in international commu-nications, anticipated the immediate postwar future of all global radio activities except one: broadcasting.

Thus, broadcasting is a peculiar phenomena that came to occupy the centerpoint of radio technology but nevertheless was not a factor that led capitalism to finally arrive in the American radio industry. The public and private policymakers who put together RCA never really considered the various possibilities that involvement in broadcasting might offer to RCA; their vision was wholly centered on control of international communications through radio technology. The dawn of radio broadcasting is associated more intimately with the amateur radio broadcaster. Of course, RCA and the American radio industry moved with the greatest haste and consummate skill to penetrate radio broadcasting and then promote their own visions of broadcast culture. At a world-systems level, this led to an ongoing dialectic still extant: short-term resistance and independence within market economies emerging around new manifestations of broadcast culture versus long-term organization and rationalization of broadcast culture according to the specific logic of global capitalism. Although capitalist expressions of media culture may often appear dominant and even oppressive, a historical analysis of capitalism and globalization of American broadcasting suggests that the struggle between capitalism's benefactors and subjects as it is manifest in the long duration of global media culture is not deterministic but instead dialectic.

Observers of the American radio industry and its Latin American activities from 1900 to 1939 need to consider historical narratives constructed around the lived past of capitalism in a global context and also historical narratives constructed around the lived past of nation-state struggles. This dual approach to history allows for a greater understanding of modern media culture. The continuing present of capitalism can be seen in conflicts of media culture over terrain such as copyrights and intellectual property. The continuing present of nation-state struggles discernible in the emergence and enunciation from third-world nations for a New International Information Order[4] is exemplary of the conflict of nation-states. Placing the New International Information Order in the realm of the nation-state does not divorce the debate from the influences of capitalism. Simply put, most scholarship (at least within the United States) that has taken up the New International Information Order debate has tended to narrate that debate along the lines of competing nation-states rather than along the lines of international capitalism operating in territory beyond the domain of the nation-state.[5] In addition, the role of the United Nations as a forum for many of the debates concerning the New International Information Order has led to those debates usually being couched in the vernacular of nation-state struggles rather than the vernacular of local market economies versus global capitalism.

In areas of concern such as technology transfer, news flow, and national sovereignty within the New International Information

Order debate, past activities of the American radio industry
continue to be visible in contemporary third-world conditions.
From the efforts of United Fruit, U.S. Rubber, and other American
corporations in the early 1900s to the beginnings of direct overseas investment by American radio manufacturers in the late
1930s, Latin American nations have faced the contradictory conditions, the benefits and problems, of communications technology
transfer from the developed to the underdeveloped world. Technology transfer seems to occasionally benefit local economic
conditions in the short term, and even temporarily spur economic
growth in local market economies. But in the long term, that
growth remains only on the cutting edge of technological developments, and attempts by Latin American and third-world nations to
continue indigenous growth in communications technology, encourage autonomous research and development, and gain a greater
measure of control over the pace and direction of technology
transfer have more often than not been unsuccessful. Actions such
as Brazil's protective attitude toward its microcomputer industry
are encouraging, but such activity should not allow analysis to
assume that the scales are now somehow balanced. Whether or not
recent events will change the long term structure of global media
culture and information economics remains to be seen.

When it comes to control over the pace and direction of international news flow, the concerted activities in the 1920s of American
public and private policymakers toward global expansion of the
American radio industry included the contributions of the American press corps. American news media still enjoy a tremendous
level of influence over the daily news consumption patterns in
Latin American and third-world nations, in both the press and in
broadcast journalism. And in the area of national sovereignty,
third-world nations still labor under the constraints and principles of decision making over the electromagnetic spectrum that
were carefully laid out by American policymakers at international
communications conferences of the 1920s and 1930s, principles
that still empower the leadership of private enterprise and disen-
franchise the nations and regions of the third world. Since the
early 1960s, the electromagnetic spectrum has been joined by
another single shared global resource used in global communications: the equatorial or geostationary orbit for communications
satellites. Although third-world nations occupy the equatorial

landmass on the earth's surface, they have little say in the allocation and use of this valuable and scarce global resource.[6]

Turning to the question of broadcasting, radio in the 1920s and 1930s became an important medium for dissemination of modern consumer culture in the United States and the world at large. The coming of international capitalism to radio, along with the rise of worldwide interest in the unforseen phenomena of broadcasting, gave the culture of the world-system a continuing dialectic. International capital would constantly be forced to search out cultural avenues of control in response to the spontaneous philosophies of cultural expression through modern media forms. The coming together of radio broadcasting with the values of the consumption ethic, although important in accounting for a large measure of capitalist control over both American and global media culture, has nevertheless not proved a strong enough ideology to change the pace and direction of a continuing story where forms of cultural expression exist beyond the interests of the architects of capitalist culture. The process of rationalization over media culture—from 1920s' broadcasting to 1980s' video—by international capitalism, both past and present, demonstrates that such rationalization is not so much action as reaction to the spontaneous exchange and independent will of local market economies.

These local market economies are the residue, the tracks, the tracings of a multitude of alternative cultural expressions beyond the bounds of economic practices. Economic history—or any history for that matter—at its best usually provides little more than the footprints of people's past lives: we know where they stood, but often still wonder how they gestured and what they thought about all they felt, heard, and saw. Like any disipline, history too has its limitations on understanding. Those limitations carry into our knowledge of the present: in the current culture of the capitalist world-system, capitalism certainly continues its movement out of the past and into the culture of the everyday, but at the same time popular expression of cultural values continues to move into territory unoccupied by the state or capital. In many instances these movements and directions away from capitalism take place off the record, away from the completeness of documentation through records of governments and corporations. The political conditions in nations such as Chile are grim testimony to the fact that even the most repressive forces cannot fully contain this popular expression, and the worldwide wave of video piracy in nations enjoying more benign political conditions suggests that a capitalist consumer culture cannot fully control societies even when the inhabitants of those societies more or less consent to that culture's powers. An analysis of the historical dialectic of capitalism, the American radio industry, and Latin American broadcasting (and by extension global media culture) suggests that revolution, like capitalism, ultimately knows no nationality.

Too often our understanding and imagery of the revolutionary process has been confined totally within the construct of the nation-state. Although this linkage of the revolution and the nation-state is undeniably critical, such total confinement ultimately becomes a sort of intellectual prisonhouse that prevents crossing the conceptual boundaries of the nation into open territory. Crossing the boundaries into open territory is the key to the long-term structure of the global revolutionary process because the open territory can provide refuge and temporary freedom so that the revolution might replenish and continue. This is a special kind of freedom not to be found in the confines of the nation-state because the synergistic relationship between the state and capitalism removes that freedom and replenishment. That synergy takes the form of power, monopoly, and repression—not everywhere on the world, but always somewhere, and almost always somewhere in the third world. Perhaps those interested in crossing the boundaries in both directions and searching for intellectual freedom as a component of social equality and global liberation will find the discussions, information, evidence, images, and questions presented in this book useful as a springboard to revolutionary thinking.

Notes

1. Lenore Franz, "Short-Wave Communications to Latin America," M.A. thesis, University of Wisconsin, Madison, 1947; Silas Bent, "International Broadcasting," *Public Opinion Quarterly* 1 (July 1937): 117–21; Karl Van Gelderland, "War in the Ether," *Nation* 12 March 1938, pp. 300–1; William Paley, "Radio Turns South" *Fortune,* April 1941, p. 77; Charles Rolo, *Radio Goes to War* (New York: Putnam, 1942); Beth Roberts, "United States Propaganda Warfare in Latin America," Ph.D. diss., University of Southern California, Los Angeles, 1943.

2. In addition to Fred Fejes, "Imperialism, Media, and the Good Neighbor: New Deal Foreign Policy and United States Shortwave Broadcasting to Latin America," Ph.D. diss., University of Illinois, Urbana, 1982, see E. Roderick Diehl, "South of the Border: The NBC and CBS Networks and the Latin American Venture, 1930–1942," *Communication Quarterly* 25 (Fall 1977): 2–12; Robert Pirsein, "The Voice of America—A History of the International Broadcasting Activities of the United States Government, 1940–1962," Ph.D diss., Northwestern University, Evanston, 1970; M. Kent Sidel, "A Historical Analysis of American Short Wave Broadcasting 1916–1942," Ph.D diss., Northwestern University, Evanston, 1976; Holly Schulman, "The Voice of History: The Development of American Propaganda and Voice of America," Ph.D. diss., University of Maryland, College Park, 1984; Douglas Boyd, "The Pre-History of the Voice of America," *Public Telecommunications Review* 2 (December 1974): 38–45; Donald Browne, "The Voice of America: Policies and Problems," *Journalism Monographs* 43 (February 1976); Howard Frederick, *Cuban-American Radio Wars: Ideology in International Telecommunications* (Norwood: Ablex, 1986).

3. "Capitalism does not invent heirarchies, any more than it invented the market, or production, or consumption; it merely uses them. In the long procession of history, capitalism is the latecomer. It arrives when everything is ready." Fernand Braudel, *Afterthoughts on Material Civilization and Capitalism,* trans. Patricia A. Ranum (Baltimore: Johns Hopkins University Press, 1976), p. 75. It is worth remembering that a portion of Braudel's everyday past life is chronicled herein; he spent a number of years in the 1920s and 1930s as a professor in Sao Paulo and was most likely a listener in the Brazilian broadcast audience.

4. Although this movement is now more often labeled as the "New World Information Order," or the "New World Information and Communication Order," I have chosen to use the term originally coined by third-world nations in the early 1970s.

5. See my discussion of dependency theory and media studies in chapter 5 for citation of some of the recent scholarship exemplifying this tendency. Also see Herbert Schiller, *Communication and Cultural Domination* (New York: International Arts and Sciences, 1976); Wilbur Schramm and Daniel Lerner, eds., *Mass Media and National Development: The Role of Information in Developing Countries* (Stanford: Stanford University Press, 1964); Kaarl Nordenstreng and Herbert Schiller, eds., *National Sovereignty and International Communication* (Norwood: Ablex, 1979); Emile McAnany, *Communication and Change in the Rural Third World: The Role of Information in Development* (New York: Praeger, 1980); Elihu Katz and George Wedell, *Broadcasting in the Third World: Promise and Performance* (Cambridge: Harvard University Press, 1977); *Many Voices, One World: Towards a New More Just and More Efficient World Information and Communication Order* (the MacBride Report) (New York: UNESCO, 1980); Tapio Varis, "The International Flow of Television Programs," *Journal of Communications* 34 (1974): 143–52; Jorge Schnitman, *Film*

Industries in Latin America: Dependency and Development (Norwood: Ablex, 1984); Jeremy Tunstall, *The Media Are American* (New York: Columbia University Press, 1977); and Douglas Boyd, *Broadcasting in the Arab World* (Philadelphia: Temple University Press, 1985).

6. Even before the first successful satellite launch in 1957 (the USSR's Sputnik) the structures of power were visible:

> As man reaches upward to the outer atmosphere, new political problems arise, the nature of which we are as yet unable to grasp. Heretofore, the relations between nations and military forces were determined by the geometry of a spheroid's curved surface. . . . Henceforth, international relations will be geared to the more difficult geometry of the interior of a large spheroid enveloping at its core a smaller and impenetrable spheroid, the earth. But even more confusing, the radius of the outer spheroid — symbolizing the aerospace of the altitude which man had reached at any given time — is expanding. The technologically most advanced nations will operate within the highest aerospace, while the spheroids circumscribing the aerial capabilities of the more backward nations will have shorter radii. Hence, in the future, the geometry of power will be described by several enveloping spheroids of different sizes. . . . Truly, a new *Weltbild* is emerging.

Stephan T. Possony and Leslie Rozenzweig, "The Geography of the Air, 1955" quoted in Edward W. Ploman, *Space, Earth and Communication* (Westport: Greenwood Press, 1984), p. 9.

Bibliography

I. Books, Journals, Dissertations, and Theses

Aitken, Hugh G. J. *The Continuous Wave: Technology and American Radio 1900–1932*. Princeton: Princeton University Press, 1985.

———. *Syntony and Spark: The Origins of Radio*. New York: John Wiley and Sons, 1976.

Anderson, Benedict. *Imagined Communities: Reflections on the Origin and Spread of Nationalism*. London: Verso, 1983.

Archer, Gleason. *Big Business and Radio*. New York: American Historical Society, 1939.

———. *History of Radio to 1926*. New York: American Historical Society, 1938.

Babcock, Glenn. *History of the U.S. Rubber Company*. Bloomington: Indiana Business Reports, 1966.

Baran, Paul. "On the Political Economy of Backwardness." In *The Political Economy of Development and Underdevelopment*, edited by Charles Wilbur. New York: Random House, 1979.

Benson, Susan Porter. *Counter Cultures: Saleswomen, Managers and Customers in American Department Stores 1890–1940*. Urbana: University of Illinois Press, 1986.

Bent, Silas. "International Broadcasting." *Public Opinion Quarterly* 1 (1937): 117–21.

Berkhofer, Robert. "Comparing Pasts and Models: Toward A Comparative Metahistory." Paper presented at the Conference on Comparative Approaches to Social History, Northwestern University, Evanston, April 1986.

Biel, Michael. "The Making and Use of Broadcast Recordings Prior to 1936." Ph.D. diss., Northwestern University, Evanston, 1977.

Bilby, Kenneth. *The General: David Sarnoff and the Rise of the Communications Industry*. New York: Harper and Row, 1986.

Bloch, Marc. *The Historian's Craft*. Translated by Peter Putnam. New York: Vintage, 1953.

Boyd-Barrett, Oliver. "Media Imperialism: Towards an International Framework for the Analysis of Media Systems." In *Mass Communications and Society*, edited by James Curren et al. Beverley Hills: Sage, 1979.

Boyd, Douglas. *Broadcasting in the Arab World.* Philadelphia: Temple University Press, 1985.

———. "The Pre-History of the Voice of America." *Public Telecommunications Review* 6 (1974): 38–45.

Braudel, Fernand. *Afterthoughts on Material Civilization and Capitalism.* Translated by Patricia M. Ranum. Baltimore: Johns Hopkins University Press, 1976.

———. *Civlilization and Capitalism 15th-18th Century.* Vol. 1, *The Structures of Everyday Life.* Vol. 2, *The Wheels of Commerce.* Vol. 3 *The Perspective of the World.* Translated by Sian Reynolds. New York: Harper and Row, 1984.

———. *The Mediterranean and the Mediterranean World in the Age of Philip II.* Translated by Sian Reynolds. New York: Harper and Row, 1972.

Browne, Donald. "The Voice of America: Policies and Problems." *Journalism Monographs* 43 (1976).

Carneal, Georgette. *Conqueror of Space: The Life of Lee DeForest.* New York: Liveright, 1930.

Carson, Gerald. *The Roguish World of Dr. Brinkley.* New York: Holt, Rinehart and Winston, 1960.

Case, Josephine Young, and Everett Needham Case. *Owen D. Young and American Enterprise.* Boston: Godine, 1982.

Chalk, Frank R. "The United States and the International Struggle for Rubber, 1914–1941." Ph.D. diss., University of Wisconsin, Madison, 1970.

Clark, Keith. *International Communications—the American Attitude.* New York: Columbia University Press, 1931.

Coon, Horace. *American Tel and Tel.* New York: Longmans, Green, 1939.

Cortina, Alfredo. *Contribucion a la Historia de la Radio en Venezuela.* Caracas: Instituto Nacional de Hipodromos, 1982.

Danielian, N. R. *ATT: Story of Industrial Conquest.* New York: Vanguard, 1939.

da Silva, Carlos Eduardo Lins. "Transnational Communication and Brazilian Culture." In *Communications and Latin American Society: Trends in Critical Research, 1960–1985,* edited by Rita Atwood and Emile MacAnany. Madison: University of Wisconsin Press, 1986.

DeForest, Lee. *Father of Radio.* Chicago: Wilcox and Follet, 1950.

DeNovo, John. "The Engigmatic Alvey A. Adee and American Foreign Relations, 1870–1924." *Prologue* 7 (1975): 68–80.

de Queiroz, Maria Isuara Pereira. "The Samba Schools of Rio de Janeiro or the Domestication of an Urban Mass." *Diogenes* 129 (1985): 1–32.

DeSoto, Clinton. *Two Hundred Meters and Down: The Story Of Amateur Radio.* West Hartford: American Radio Relay League, 1936.

Diehl, E. Roderick. "South of the Border: The NBC and CBS Networks and the Latin American Venture, 1930–1942." *Communication Quarterly* 25 (1977): 2–12.

Douglas, Susan. *Inventing American Broadcasting 1899–1922.* Baltimore: Johns Hopkins University Press, 1987.

———. "The Navy Adopts the Radio, 1899–1919." In *Military Enterprise and Technological Change,* edited by Merritt Roe Smith. Cambridge: MIT Press, 1985.

DuPlessis, Robert. "The Partial Transition to World-Systems Analysis in Early Modern European History." *Radical History Review* 39 (1987): 8–35.

Eckert, Charles. "The Carole Lombard in Macy's Window." *Quarterly Review of Film Studies* 3 (1978): 3–21.

Evans, Peter. *Dependent Development: The Alliance of Multinational, State and Local Capital in Brazil.* Princeton: Princeton University Press, 1979.

Federico, Maria Elvira Bonavita. *Historia da Comunicacao Radio e Television no Brasil.* Petropolis: Vozes, 1982.

Fejes, Fred. "Imperialism, Media and the Good Neighbor: New Deal Foreign Policy and United States Shortwave Broadcasting to Latin America." Ph.D. diss., University of Illinois, Urbana, 1982.

———. "Media Imperialism: An Assessment." *Media Culture and Society* 3 (1981): 281–88.

Feldman, Mildred. *The United States in the International Telecommunications Union and Pre-ITU Conferences.* Published privately, 1975.

Fessenden, Helen M. *Fessenden.* New York: Coward-McCann, 1940.

Fowler, Gene, and Bill Crawford. *Border Radio.* Austin: Texas Monthly Press, 1987.

Fox, Richard W., and T. J. Jackson Lears, eds. *The Culture of Consumption: Critical Essays in American History 1880–1980.* New York: Pantheon, 1983.

Frank, Andre Gunder. "The Development of Underdevelopment." In *Imperialism and Underdevelopment,* edited by R. I. Rhodes. New York: Monthly Review Press, 1970.

Franz, Lenore. "Short-Wave Communications to Latin America." M.A. thesis, University of Wisconsin, Madison, 1947.

Frederick, Howard. *Cuban-American Radio Wars: Ideology in International Telecommunications.* Norwood: Ablex, 1986.

Furtado, Celso. *The Economic Growth of Brazil.* Berkeley: University of California Press, 1965.

Glover, John G., and William B. Cornell, eds. *The Development of American Industries.* New York: Prentice-Hall, 1941.

Godfried, Nathan. "The Origins of Labor Radio: WCFL, the 'Voice of Labor,' 1925–1928." *Historical Journal of Film, Radio and Television* 7 (1987): 143–59.

Griffin, Keith. *Underdevelopment in Spanish America.* Cambridge: MIT Press, 1969.

Guback, Thomas, and Stephen Hill. "The Beginnings of Soviet Broadcasting and the Role of V.I. Lenin." *Journalism Monographs* 26 (1972).

Gustafson, Milton O., ed. *The National Archives and Foreign Relations Research*. Athens: Ohio University Press, 1974.

Haley, P. Edward. *Revolution and Intervention: The Diplomacy of Taft and Wilson with Mexico, 1910–1917*. Cambridge: MIT Press, 1970.

Hall, Henry, ed. *America's Successful Men of Affairs*. New York: New York Tribune, 1895.

Harbord, James. "America's Position in Radio Communication." *Foreign Affairs* 4 (1926): 465–74.

Herring, James, and Gerald Gross. *Telecommunications: Economics and Regulations*. New York: McGraw-Hill, 1936.

Hill, Lawrence W. *Diplomatic Relations Between the United States and Brazil*. Durham: Duke University Press, 1932.

Hilmes, Michele. *Hollywood and Broadcasting: From Radio to Cable*. Urbana: University of Illinois Press, 1990.

Hoffer, Thomas. "Norman Baker and American Broadcasting." M.A. thesis, University of Wisconsin, Madison, 1969.

Hogan, Michael. *Informal Entente: The Private Structure of Cooperation in Anglo-American Economic Diplomacy, 1918–1928*. Columbia: University of Missouri Press, 1977.

Hufton, Olwen. "Fernand Braudel." *Past and Present* 112 (1987): 208–13.

Hughes, Brady A. "Owen D. Young and American Foreign Policy, 1919–1929." Ph.D. diss., University of Wisconsin, Madison, 1969.

Hunt, Lynn. "French History in the Last 20 Years: The Rise and Fall of the *Annales* Paradigm." *Journal of Contemporary History* 21 (1985): 209–24.

Huntford, Roland. *Scott and Amundsen*. New York: Putnam, 1979.

Jewell, Richard. "Hollywood and Radio: Competition and Partnership in the 1930s." *Historical Journal of Film, Radio and Television* 4 (1984): 125–41.

Katz, Elihu, and George Wedell. *Broadcasting in the Third World: Promise and Performance*. Cambridge: Harvard University Press, 1977.

Kirwin, Harry. "The Federal Telegraph Company: A Testing of the Open Door." *Pacific Historical Review* 22 (1953): 271–86.

Kucera, Geoffrey. "Broadcasting in Africa: A Study of Belgian, British and French Colonial Policies." Ph.D. diss., Michigan State University, East Lansing, 1968.

LaFeber, Walter. *Inevitable Revolutions: The United States In Central America*. New York: Norton, 1982.

———. *The New Empire: An Interpretation of American Expansion 1860–1898*. Ithaca: Cornell University Press, 1961.

Lawrence, James. *The World Struggle With Rubber 1905–1931*. New York: Harper and Row, 1952.

Le Goff, Jacques, and Pierre Nora, eds. *Reconstructing the Past: Essays in Historical Methodology*. Cambridge: Cambridge University Press, 1985.

Lears, Jackson. "The Concept of Cultural Hegemony: Problems and Possibilities." *American Historical Review* 90 (1985): 567–93.

———. "Radical History in Retrospect." *Reviews in American History* 14 (1986): 17–24.

Lee, Chin Chuan. *Media Imperialism Reconsidered: The Homogenizing of Television Culture.* Beverley Hills: Sage, 1980.

Lent, John. *Third World Mass Media and Their Search for Modernity.* Cranbury: Associated University Presses, 1977.

Levine, Robert M. "Elite Intervention in Urban Popular Culture in Modern Brazil." *Luso-Brazilian Review* 21 (1984): 9–22.

Lichty, Lawrence Wilson. "The Nation's Station: A History of Radio Station WLW." Ph.D. diss., Ohio State University, Columbus, 1964.

Maclaurin, Rupert. *Invention and Innovation in the Radio Industry.* New York: Macmillian, 1949.

Mance, Sir Osborne. *International Telecommunications.* London: Oxford University Press, 1944.

Marchand, Roland. *Advertising the American Dream: Making Way for Modernity, 1920–1940.* Berkeley: University of California Press, 1985.

Matellart, Armand. *Transnationals and the Third World: The Struggle for Culture.* South Hadley: Bergin and Garvey, 1983.

Mattelart, Armand, and Seth Siegelaub, eds. *Communication and Class Struggle.* Vol. 2. New York: International General, 1983.

Mayr, Otto. *Authority, Liberty, and Automatic Machinery in Early Modern Europe.* Baltimore: Johns Hopkins University Press, 1986.

McAnany, Emile. *Communication and Change in the Rural Third World: The Role of Information in Development.* New York: Praeger, 1980.

McCann, Frank D. *The Brazilian-American Alliance 1937–1945.* Princeton: Princeton University Press, 1973.

McCormick, Thomas. *China Market: America's Quest for Formal Empire, 1890–1913.* Chicago: Quadrangle, 1967.

———. "Corporatism: A Reply to Rossi." *Radical History Review* 33 (1985): 53–59.

———. "Drift or Mastery? A Corporatist Synthesis for American Diplomatic History." *Reviews In American History* 10 (December 1982): 318–30.

Miller, Richard S., ed. *American Imperialism in 1898: The Quest for National Fulfillment.* New York: John Wiley and Sons, 1980.

Moran, Philip, ed. *Warren G. Harding, 1865–1923.* Dobbs Ferry: Oceana, 1970.

Nerlich, Michael. *Ideology of Adventure: Studies in Modern Consciousness, 1100–1750.* Translated by Ruth Crowley. Minneapolis: University of Minnesota Press, 1987.

Noble, David F. *America By Design.* New York: Knopf, 1977.

Noble, David W. *The End of American History: Democracy, Capitalism, and the Metaphor of Two Worlds in Anglo-American Historical Writing, 1880–1980.* Minneapolis: University of Minnesota Press, 1984.

Noguer, Jorge Eduardo. *Radiodifusion en la Argentina*. Buenos Aires: Editorial Bien Comun, 1985.

Nordenstreng, Kaarl, and Herbert Schiller, eds. *National Soverignty and International Communication*. Norwood: Ablex, 1979.

Nutter, Thomas. "American Telegraphy and the Open Door Policy in China." Ph.D. diss., University of Missouri, Columbia, 1974.

Nye, David E. *Image Worlds: Corporate Identities at General Electric*. Cambridge: MIT Press, 1985.

Oakenfull, J. C. *Brazil in 1911*. London: Butler and Tanner, 1912.

Oliven, Ruben George. "The Production and Consumption of Culture in Brazil." *Latin American Perspectives* 40 (1984): 103–15.

Page, Leslie J. "The Nature of the Broadcast Receiver and its Market in the United States from 1922 to 1927." In *American Broadcasting: A Source Book on the History of Radio and Television*, edited by L. Lichty and M. Topping. New York: Hastings House, 1975.

Panitch, Leo. "The Development of Corporatism in Liberal Democracies." *Comparative Political Studies* 10 (1977): 61–90.

Pareja, Reynaldo. *Historia de la Radio en Colombia 1929–1980*. Bogota: Servicio Colombiano de Communication Social, 1984.

Perrini, Carl. *Heir to Empire: United States Economic Diplomacy 1916–1923*. Pittsburgh: University of Pittsburgh Press, 1969.

Pirsein, Robert. "The Voice of America—A History of the International Broadcasting Activities of the United States Government, 1940–1962." Ph.D. diss., Northwestern University, Evanston, 1970.

Ploman, Edward W. *Space, Earth and Communication*. Westport: Greenwood Press, 1984.

Prada, Raul Rivadeneira. *La Television en Bolivia*. La Paz: Editorial Quipus, 1986.

Preito, Jorge Mejia. *Historia de la Radio y la Television en Mexico*. Mexico: Editores Associados, 1972.

Reich, Leonard S. *The Making of American Industrial Research: Science and Business at G.E. and Bell, 1876–1926*. Cambridge: Cambridge University Press, 1985.

Renaud, J. L. "The Changing Dynamics of the International Telecommunications Union: An Historical Analysis of Development Assistance." Ph.D. diss., Michigan State University, East Lansing, 1986.

———. "U.S. Government Assistance to Associated Press's World-Wide Expansion." *Journalism Quarterly* 62 (1985): 10.

Resler, Ansel Harlan. "The Impact of John R. Brinkley on Broadcasting in the United States." Ph.D. diss., Northwestern University, Evanston, 1958.

Ridings, Eugene W. "Business Interest Groups and Communications: The Brazilian Experience in the Nineteenth Century." *Luso-Brazilian Review* 20 (1983): 241–57.

Roberts, Beth. "United States Propaganda Warfare in Latin America." Ph.D. diss., University of Southern California, Los Angeles, 1943.

Rolo, Charles, *Radio Goes to War*. New York: Putnam, 1942.

Rosen, Philip T. *The Modern Stentors: Radio Broadcasters and the Federal Government 1920–1934*. Westport: Greenwood Press, 1980.

Rosenberg, Emily S. "Anglo-American Economic Rivalry in Brazil During World War 1." *Diplomatic History* 2 (1978): 131–52.

———. *Spreading the American Dream: American Economic and Cultural Expansion 1890–1945*. New York: Hill and Wang, 1982.

Rossi, John P. "A 'Silent Partnership'?: The U.S. Government, RCA, and Radio Communications with East Asia, 1919–1928." *Radical History Review* 33 (1985): 32–52.

Saroldi, Luiz Carlos, and Sonia Virginia Moreira. *Radio Nacional O Brasil em Sintonia*. Brasilia: FUNARTE, 1984.

Schiller, Herbert. *Communication and Cultural Domination*. New York: International Arts and Sciences, 1976.

———. "Decoloniation of Information." *Latin American Perspectives* 5 (1978): 35–48.

———. *Mass Communication and the American Empire*. Boston: Beacon, 1969.

Schmitter, Phillipe. "Still the Century of Corporatism?" In *The New Corporatism*, edited by Frederick Pike and Thomas Stritch. Notre Dame: University of Notre Dame Press, 1974.

Schnitman, Jorge. *Film Industries in Latin America: Dependency and Development*. Norwood: Ablex, 1984.

Schramm, Wilbur, and Daniel Lerner, eds. *Mass Media and National Development: The Role of Media In Developing Countries*. Stanford: Stanford University Press, 1964.

Schreiner, George A. *Cables and Wireless and Their Role in the Foreign Relations of the United States*. Boston: Stratford, 1924.

Schubert, Paul. *The Electric Word: The Rise of Radio*. New York: Macmillian, 1928.

Schulman, Holly. "The Voice of History: The Development of American Propaganda and the Voice of America." Ph.D. diss., University of Maryland, College Park, 1984.

Schwoch, James. "The American Radio Industry and International Communications Conferences, 1919–1927." *Historical Journal of Film, Radio and Television* 7 (1987): 289–309.

———. "The Information Age, the AT&T Settlement: Corporatism-In-the-Making?" *Media Culture and Society* 6 (1984): 273–88.

———. "The United States and the Global Growth of Radio, 1900–1930: In Brazil and in the Third World." Ph.D. diss., Northwestern University, Evanston, 1985.

Segal, Howard. *Technological Utopianism in American Culture*. Chicago: University of Chicago Press, 1985.

Sidel, M. Kent. "A Historical Analysis of American Short Wave Broadcasting 1916–1942." Ph.D. diss., Northwestern University, Evanston, 1976.

Sinclair, John. "Dependent Development and Broadcasting: the Mexican Formula." *Media Culture and Society* 8 (1986): 81–101.

Sklar, Martin J. "Woodrow Wilson and the Political Economy of Modern United States Liberalism." In *A New History of Leviathan*, edited by Ronald Radosh and Murray Rothbard. New York: Dutton, 1972.

Smith, Anthony. *The Geopolitics of Information: How Western Culture Dominates the World*. London: Oxford University Press, 1980.

Smythe, Dallas. *Dependency Road: Communications, Capitalism, Consciousness, and Canada*. Norwood: Ablex, 1981.

———. "The Structure and Policy of Electronic Communications." *University of Illinois Bulletin* 54 (1957).

Sobel, Robert. *The Curbstone Brokers*. New York: Macmillian, 1970.

Spry, Graham. "A Case for Nationalized Broadcasting." *Queen's Quarterly* 38 (1931): 151–69.

Stephens, John D. "Islands, Ether and Echoes." *Pacific Islands Communications Journal* 12 (1983): 79–87.

Tarbell, Ida. *Owen D. Young: A New Type of Industrial Leader*. New York: Macmillian, 1932.

Thomas, Irwin. "The Beginnings of Broadcasting in the British West Indies." Ph.D. diss., University of Missouri, Columbia, 1977.

Tichi, Cecelia. *Shifting Gears: Technology, Literature and Culture in Modernist America*. Chapel Hill: University of North Carolina Press, 1987.

Tolstedt, Mark. "Micronesian Broadcasting and U.S. Strategic Interests: The Evolution of a Dependency." Ph.D. diss., Northwestern University, Evanston, 1986.

Tribolet, Leslie. *The International Aspects of Electrical Communications in the Pacific Area*. Baltimore: Johns Hopkins University Press, 1928.

Tuchman, Barbara. *The Zimmermann Telegram*. 1958. Reprint. New York: Ballantine, 1979.

Tulchin, Joseph. *The Aftermath of War: World War 1 and U.S. Policy Toward Latin America*. New York: New York University Press, 1971.

Tunstall, Jeremy. *The Media Are American*. New York: Columbia University Press, 1977.

Tyne, Gerald. *Saga of the Vacuum Tube*. Indianapolis: Howard W. Sams, 1977.

Varis, Tapio. "The International Flow of Television Programs." *Journal of Communications* 34 (1974): 143–52.

Waldrop, Frank C., and Joseph Borkin. *Television: The Struggle for Control*. New York: Morrow, 1938.

Wallerstein, Immanuel. *Historical Captalism*. London: Verso, 1983.

———. *The Modern World-System: Capitalist Agriculture and the Origins of the European World-Economy, 1600–1750*. New York: Academic Press. 1974.

———. *The Modern World-System II: Merchantilism and the Consolidation of the European World-Economy, 1600–1750*. New York: Academic Press, 1980.

Weinstein, James. *The Corporate Ideal in the Liberal State 1900–1918*. Boston: Beacon, 1968.

Werking, Richard. *The Master Architects: Building the United States Foreign Service 1890–1913*. Lexington: University Press of Kentucky, 1977.

Westman, John. "Modern Dependency: A 'Crucial Case' Study of Brazilian Government Policy in the Minicomputer Industry." *Studies in Comparative International Development* 20 (1985): 25–47.

Williams, William Appleman. *Empire as a Way of Life*. New York: Oxford University Press, 1980.

———. *The Tragedy of American Diplomacy*. New York: Dell, 1959.

Williamson, Peter J. *Varieties of Corporatism: A Conceptual Discussion*. Cambridge: Cambridge University Press, 1985.

Winkler, J. T. "Corporatism." *European Journal of Sociology* 17 (1976): 100–36.

Wise, George. *Willis R. Whitney, General Electric, and the Origins of U.S. Industrial Research*. New York: Columbia University Press, 1985.

Wolf, Howard. *Rubber*. New York: Convici—Friede, 1936.

Year Book of Wireless Telegraphy and Telephony 1915. London: Wireless Press, 1915.

Zunz, Olivier. "Problem-Oriented History: A French-American Dialogue." *Reviews in American History* 14 (1986): 175- 80.

II. Newspapers, Magazines, and Trade Press

Bothelho, Antonio Jose. "Brazil's Independent Computer Strategy." *Technology Review*, May-June 1987, p. 36.

"Broadcasting Above the Clouds in Brazil." *Current Opinon* 74 (1923): 605.

"Freedom of the Air." *Saturday Evening Post*, 16 November 1929.

"Harbord Reviews His South American Trip." *World Wide Wireless*, May 1925, p. 6.

"Illegal Homevid in Latin Orbit." *Variety*, 7 March 1985.

"Intelsat Approves System Coordination." *Broadcasting*, 2 March 1987, p. 76.

"Intelsat OK's PANAMSAT Plan." *Broadcasting*, 15 December 1986, p. 50.

Lubell, Samuel. "Magnificent Failure." *Saturday Evening Post*, 17, 24, and 31 January 1942 (three-part series).

"The Monster with Two Heads." *Forbes*, 8 April 1985.

New York Journal of Commerce, 17 July 1913; 26 April 1915.

New York Times, 22 August 1922; 22 May 1927; 31 July 1927.

Paley, William. "Radio Turns South." *Fortune*, April 1941, p. 77.

"PANAMSAT Bemoans Competitive Position Vis-a-Vis INTELSAT." *Broadcasting*, 23 November 1987, p. 82.

"PANAMSAT Cleared for Launch in '88." *Satellite Communication*, December 1987, p. 15.

"Piracy Laws Hit Brazil." *Variety*, 17 October 1983.

"Piracy Still Cutting Home Video Profits: Illegal Tapes Rush Latin American Markets." *Variety*, 23 November 1985.

"U.S., Intelsat Wrestle with PANAMSAT Application." *Broadcasting*, 13 October 1986, pp. 62–63.

Van Gelderland, Karl. "War in the Ether." *Nation*, 12 March 1938, pp. 300–01.

Willoughby, Raymond C. "Radio, a Test of Democracy." *Nation's Business*, January 1928, p. 36.

"Yanks Ready Legal Grip on Argentine Home Video." *Variety*, 9 May 1984.

III. Government and Corporate Publications

Berthold, Victor. *The History of the Telephone and Telegraph in the Argentine Republic 1851–1921*. New York: American Telephone and Telegraph. 1921.

——. *The History of the Telephone and Telegraph in Brazil 1851–1921*. New York: American Telephone and Telegraph, 1922.

——. *The History of the Telephone and Telegraph in Chile 1851–1922*. New York: American Telephone and Telegraph, 1924.

——. *The History of the Telephone and Telegraph in Colombia 1865–1921*. New York: American Telephone and Telegraph, 1921.

——. *The History of the Telephone and Telegraph in Uruguay 1886–1923*. New York: American Telephone and Telegraph, 1925.

EU-F-GB-I Radio Protocol (of August 25, 1919) as Modified and Commented upon by a Committee Appointed by the Secretary of Commerce. Washington: Government Printing Office, 1920.

Geiger, Theodore. "The General Electric Company in Brazil." *National Planning Association Studies of United States Business Performance Abroad*. Washington: National Planning Association, 1961.

Howeth, L. S. *History of Communications—Electronics in the United States Navy*. Washington: Government Printing Office, 1963.

Many Voices, One World: Towards a New More Just and More Efficient World Information and Communication Order (The MacBride Report). New York: UNESCO, 1980.

"Memorandum of Tropical Radio Telegraph Company Respecting the Proposed Universal Electrical Communications Union." Pamphlet, United Fruit Company, 23 May 1921.

National Resources Committee. *Technological Trends and National Policy*. Washington: Government Printing Office, 1937.

Pan American Union. *Descriptive Data: Brazil, 1914*. Washington: Government Printing Office, 1914.

——. *First Conference of Pan American Journalists*. Washington: Government Printing Office, 1926.

——. *Memorandum Concerning Cable and Radio-Telegraphic Communication with Mexico, Central and South America, and the West Indies, Second Pan American Conference, 19–24 January 1920*. Washington: Government Printing Office, 1920.

"Permanent Control of Radio in U.S. by Navy Urged by Secretary Daniels at Hearing Before House Committee." *Official U.S. Bulletin*, 13 December 1918.

Schultz, George P. "The Shape, Scope and Consequences of the Age of Information." Address before the Stanford Alumni Association's First International Conference, Paris, 21 March 1986.

United Fruit Company. *Annual Report*, 1900–1929.

U.S. Congress. Office of Technology Assessment. *Intellectual Property Rights in an Age of Electronics and Information.* Washington: Government Printing Office, 1986.

U.S. Department of Commerce. *Direct Broadcast Satellites: Policies, Prospects, and Potential Competition.* Washington: Government Printing Office, 1981.

———. Trade Information Bulletin no. 771. "Broadcast Advertising in Latin America." Washington: Government Printing Office, 1931.

———. Trade Information Bulletin no. 536. "Market for Electrical Equipment in Argentina." Washington: Government Printing Office, 1928.

———. Trade Information Bulletin no. 487. "Market for Electrical Equipment in Australia." Washington: Government Printing Office, 1927.

———. Trade Information Bulletin no. 563. "Market for Electrical Equipment in Central America." Washington: Government Printing Office, 1928.

———. Trade Information Bulletin no. 515. "Market for Electrical Equipment in Chile." Washington: Government Printing Office, 1928.

———. Trade Information Bulletin no. 511. "Market for Electrical Equipment in Colombia and Venezuela." Washington: Government Printing Office, 1927.

———. Trade Information Bulletin no. 513. "Market for Electrical Equipment in India." Washington: Government Printing Office, 1927.

———. Trade Information Bulletin no. 505. "Market for Electrical Equipment in Japan." Washington: Government Printing Office, 1927.

———. Trade Information Bulletin no. 519. "Market for Electrical Equipment in Mexico." Washington: Government Printing Office, 1928.

———. Trade Information Bulletin no. 727. "Market for Electrical Equipment in the Netherlands East Indies." Washington: Government Printing Office, 1930.

———. Trade Information Bulletin no. 508. "Market for Electrical Equipment in Peru." Washington: Government Printing Office, 1927.

———. Trade Promotion Series no. 101. "Market for Electrical Equipment in the Union of South Africa." Washington: Government Printing Office, 1930.

———. Trade Promotion Series no. 109. "Radio Markets of the World, 1930." Washington: Government Printing Office, 1930.

———. Trade Promotion Series no. 23. "Rubber Production in the Amazon Valley." Washington: Government Printing Office, 1925.

U.S. Department of Navy. "History of the Bureau of Engineering—Navy Department—During World War." Washington: Government Printing Office, 1922.

U.S. Department of State. *International Telecommunications Conference Cairo 1938, Report to the Secretary of State by the Chairman of the*

American Delegation, with Appended Documents. Publication no. 1286, Conference Series no. 39. Washington: Government Printing Office, 1939.

U.S. General Accounting Office. *International Trade: Strengthening Worldwide Protection of Intellectual Property Rights*. Washington: Government Printing Office, 1987.

U.S. International Communications Agency. *The United States and the Debate on the World 'Information Order'*. Washington: Government Printing Office, 1979.

U.S. Rubber Company. *Annual Report 1904*.

U.S. Senate. *International Telecommunications and Information Policy: Selected Issues for the 1980s*. 96th Cong., 1st sess. Washington: Government Printing Office, 1983.

"The Universal Electrical Communications Union." Pamphlet, Radio Corporation of America, 23 May 1921.

"The Universal Electrical Communications Union." Pamphlet, Tropical Radio Telegraph Company, 23 May 1921.

IV. Archival and Manuscript Collections

Azcarraga, Emilio. Biography. State Historical Society of Wisconsin, Madison.

Davis, Norman. Papers. Library of Congress Manuscript Division, Washington.

Fabbri, Allessandro. Papers. Library of Congress Manuscript Division, Washington.

Hoover, Herbert. Commerce Papers of Herbert Hoover. Herbert Hoover Presidential Library, West Branch, Iowa.

National Broadcasting Company. Central Office Files. State Historical Society of Wisconsin, Madison.

Royal, John. Papers. State Historical Society of Wisconsin, Madison.

U.S. Commission to the Brazil Centennial Exposition. Final Report. Library of Congress Manuscript Dvision, Washington.

U.S. Department of Commerce, Bureau of Foreign and Domestic Commerce. Record Group 151. National Archives, Washington.

U.S. Department of Commerce. Record Group 40. National Archives, Washington.

U.S. Department of State. Record Group 59. National Archives, Washington.

U.S. Post Office Department, Bureau of the Second Assistant Postmaster General, Division of Air Mail Service. Record Group 28. National Archives, Washington.

Wells, Fay Gillis. Oral History. Broadcast Pioneers Library, Washington.

White, Wallace. Papers. Library of Congress Manuscript Division, Washington.

Young, Owen D. Papers. Van Hornesville, N.Y.

Index

About the Author

James Schwoch was born in 1955 in Milwaukee. He received his B.A. from the University of Wisconsin in 1976, his M.A. from Northwestern University in 1980, and his Ph.D. from Northwestern University in 1985. He has written on media history, broadcasting, and telecommunications for several scholarly journals. Currently a visiting assistant professor in the Department of Radio/TV/Film at Northwestern University, Schwoch lives in Evanston, Illinois with his wife, Mimi White, and their son Travis.

$24.95